JOHN WIMBER'S PASTORAL LETTERS

Compiled & edited by

Derek Morphew

PUBLICATION DETAILS

Vineyard International Publishing
84 Starke Road, Bergvliet, 7945, South Africa
Copyright © The Association of Vineyard Churches, 5115 Grove West Blvd, Stafford, Texas 77477, 2019.

All rights reserved. No part of this publication may be reproduced, stored in a retrieval system or transmitted, in any form or by any means, electronic, mechanical, photocopying, recording, or otherwise, without the prior written permission of the copyright owner.

Use of the material by John Wimber was obtained from the Association of Vineyard Churches, USA, who are the owners of the copyright for the John Wimber archives.

Scripture quotations, unless otherwise specified are taken from The Holy Bible, New International Version® NIV®
Copyright © 1973 1978 1984 2011 by Biblica, Inc. TM
Used by permission. All rights reserved worldwide.

ISBN: 9798624494329

ABBREVIATIONS

AVC—Association of Vineyard Churches
NICNT—New International Commentary on the New Testament
TAV—Toronto Airport Vineyard
VMG—Vineyard Music Group
VMI—Vineyard Ministries International

TABLE OF CONTENTS

Foreword By Phil Strout I

Introduction 2

Who Are We And Where Are We Going? (Part I) 5

Who Are We And Where Are We Going? (Part Ii) 19

Leading And Developing Foot Soldiers 32

The Vineyard Movement 45

A Leadership Shopping List 64

Liberating Women For Ministry And Leadership 74

Season Of New Beginnings 86

Refreshing, Renewal, And Revival 98

An Unchanging Destination 110

Learning From Our Elders 122

Board Report 131

John Wimber Responds To Phenomena 138

Facing The Fires Of Fanaticism – Part I 142

Facing The Fires Of Fanaticism – Part 2 152

Staying Focused: The Vineyard As A Centered Set 159

Unity And Withdrawal 168

The Five-Fold Ministry 177

Disciplining Fallen Leaders 202

Select Bibliography 212

Bibliography 214

FOREWORD BY PHIL STROUT

I have always been so thankful for the mentors throughout my life and ministry. Some of the people that have had a great impact on my life are those I never met but read and then there are those that I have had relationships with. Derek has done a great favor in collecting and editing many of the pastoral letters and articles that came from the pen of John Wimber. Many that will read this book never met John Wimber but have heard him referenced for so many years. Others, who knew him, will enjoy the access that this edition brings in a way of remembering so many thoughts, teachings and stories. In a humorous way, it has been interesting to hear people say, "John said this, and John said that" and at times there seems to be differing points of view. Here we have many of the teaching and thoughts from the very material that the Vineyard produced regarding ministry, worship, social issues, theology and many practical tips for what church could and should be.

I highly recommend this volume to be used to help people who did not get the chance to know John, to take the time to consider what he said and did. For those that did know and heard John, use this as a reminder and be encouraged to pass this on to the people that you may be discipling at this point of your life.

Thank you Derek, for the hard work and service to the body of Christ.

INTRODUCTION

INTRODUCING JOHN WIMBER

John Wimber was the first International Director of the Vineyard movement and had a formative influence on renewal movements in England among Anglican churches, particularly New Wine, launched from St. Andrews', Chorleywood, and Holy Trinity Brompton. Apart from these church groupings he had a remarkably far-reaching influence on the international Christian community of almost every denomination. His contribution was primarily in the emphasis on equipping ordinary church members to do works of ministry ("doing the stuff"), and therefore on transferable models of healing.

John was the manager of the 1960's Rock band "The Righteous Brothers", but his career in music was soon abandoned in favor of his calling to Christian ministry. The gathering of people, which later became the *Yorba Linda Vineyard Christian Fellowship,* was born in a context of new Worship songs. This led to John registering *Mercy Music* in order to document the worship of the fledgling movement. *Vineyard/Mercy Music*1 became one of the best-known Christian Praise and Worship music labels, operating in six nations.

During his career he was a Quaker pastor, a lecturer in the Fuller Theological Seminary School of World Missions, a Church Growth consultant, founding pastor of the *Anaheim Vineyard Christian Fellowship,* a well-known author (his best known works being *Power Healing* and *Power Evangelism*), an international conference speaker and a father figure to many church leaders in many countries, who regarded him as their primary mentor. *Christianity Today* magazine featured him in one of its cover stories, naming him as one of the leading Christian figures of the last century.

1*Mercy Music* later changed its name to *Vineyard Music Group,* or VMG.

INTRODUCING THE LETTERS

The *John Wimber's Pastoral Letters* is a compilation of his letters published by the *Association of Vineyard Churches*, USA, as *Vineyard Reflections*.

I can recall, when doing my undergraduate studies in theology, how the Methodist students on campus were required to study John Wesley's sermons. John Wimber saw Wesley as one of his historic role models. Should we not require our emerging leaders to study Wimber's pastoral letters? Because we are in the Vineyard, we may tend to want to exaggerate the role history will reserve for Wimber, since we hold him in such high regard. Yet enough has been written already, by those outside the movement, to justify offering his pastoral reflections as required reading for succeeding generations of Vineyard leaders. Such is the crucial and seminal influence John had on the founding generation. As a volume it will stand alongside Carol Wimber's *The Way It Was*,[2] Bill Jackson's *Quest for the Radical Middle*,[3] the Vineyard *Position Papers*,[4] and Alexander Venter's *Doing Church*,[5] as essential literature to truly understand what the Vineyard is and what its real values are. It will stand alongside them, but since John really was the primary founding Father of the movement, it should really take priority of place.

Here are some of the significant points to emerge.

- You will be impressed by John's wisdom, balance, and breadth of vision—the way he weighed difficult issues, the way he "made the main thing the main thing".

- You will be impressed by his passion, his humility and his graciousness. However deeply John felt the pain or hurt of those who criticized or attacked him, his public stance was always generous and gracious.

- You will learn his angle on the difficult times the Vineyard lived through, its peculiarly controversial nature, as a young movement, and the nerve it took to steer the ship through the stormy waters.

---

[2]Carol Wimber, *The Way It Was*, Hodder and Stoughton, 1999.

[3]Bill Jackson, *The Quest for the Radical Middle*, Vineyard International Publishers, Cape Town, 2000.

[4]Available from AVC USA.

[5]Alexander Venter, *Doing Church: Building from The Bottom Up*, Vineyard International Publishers, Cape Town, 2001.

- Most important of all, you will hear from John, the founding Father, on our values, priorities and philosophy of ministry.

As the movement grows into many countries, and as it reaches succeeding generations, the need to relate to these historical origins will increase. These materials will be of primary interest "in house", but many of our friends, and perhaps a few of our critics, will find them helpful as well.

Derek Morphew
Editor/producer
February 2020

WHO ARE WE AND WHERE ARE WE GOING? (PART I)

April/May 1993, Volume 1, Issue 1

The National board of the Association of Vineyard Churches asked me to write a newsletter. It's something I wanted to do for some time, but it was simply more that I could handle because of other commitments. But the Board has graciously given me Jon Panner as an assistant who will help me put together a bi-monthly leadership letter.

My purpose in writing the letter is threefold:

1. To communicate my views on issues that currently affect Vineyard pastors and our friends,

2. To communicate the values, vision and mission of the Vineyard as I see it, and

3. To make known various and sundry things that are going on around the world that are of interest to us as our movement expands.

I hope this leadership letter encourages you and provides a higher level of communication.

By the way, I want every Vineyard pastor to receive his own copy of *Vineyard Reflections*; please give us any information on any staff members we overlooked with this our first issue.

WHO ARE WE AND WHERE ARE WE GOING?

In recent months there has been a need here at Anaheim to clarify our vision. It was somewhat obscured as a result of our interaction with the prophetic and the coming and going of staff members over the past few years. So I did a six week sermon series entitled, "The Church I Would Start" capped off by a three hour leaders seminar called, "Who Are We and Where Are We Going?" to communicate my vision for the Anaheim Vineyard. I thought you might enjoy a summary of this material. We are going to publish portions of it here in our leadership letter in several installments. Here is the first.

OUR FOUNDATION

What We Stand On

The Anaheim Vineyard is founded on the Word of God. We are first and foremost evangelicals that believe the Bible to be the literal inerrant Word of God. As such it is the standard for our faith and practice and the yardstick by which we measure all of our activity. It is the principle resource from which we draw our understanding of what the church is to be about.[6]

In our case, one helpful interpretive key to understanding the Bible is the teaching of George Eldon Ladd on the kingdom of God. The discovery of Dr. Ladd's teaching was a monumental experience for me. It was the principle turning point in my ministry. Dr. Ladd's teaching concerning the "already-and-the-not-yet" of the kingdom dramatically influenced our understanding of our daily activity in Christ. Though I am sure Dr. Ladd would not have made all the applications we have, we think the Bible allows for the emphasis of the *word* and the *works* in combination.

As we've said many times in the past, we believe the word of God is essential for illumination and the works of God, i.e., deliverance, healing, ministry to the poor, etc., are helpful for illustration. We need both the illumination and the illustration if we're to see the kingdom of God done on earth today. We are, of course, aware that the kingdom is not yet consummated and will not be until the second coming of Jesus. Until that day however, we can borrow from that which will be, through faith and prayer, even as Jesus encouraged us to ask for "tomorrows bread" today in his instruction to the apostles concerning prayer.

---

[6]For a fuller discussion of this area, John Wimber & Kevin Springer, *Power Points*, London, Hodder & Stoughton, 1990.

Building A Local Body

Two legs: Worship and Compassion

We are building a body, a local expression of the church. As such, we link to the church throughout the world. The Anaheim Vineyard is gifted by God with two major emphases: *worship* and *compassion.*

Worship is the highest priority of the Vineyard. We believe that we live to worship God and rescue men. We practice our worship throughout the week in a subservient attitude towards the purposes and person of God. The Lord Jesus Christ is worthy of our worship and we do so by singing songs, praying prayers, meditating on the scripture, congregating and building one another up in fellowship, as well as by healing the sick, casting out devils, ministering to the poor, the bereaved, the widowed, etc. Our worship expresses love upward towards God and outwards towards men. Worship leads us to compassion, the second emphasis or "leg" the Lord has given us.

Compassion in the New Testament was a work of the Spirit that precipitated or preceded a major portion of the miracles found in Scripture. Jesus was filled with compassion before he encouraged the apostles to pray to the Master of the harvest to send out workers. It was compassion that caused him to preach the Sermon on the Mount, to raise the Widow of Nain's son from the dead, to heal the sick and the demonized. Compassion (and obedience) seems to be a primary motivation for everything he did.

We feel blessed here at the Anaheim Vineyard when God endues us with compassion. That is not to say that we think compassion dwells within us, like some human resource such as sympathy or empathy. Compassion is an unction of the Spirit that comes from time to time, that motivates us to minister, and I believe we follow Jesus' example when we minister from hearts brimming over with compassion. However, this is not to say that we only minister when we "feel" compassionate. We minister out of obedience. Compassion is not devoid of feeling, but it is more than feelings. Compassion is placed within the bowels of the body of Christ by the Holy Spirit and so reflects God's heart of justice and mercy towards a broken world.

The Torso

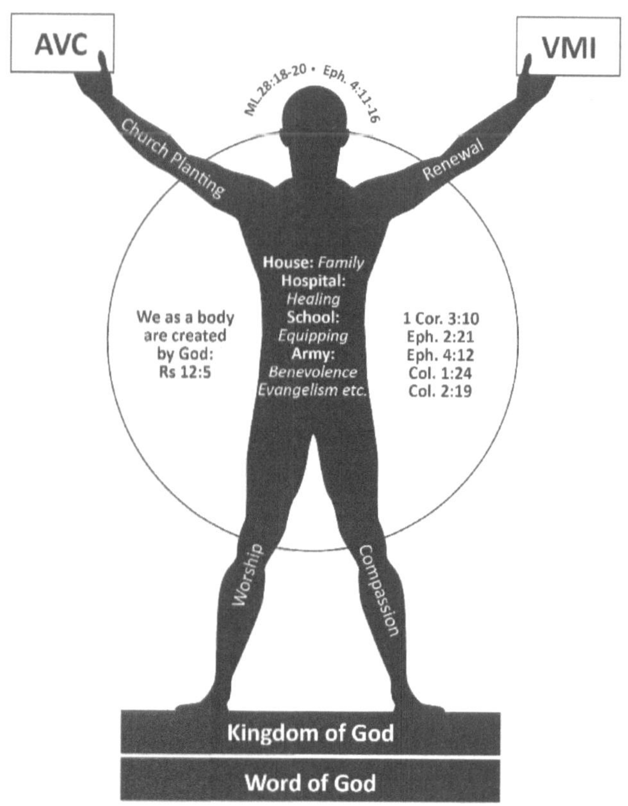

Four Facts about the Body

It is my impression that God calls our local church to express four facts of the body of Christ. They are: the church as a House, Hospital, School and Army. These are not the only biblical metaphors one could use (some count as many a sixty-seven in the New Testament) but they are the ones that I believe God wants to mature in us. When we see our local body in full expression, it should function maturely in these aspects.

House or Family

We are called to be a house, a household, or family. This, of course, is the fruit of being reborn and converted into the body of Christ. We are in good standing as members of the family of God because of the finished work of Christ on our behalf – this plus nothing else! – has established us in the body of Christ and in the family of God. As such we are the spiritual household of God and Christ is the foundation and cornerstone.

Hospital

At Anaheim, we find that many who come to Christ arrive terribly wounded, either by their sin or other's sin against them. They need a significant amount of healing in the aftermath of their conversion experience. Though all things have become new in Christ, the reality of yesterday's pain sometimes lingers on because it is not dealt with in the context of the declarations and ministries of the church. Our sins are forgiven at the cross, yet we sometimes do not deal adequately with sin's effects in our lives. We need to allow the reality of the cross and the truth of the scripture to expose the lies we believe. We need to cast our cares upon Christ and allow the Holy Spirit to cleanse and transform us. And so we find that many people who are in the family of God are also in need of special pastoral care. Though sanctification and mortification of the flesh is a lifelong process, healing and "hospitalization" is hopefully but for a season.

School

At Anaheim, we felt the need to provide a form of schooling to equip our people for both life and ministry. First, we believe scripture enjoins us to equip the saints and so it behooves us as leaders to train them in basic ministerial skills: teaching, counseling, evangelism, etc. But that is not the end. We must also equip people for life and teach them the kinds of things that would reflect the whole counsel of God relating to the nurture of their family, finances, vocations and social relations. The whole of life's experiences ought to be, in one way or another, addressed by the gospel. The church is entrusted with the task of bringing God's wisdom to bear in working out the issues of life while leaving freedom for people to make choices and direct their lives as they respond to God's word and the Holy Spirit.

Army

Is there any question of a need for an army of God in our dark era? We are a house, a hospital, a school – but God also releases us into his work force to advance the reign of his kingdom in the lives of dying men and women. God sovereignly prepares us, through our new birth in Christ, the ministry of his healing hand and the equipping of pastors and leaders, to do the work of the kingdom: preaching the gospel, healing the sick, caring for the poor, etc.

The Head of the Body: Our Aims

The head of the body is the Lord Jesus Christ. It is Jesus who gives us our aims and that is why we chose to position them here. Simply stated, our mission is to fulfill the Great Commission through evangelism and to equip, grow and mature a body of believers.

First, evangelism. As Peter Wagner has pointed out, people often confuse decision with discipleship. Effective ministry in the local church requires not only catching but cleaning the fish: we must not only harvest, but also process the fruit. Fish left uncleaned and harvests not processed represent an incomplete picture of the evangelistic endeavor. We must disciple those who pray and make decisions for Christ.

The essential nature of equipping, touched on in the previous section related to the school, is to repair and prepare a people to do kingdom ministry. God has prepared good works for us to walk in and he has set leadership in the Church to train us how to walk. But, unfortunately, a great deal of the body of Christ is underdeveloped in this regard.

Many maintain some of the basis organizational disciples. These are: attendance at most services, general assent to creedal or doctrinal emphases, a modicum of service to the local body whenever conscripted, and giving on a regular or irregular basis when motivated by church leadership. These four practices qualify you for membership in almost any church in America. Yet none of the above truly represent the New Testament picture of the body of Christ in action. That is not to say that these practices are unimportant or that the Early Church didn't encourage them. The body should always gather, give, believe and serve. But the body must be equipped to do more than minimum requirements for organizational membership. And this is where our training emphasis comes into play.

The Arms of the Body: Renewal

Notice that our figure has two arms. The first is our renewal involvement (keep in mind that we're talking about the local church at Anaheim). In renewal, the church at Anaheim has three priorities.

The first is to encourage the body of Christ in unity (John 17:21). As I've said numerous times, this is the most difficult command of God that I ever tried to work out. It is very awkward to affirm believers in Christ who have doctrinal or aberrational practices that seem at variance from the scriptural norm. This, of course, is consistent with the Post-Reformation Protestant milieu in that we have parted and departed from the brethren for several hundred years now over such issues. If we take seriously the commandment to love the brethren, so that Jesus is communicated to the world in a wholesome way, we must learn to build bridges and make relationships with people who previously we were not able to relate to. One way, of course, is to affirm what we can, in an open and honest way, and keep our criticism to ourselves while not pretending that the differences do not exist.

The second aspect of our renewal ministry is to call the Church back to Christ. By that I mean to make Jesus Lord over the local church, the local body of Christ, even as He is Lord over the spiritual Body of Christ. Unfortunately, this simple call challenges the mindset of many Christians today who think ownership of the church is theirs by birthright, divine fiat, or tithe total. We see this attitude when people refer to the local body as "our" church. I think it is important in the Vineyard that we affirm repeatedly that it is not "our" local church. It is "His" Church the world over, throughout the ages, from Pentecost to the Parousia. The Church always has been and always will be "His".

Third, we are called to minister and release the empowerment and gifts of the Holy Spirit in the Church at large. And we are called to take the hype and mysticism out of much that is labeled the ministry of the Spirit today. Instead, we want to minister in power, simplicity and with a loving heart as we seek to edify the body through the gifts of the Spirit. This has been the easiest of the three emphases that God gave to us to give to the Church at large.

Church Planting

The other arm of our figure shows our linkage with the *Association of*

Vineyard Churches and our commitment to plant churches. This will be done as the opportunity presents itself, the leaders and finances are made available, and in cooperation with our national, regional and area plans. We thank God for linking us to a growing movement of churches being planted in the United States and now internationally in eleven countries.

This introduces you to the basic vision of our local body at Anaheim. Most of it came out of the crucible of interaction with the scripture, burdens of the Holy Spirit and occasions of God giving specific leading. I never had a clear vision or "ten step plan" of what God was doing until such a time as he had done it. Unlike some, I've not had the privilege of looking out into the future and knowing what was coming with any great clarity. However, I do believe that God led us to establish a local church here at Anaheim. This local body has had its impact not only in our community, but across the nation and around the world. This is part of "who we are" and will remain the direction of "where we are going" – until Jesus leads otherwise.

THE IMPORTANCE OF SMALL GROUPS IN THE CHURCH

A young pastor in the Vineyard recently asked me, "Do you value small groups?" My immediate response was to laugh. Then I realized that he was serious, which almost brought me to tears. What a surprise that someone in the Vineyard – especially a leader – thought I did not value small groups. I think it might help to clarify my personal history and view on this vital subject.

I converted in a small group. The group started for the purpose of evangelizing my wife and I. There were only seven in the group and it went for several months. As we interacted over the scriptures the Holy Spirit was drawing us to Jesus. The result was both my wife's and my conversion. Furthermore, the same man that led me to Christ equipped me in the basic ministry of evangelism through small groups. So as a new convert I began to continually share my faith with people in the Southern California basin. This came as a direct result of watching my mentor, Gunner Payne, interact with and answer questions concerning scripture. Soon I could give all the answers that Gunner gave and tell all the stories that he told. I just simply mimicked the behavior, attitude and practice that he modeled.

Gunner also discipled me in church life. He was not only active throughout the week in winning people to Christ – sometimes as many as seven nights a week – but he was very active in the church. Gunner's example taught me a great deal concerning love for the church. So, from the outset of my Christian walk I made three commitments: first, to Christ; second, to His church; and third, to His cause – the reconciliation of men and women to Himself. And through Gunner's modeling and mentoring from a wealth of experience, I learned the value of small groups. Small groups can help deepen a threefold commitment to Christ, His cause, and His church.

During the 1970's small groups were a vital part of my life and ministry. I started hundreds of groups myself and many reproduced. As a consultant I helped hundreds of churches begin small group ministries. I also helped plant churches from "the bottom up" by beginning with small group infrastructures. My own church was planted this way and today we have over one hundred small groups. But enough about my history. Let's consider the issue at hand. I'd like to answer two basic questions from my own knowledge and experience: What are small groups for? Are there different kinds of groups?

Four Functions

Small groups can play many roles and there are several categories of small groups. Generally, most small groups have at least one of these four functions: evangelism, integration, discipling, and maturing.

First, small groups provide one of the best places for *evangelism*. A congenial atmosphere of friendly dialog over the person and work of Christ can produce high dividends in winning people.

In our evangelical sub-culture we place such a high value on the individual's personal relationship with Christ we often forget the importance of our corporate relationship with the body of Christ. But remember Christianity is not a solo flight! Small groups provide an environment to undermine the bias toward individualism that runs so deep in our culture. Small groups can help to teach people to love one another in a way that exemplifies a New Testament lifestyle. A loving community is a powerful tool and witness to the world. From the Book of Acts, we get a glimpse of the effectiveness of this corporate witness (2:44; 4:32). The messianic community of the King broke into first century life and was a foretaste of the banquet table to come. Surely the lavish love for one another expressed by the early church was a sign and a wonder to unbelievers that was as powerful as the healing of crooked legs!

Second, small groups *integrate people* into the Christian community of the group itself and the larger corporate community of the local church. And, in fact, where groups do not see the importance of being a bridge to bring people into the church, they often will turn into themselves, spoil, and become a problem in the church.

Third, small groups are one of the most powerful *discipling mechanisms* in the church. The primary way people are discipled in groups is through modeling. What they do and how they do it and why they do it and the attitude with which they do it becomes the norm for the new convert or the new member of the group. Newcomers soon take on the behavior, lifestyle, and patterns – for good or bad - of the rest of the group.

Another form of small group discipling is informal teaching. Informal teaching uses real life situations to train group members. A financial crisis of one member becomes an opportunity to mature the whole group in biblical values of giving and stewardship. A couple with children in adolescent rebellion can be encouraged by other members who have been down that road before.

Many small groups do formal teaching (curricula abound). Whatever the level of formal interaction, the informal interaction among the group influences how they receive that teaching, what application they make, the attitude with which they relate to the teacher and his or her message.

A fourth function of small groups is the *maturing* dynamic so encouraged in the New Testament. Small groups help to repair and prepare people for works of service.

Are There Different Kinds of Small Groups?

The answer is yes. In our church we have several subcategories of groups that I think every church ought to consider.

First, we have a category we might call *task-related groups*. Their purpose for gathering is usually to perform a service. But there are by-products to working together. I use the word by-product not in a derogatory way but rather to point out the primary intent of the group is a task, not relationship. But people who work together bond together. In fact, most people bond better if they share a common activity or goal. Groups that go out and minister to the poor or prisoners, groups organized for evangelism, groups who minister pastoral care to the sick, the aged, the widows or divorced, groups designed specifically for prayer and intercession - all these can both perform a task and develop a bonded community with a high degree of love and acceptance for one another. These groups can be very satisfying for participants. Often unbelievers and nominal Christians (and people who can't sit still) find a home in task-related groups where service is the goal.

Another kind of group I call *training group*. These groups usually are short-term groups put together for training in specific ministry skills. A group working on leadership issues is a good example. Such a group might meet for two or three months to work on biblical teachings of character formation, spiritual development and leadership gifts. Hopefully, as a natural by-product, the group will bond and relate closely enough so social and emotional needs are met as well.

Short-term training groups for new converts can be fun especially when the group does a baptism celebration together. The goal here is to train members in basic Christian doctrine and to initiate and prepare them for deeper participation in church life. Other types of training groups include pre-marital, new parent, and marriage renewal or communication group.

Specialized training groups to prepare church planters, is a group we sometimes employ. In this setting an experienced church planter or supervising pastor shares wisdom and information, and involvement in ministry is evaluated. In this training group bonding and relationship building occurs as well. In fact, the supportive network that develops between prospective planters may be the most beneficial aspect of such a group. Long after the information rots away in a notebook the relationships can be a vibrant resource.

Another category is *integration groups*. These groups help people get into the life of the local church. Solid relationships are the key to assimilating newcomers into any church. Remember, people come to churches for many reasons, but usually stay because they've made a close friend or two in the church. Integration groups have several functions: evangelism, assimilation and discipling, but their primary purpose is to be a bridge from the community into the church. These relationships will continue to nurture, support and encourage the individuals that participate.

A word about transition

Small groups are essential to a healthy growing church. When I speak to young pastors who want to plant a church, I always encourage them to "build from the bottom up" and resist the people's pressure to go public before infrastructure is established. Some of our newer leaders in the Vineyard are evidently not exposed to those ideas.

For pastors leading churches without small group ministries, identifying leaders and releasing small groups is one of the most vital steps you can take. Yet there are dangers in this process, and I'd like to just cite four things you ought to be aware of if this is your situation.

First, depending on the nature and the activity of the group, you run the risk of violating some basic Vineyard values. For instance, if the small group model you employ excludes worship or fellowship or gifts ministry, that model - right from the start - will violate three essential values of the Vineyard. Whatever type of small group you start ought not to violate these values.

Second, if you take small group training models from the church catalog milieu, you may run the risk of getting into a situation like David encumbered with Saul's armor. Whereas the program worked for the originator, it won't always work for you. Some programs won't fit certain kinds of churches. This is because many models have to be contextualized. For example, people working in a "blue collar" kind of setting may need more structure and definition in their groups than executives working in a "white collar" setting.

Third, some pastors assume that every person who attends Sunday services ought to participate in a small group. By everyone they mean, *everyone*. It's been my experience however, that this is a naïve assumption. Young people tend to want a high quantity of relationships as well as a few quality ones. Therefore, they are very amenable to being involved in small group. But the older they get they tend to want fewer relationships with higher quality. People, older than 50, are less likely to involve themselves in small groups that are large and have turnover. It just simply isn't easy for them to undergo so much social change. Of course, the exception is someone who's been in a small group from the time they were young. My brother-in-law, Bob Fulton, converted in a small group. He's now very old - in his fifties! - and has never been outside of one. So small group life *is* church life for him.

The initiation of small groups as a program in a church ought to be done over a period of time, giving people lots of room to opt in or out. To suddenly announce, "beginning next month, we're going to divide everybody in the church into new groups" can be very hurtful and disruptive. I think it wise from both a leadership and fellowship standpoint to give at least a year to that process. Let people try some small groups with those that are the most responsive. Share some literature with leaders in the church so they can get acquainted. Let them visit other churches that have small groups and then let them get involved in designing their own small groups so they can do something that reflects their own values.

These then, are the kinds of suggestions I make to pastors attempting to start (or restart) small groups in the local church.

Summary

In summary, the purpose of small groups is to make and nurture disciples who evidence a growing commitment to Christ, his Cause, and his Church. The training elements of modeling, and formal and informal teaching, produce a powerful dynamic for maturing believers.

At first groups may be fairly homogenized and reflect the style of the founding pastor. As the church grows others needs will surface and other leadership styles will emerge to meet those needs. In our church we place groups in three broad categories: task, training and integration.

Every Vineyard should have vibrant small group life. It is difficult for me to think of exceptions. I value them so much because the Lord has met me there so many times. If you are just starting (or restarting) small group ministry in your church, then I encourage you to listen to what the Holy Spirit wants to do in your context. I know he will bless you and your people on your journey together toward him.

VINEYARD PROTOCOL AND VALUES

In introducing new ideas to the Vineyard movement, it is "Vineyard protocol" to let ministries mature to a tried and proven level before I encourage pastors to share them outside the local church. This is especially true of any new program that significantly alters the "genetic code" of the Vineyard. Clearly, there needs to be time for the maturing process to occur, for new models to be "Vineyardized" so as not to conflict with our values and practices. To use my friend Tom Stipe's phrase, it is Vineyard protocol to "show fruit - not seeds".

In introducing new ideas to your church, I encourage you to communicate your vision or message with the following in mind:

- Never denigrate the Bride of Christ for who the Lord shed His precious blood by comparing your new program with the "old wineskin" of other churches or movements. We value the whole Church - even though it is (as we are) immature and ineffective in many places.

- Ruthlessly assert the Vineyard value of no-hype in all communications. Avoid pumping people up for the "new thing God is doing." Demystify new emphases even as the Vineyard has attempted to demystify spiritual gifts. Understatement is a key Vineyard value I hope will flourish among us for years to come.

- Pay careful attention to language that is offensive to some, due to the theology embedded in it or the baggage attributed (rightly or wrongly) to it.

- Don't offer simplistic solutions to complex problems like leadership development and pastoral care.

- Make every effort to contextualize, "Vineyardize," and adapt new emphases rather than adopt someone else's values in a wholesale manner.

- Ensure adequate safeguards against the specter of authoritarianism. Don't assume people are rebellious just because they don't like the direction of your new philosophy of ministry, emphasis or program.

WHO ARE WE AND WHERE ARE WE GOING? (PART II)

June/July 1993, Volume 1, Issue 2

My purpose in sending you *Vineyard Reflections* is to encourage you through communicating:

- My views on issues that currently affect Vineyard pastors,

- The values, vision and mission of the Vineyard as I see it,

- Various news items from around the world of interest to the movement.

By the way, I want every Vineyard leader to receive his own copy of Vineyard Reflections; please give us the addresses of any staff members or interns we overlooked.

As most of you are already aware, the doctors diagnosed me as having an undifferentiated carcinoma tumor. This cancerous tumor is small (3.2 centimeters) and resides in the left side of my nasal pharynx. I am currently undergoing treatment at Loma Linda University Medical Center. The treatment consists of a combination of X-ray and proton radiology and has some limited side effects such as nausea, dizziness, extreme fatigue, dry mouth, sore throat, etc. The duration of the treatment is approximately three months (May to August) but could be less. Recovery will take a little longer. The prognosis for recovered health is good. There is an 85% probability for full recovery (because the tumor is small and self-contained) and for no cancer to reoccur in the next five years. After extensive tests, they found no cancer in any other areas. I will not know definitively how well the treatment is working until the physicians examine the tumor's size in early June. Though any cancerous tumor is serious, I have every reason to believe that this one will shrink and that I will be working more actively in the autumn and winter.

Finally, I want to remind those of you who have not signed up yet for the international Vineyard pastor's conference to do so soon since the deadline approaches. I am looking forward to an excellent time of ministry and renewal for leaders in the Vineyard movement.

Hope to see you next month!
Sincerely,
John Wimber.

In the last issue of *Vineyard Reflections* I began a series of articles that summarizes the vision of the Vineyard here in Anaheim. I posed the question, "Who are we and where are we going?" to our church at a time when our genetic code needed rediscovery. You may recall that I used the biblical metaphor of the body as a controlling image. The way this applies to our fellowship was diagrammed in what was affectionately dubbed around here as "The lilt man". My staff has seen it so many times they complain that they could draw it in their sleep. Exactly my point. For vision to take root, it must be from God, and you must sow it generously.

I must also remind you: these are aspects of one local church's vision. It does not adequately cover the Vineyard movement. Hopefully no single vision can. But I will have more to say on that broader subject in future issues.

This month I want to continue the series, further defining who we are and where we are going, while changing metaphors to the modern notion of a team involved in a game. The questions I want to answer in this issue are: *What game does Team Vineyard play – and how will we know if we are winning?*

TEAM VINEYARD

We sometimes forget that, regardless of our position on the team, it is important for the team to win. Furthermore, wherever you work, whether as a parking lot attendant at the stadium or a general manager, you have an interest in the team winning. If nothing else, it makes selling hot dogs more fun if the team advances toward a winning season.

How distinctives can become distortions: the "pig in the python" syndrome

The Vineyard is more than music, more than healing, more than power or prophecy, more than ministry to the poor, more than evangelism. But if you come to the Vineyard when one of these ministries is particularly emphasized, or if you thoroughly invest in one of these ministries, you might not see the whole nature of the game. You might mistake the bulge of a newly eaten pig (a new ministry emphasis) for the whole python. People often reduce the Vineyard to a particular conference theme that they enjoyed or a ministry that excites them. But the nature of the game we play is larger than any single ministry focus.

The name of the game: evangelize & equip

Though game rules occasionally modify (e.g., adding a three-point line in basketball or a designated hitter in baseball), the nature of the game remains much the same season to season. Opponents change. Teammates change. Game sites change. But the rules stay basically the same. If you see film clips of games from the 1940's, you can instantly identify and follow the game. The objectives of Team Vineyard's game remain constant, but the methods for achieving our aims and the style of game we play may change.

The name of the game for Team Vineyard is the kingdom of God. This game has two primary aims: *evangelize* and *equip*. The objectives are related processes that form a kingdom ministry continuum (see figure 1):

Kingdom Ministry Continuum

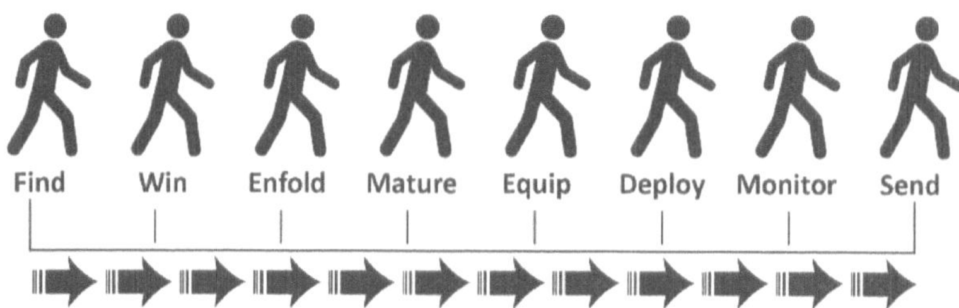

The Holy Spirit empowers us to do all these activities. Different people come – and go – at different places on the continuum. To initiate the process, we need to find and enfold people ripe for the kingdom. Jesus commissions the church to continue his kingdom ministry. Our authority and mandate to disciple the nations is clearly seen in the Great Commission text.

Commissioned to evangelize (Matthew 28:16 ff.)

After the Lord rose from the dead, an angel who looked like lightning appeared to the women at the tomb and gave instructions for the disciples to go to Galilee. The disciples *obeyed* Jesus' directive and went "to the mountain where Jesus had told them to go" (Matthew 28:16). "When they saw him, they *worshiped* [fell prostrate before] him, but some doubted" (v. 17). From a distance the eyes of faith "saw" Jesus – and believed. Others doubted. But Jesus drew closer and revealed himself more fully. Thus, the great commission springs from a context of revelation ("seeing" the risen Jesus) and worship. Our commission too is given in a similar context of worshiping the Risen Lord with the expected response of obedience to His command as recorded in Scripture.

"Then Jesus came to them and said, 'all authority in heaven and on earth has been given to me...'" (v. 18). The Father gave Jesus absolute, sovereign power and jurisdiction over all creation. This authority is the basis for continuing his kingdom works and it is the authority that directs Team Vineyard.

"Therefore go and make disciples of all nations, baptizing them..." (v.19). We must keep the *go* in the *go*spel and both go to our neighbors and the nations. From Pentecost to the *Parousia*, we are called to be worshippers of God and rescuers of men. This is a call outward to make disciples of Christ (not just decisions about Christ) and to fully initiate them into the church and into the Holy Spirit. Discipleship is following Jesus by being, believing and doing like Him. It involves not only right doctrine, but right hearts and right practices (James 2:14-26).

"[And] teaching them to obey everything I have commanded you. And surely I am with you always, to the very end of the age" (v. 20). The goal of teaching is ethical obedience and love, not intellectual stimulation; it is transformation, not just information. The Bible never divorces teaching from ethics the way the world does. Through this whole process, Jesus promises to be with us, helping to fulfill the charge He has given.

Commissioned to equip for life and ministry (Ephesians 4:1-16)

Imbedded in the Vineyard genetic code is the desire to see a team-centered ministry made up of the royal priesthood rather than a stage-centered ministry where only a few key players get into the game. This desire to equip the saints – not just the stars – is rooted firmly in the familiar Ephesians 4:11 ff. text.

In order to continue to make and nurture disciples, the risen Lord gave leadership roles (or functions) to some in order to equip the whole body to continue the kingdom ministry of Jesus.

In Ephesians 4:1-7, Paul exhorts us to keep unity. We must recognize that our unity of status, purpose and position in the universal church already exists in Christ. The reality of our "unity" (v. 3) and "oneness" (vs. 4-6) in status holds in tension the reality of our diversity of functions: "but to each one of us grace had been given as Christ apportioned it…It was he who gave some…(v. 7, 11).

In verses 11-12, the role of leadership is to equip the body for works of service. The connotation is that leaders repair and prepare the people of God, corporately and individually, for delegated tasks. The preparation is primarily functional rather than qualitative and so can be measured by asking the question, "Is it working? Is the task being accomplished?"

In verses 13-16 Paul's concern for qualitative growth or fruit can be seen. Works of service will result in "unity," "faith," and "knowledge of the Son of God… So that we become mature [complete; doing what we are designed for]" and "built up in love, as each part does its work."

Paul's argument goes like this: In Christ, you're unified. So keep your unity. The Risen Christ gives different giftings, roles of ministry functions to servant-leaders. Their purpose is to equip you to do works of service, so that you become *more* completely unified and mature, so that you can become who you are in Christ.

The implication is that leaders (chosen by God) prepare the whole body in love. God trains and equips the body through the ministry of servant-leaders so that the saints are prepared to do what each part or member is designed to do. Then quantitative *and* qualitative fruit will result. This equipping is not just for ministry, but for living the whole of one's life under the lordship of Christ, who is not only Head of the Church (v. 15) but Head over Heaven and earth (v. 10).

The Future of the Game (Matthew 16:18)

"I tell you that you are Peter, and on this rock I will build my church, and the gates of Hades will not overcome it" (Matthew 16:18).

The "gates of hell" may be defined as the strategies, lies, counsels or decisions of the enemy. The Church has the assurance that the gates of Hell will not prevail against its advance (see also 2 Corinthians 10:3-5). The church is built on the apostolic witness and confession represented by

Peter (the primary spokesman of the disciples) that Jesus is the Messiah, the Anointed One, who is the righteous fulfillment of the prophetic, priestly, and kingly types of the Old Testament (Ephesians 2:20). This witness is both a sure foundation and an advancing force in the earth: "for the reason the Son of God appeared was to destroy the devil's work" (1 John 3:8). The church is to continue working out or applying the kingdom ministry of Jesus (Matthew 28:16; John 14:12).

Though we want to avoid the extreme errors of triumphalism, dominion theology or theonomy, clearly the church has authority to take back territory by making disciples. In fact, the evidence shows that this is exactly what is happening. The percentage of bible-believing Christians as a percentage of total world population is increasing (see figure 2):

Percentage of world-wide population that is Christian

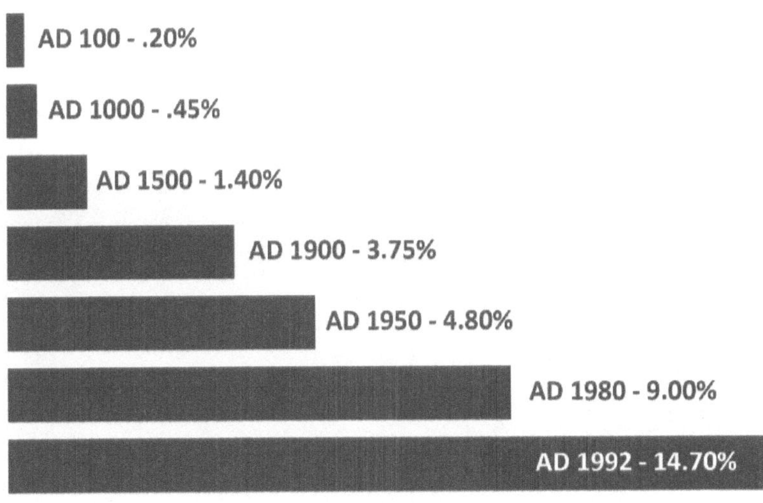

Source: Dr. David B Barrett in *Christianity Today*

God is working out his purposes in redemptive history. Remember that in John's vision, the Bridegroom marries a "big Bride" comprised if a "great multitude that no one could count, from every nation, tribe, people and language" (Revelation 7:9). In our time, we are continuing to see the fulfillment of God's promise to redeem a people from all the nations. Indeed, the center of world Christianity is moving "south and east." The center of the world's Protestants living in Asia, Africa and Latin America is also increasing (see figure 3).

Whereas fewer than 10% of the citizens of the United Kingdom attend church on any given Sunday (an increase from the "70"s), and only 7% of Australians, more than 24% of the citizens of Korea attend church regularly.

Percentage of world's Protestants living in Aisa, Africa & Latin America

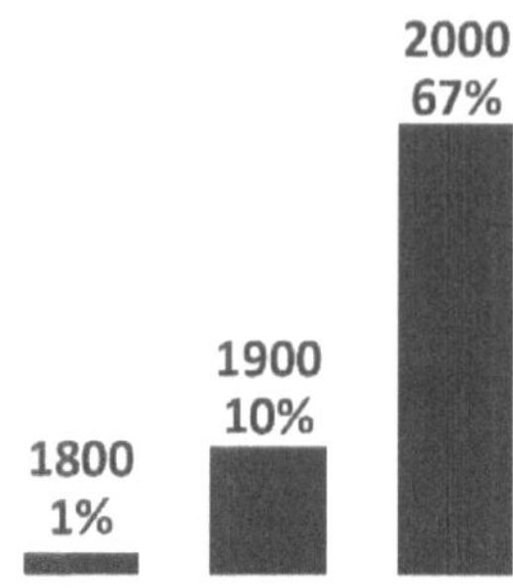

Source: Dr. Paul E Pierson in *Christianity History,* issue 36 (vol. XI No.4), p 221

Putting Up the Scoreboard

The scoreboard: measuring the progress of the game

If the name of the game for Team Vineyard is continuing the kingdom ministry of Jesus, especially in evangelism and equipping, then how do we keep score? How do we measure progress? Team Vineyard's game is scored through a combination of *quantitative* and *qualitative* sub-scores.

It is helpful to think of the team divided into two platoons. This is simply for illustration; these are not exclusive categories. Much overlap exists between the tasks of evangelism and equipping, conversion and discipleship. Indeed, sanctification is an ongoing work of conversion to the Lordship of Christ. But for our purposes it is helpful to think of Team Vineyard as having two platoons.

The "evangelism platoon" will focus on disciples – not just decisions. There are many measurable indicators worth examining. I keep track of the *quantitative* score by looking at the numbers of:

- Conversions
- Baptisms
- Those enfolded into groups
- Worship attendance
- Giving
- New, consistent givers

I measure the *qualitative* score of Team Vineyard and the work of our "evangelism platoon" more subjectively. Qualitative growth is measured by looking for such things as:

- Increased boldness and zeal in evangelism
- Widespread genuine joy and excitement in the gospel
- A winsome and contagious witness among a cross section of people
- The aroma of Christ and the presence of the Holy Spirit

I measure the "equipping platoon" by how well people are repaired and prepared for the works of service. This is done through measuring the numbers of:

- Home Fellowships/small groups
- Involvement in ministries and outreaches
- Attendance and quality of training events
- Works of healing done through the saints (physical, emotional, spiritual, relational)

I measure qualitative growth in equipping (again, more subjectively) by examining

- Obedience to the Word of God
- The fruit of the Spirit and attitude of the church
- Whether there is humble willingness to follow leadership
- Eagerness to do works of service
- Receptivity to non-Christians
- Unity, maturity, zeal, faith, hope, love, etc.

Jesus said, "the kingdom of heaven has been forcefully advancing, and forceful men lay hold of it" (Matthew 11:12). Every time we put a marriage back together, every time a kid gets converted, every time a demonized person is set free, a sick body healed, or the people of God become like Jesus, the kingdom of God advances and Team Vineyard makes measurable progress.

A good team always plays to win. A good player-coach – a Vineyard pastor – works to ensure that the teammates he leads are well prepared and play their best so that the goals of the team advance. And this requires servant-leadership.

In the other article in this issue of *Vineyard Reflections*, I share what I believe are some key leadership values and principles that make a good player-coach.

VINEYARD VALUES FOR LEADERSHIP

1. Spiritual leaders are lovers of God

The core motivation of Vineyard leaders must be to fulfill the greatest commandment which is to love God with heart, soul, mind, and strength (Mark 12:30). Psalm 42:1-2 beautifully expresses this ardent love which leaders are given as a gift from God: "As the deer pants for water, so my soul thirsts for you, O God. My soul thirsts for the living God. Where can I go and meet with God?"

2. Leaders must be saturated in the Word of God

Paul admonished Timothy to, "Do your best to present yourself to God as one approved, a workman who does not need to be ashamed and who correctly handles the word of truth" (2 Timothy 2:15). Those who lead in the Vineyard must know the Holy Scripture, the inerrant Word of God, our only infallible rule for faith, life and practice. Not only must leaders have a high view of Scripture, giving it positional or doctrinal authority, they must also allow Scripture to have functional authority in their daily lives. It is not enough to give mere mental assent to bible information. Leaders must seek formation and spiritual transformation through a deep knowledge of the Word.

3. Leaders are called to a life of service and self-sacrifice

In the Vineyard, we perceive leadership not as a position, or title, or power, or authority, or respect, or privilege but rather an obligation to service and self-sacrifice. This was Jesus' model:

> Whoever wishes to become great among you shall be your servant and whoever wishes to be first among you shall be slave to all. For even the Son of Man did not come to be served, but to serve, and to give His life as a ransom for many (Mark 10:43-45).

Both a leader and his wife should sense a call to service. This is because the family is the smallest guerrilla outpost of the kingdom and the basic building block of Christian community. Some leaders have become casualties because their spouse did not willingly share their commitment to be on the front lines.

4. Leaders must be full of the Spirit, good character, wisdom and faith

Leaders must be people of good reputation who demonstrate fullness of the holy spirit, wisdom and faith. Leaders must be trusted enough to be put in charge of designated tasks.

> But select from among you, brethren, seven men of good reputation, full of the Spirit and wisdom, whom we may put in charge of this task...and they chose Stephen, a man full of faith and of the holy Spirit (Acts 6:3,5).

Leaders must be capable and respected, mature in the faith, tested in character with proven ministry ability.

> An overseer, then, must be above reproach, the husband of one wife, temperate, prudent, respectable, hospitable, able to teach, not addicted to wine or pugnacious, but gentle, uncontentious, free from the love of money. He must be one who manages his own household well, keeping his children under control with all dignity...not a new convert...and he must have a good reputation with those outside the church (1 Timothy 3:2-7).

Mature leaders are trustworthy. They resist being bribed or bought. Their spiritual immune system is healthy enough to fight off the infection of greed that so pervades our culture. "Select out of all the people able men who fear God, men of truth, those who hate dishonest gain" (Exodus 18:21a).

5. Wise leaders are accountable, able to accept reproof, and willing to repent

Willingness to be judged by strict standards and to accept reproof is a sure sign of a maturing leader. "Let not many of you become teachers, my brethren, knowing that as such we shall incur a stricter judgment" (James 3:1).

Perhaps no biblical leader demonstrated this accountability to other leaders with readiness to repent more completely than King David. David made horrendous violations of God's Holy Law when he coveted Bathsheba. He was guilty of adultery, murder and a cover-up – but he repented so well! Though his repentance did not eliminate all the consequences of sin, in David's case God ameliorated a more severe judgment:

> Then David said to Nathan, "I have sinned against the Lord." And Nathan said to David, "The Lord also has taken away your sin; you shall not die" (2 Samuel 13:13).

6. Leaders who are true shepherds have a God-given love for people

Remember the Lord's restoring words to Peter after his miserable failure and lack of loyalty? "Jesus said to him, 'Tend my sheep'" (John 21:17). But leaders who persist in denying the Lord end up like malevolent wolves among the sheep. The Lord has harsh words for these:

> Woe to the shepherds of Israel who only take care of themselves! Should not shepherds take care of the flock! I am against the shepherds and will hold them accountable for my flock. I will remove them from tending the flock so that the shepherds can no longer feed themselves. I will rescue my flock from their mouths, and it will no longer be food for them (Ezekiel 34:2;10).

7. Good leaders are humble team players

A leader must be willing to be "team player". Good leaders make it their aim to equip their associates so that they succeed in fulfilling their calling. A leader who understands Team Vineyard is secure enough to let others play what would normally be his position – even if the new guy does not play it as well. Team players are thankful – not jealous – when God raises up a star player to lead the team for a season; they understand that when one player shines the *whole* team advances.

> Do nothing from selfishness or empty conceit, but with humility of mind let each of you regard one another as more important than himself; do not merely look out for your own personal interests, but also for the interests of others (Philippians 2:3-4).

LEADING AND DEVELOPING FOOT SOLDIERS

August/September 1993, Volume 1, Issue 3

Many of you have inquired about my health. Thank you for all your prayers and encouragement. I have been so affirmed and strengthened by your concern during this difficult time. The radiation and proton treatment is over now – hallelujah! I will not know definitely for some time whether the treatment was totally successful in eradicating all potential cancerous growths, but I have every reason to believe it was. For the next few months I will continue to rest and will work periodical as I regain my strength. Carol and I thank you again for all your prayers and many kindnesses over the past four months.

In this issue of *Vineyard Reflections*, I look to Jesus' pattern of leadership development as the paradigm for the Vineyard to follow. The Church is in desperate need of servant-leadership! I have attempted to follow His model in my own church and across the Vineyard movement. My hope is that this issue helps you, in a small way, to lead and develop the foot soldiers in your own church so that the harvest of these last days may be brought in.

In the gospels, we see the Father drawing followers (simple fishermen, a tax man, etc.) to Jesus in order to redeem and empower them as witnesses of the resurrection and messengers of the gospel. God chose apostles as unique vessels through whom he displayed His glory. The role they played in redemptive history will never be repeated.

So, when I consider Jesus' model of leadership development, I am careful to remember that He is the Divine Son of God and the Father's treasure. My meager attempt to follow His disciple-making model is woefully incomplete. Though we are not discipling apostles, we are still in the business of leading and developing humble foot soldiers, men and women who obediently follow their Leader. God is *still* making disciples and astonishing the world by using "unschooled, ordinary men" (Acts 4:13) - like you and me - to make His name famous throughout the earth.

With these cautions in mind, then, there is nonetheless much wisdom to mine from Jesus' model that we can employ today.

JESUS SELECTED

Come and see

> Turning around Jesus saw them [Andrew and another of the Baptist's disciples] and asked, "What do you want?" They said, "Rabbi (which means Teacher) where are you staying?" "Come," he replied, "and you will *see* [in John's gospel, literally *and* spiritually]. So they went and *saw* where he was staying, and spent the day with him" (John 1:38-39).

Jesus *recruited* leaders – but differently than the world does! The normal pattern in the Ancient Near East was for disciples to choose their rabbi. But Jesus chose his disciples from those who were drawn to him by the Father. The disciples responded as their hearts were stirred and as the Holy Spirit enabled them to perceive – at least in part – that *their* Rabbi was unique.

Jesus recognized the innermost desires of those drawn to Him. His question to them is a loaded one, "What do you want?" Their response displayed their hearts: "Where are you staying?" They desired to be with Jesus and be taught be this amazing Rabbi. Jesus still says, "Come and *see*" to all those who are drawn to Him.

We need to ask the same question Jesus did of young leaders whom God gives us to develop: "What do you want?" Our task of developing disciples requires that they come and see Jesus and remain there with Him. I cannot stress enough that our job is not to make disciples of ourselves – we are far too flawed for that! Our job is to help them come to Jesus in ever-greater dependence and see Him for who He is. Jesus is *the* Teacher, *the* Mentor, and *the* Disciple-maker. To follow anyone else is idolatry.

In practical terms, *come and see* is surely the best method of training. We need to say to young leaders, "Come alongside; come with me and take a look. Do what I do. See what I see." We extend an "invitation to the party" and to relationship to those who are drawn towards us by the Spirit.

And when we do, we often see the ministry of Jesus develop more maturely in them. This call to "come and see" is not a call into a vacuum, but into a vital ministry that is in progress.

From time to time over the years, I have called a Vineyard leader up and said, "I want you to go with me to such-and such country," or "I want you to do thus-and-so with me." Usually they're startled. The invitation is given at the initiative of the Spirit. The Spirit will speak to my heart, "Call that person – tell them to come." People who don't know this pattern are meanwhile waiting impatiently thinking: "Why doesn't Wimber ever call me? I've got a solid church. I'm a good teacher." They don't understand that I am not operating on the basis of one's visibility, gifts or ministry. I am operating on the basis that there are some men who are supposed to be drawn close to me at certain times, and some who are not. And when the time comes that the Spirit leads, then I will call – but I will not call until then. There is safety in that for younger leaders. I have made the mistake of drawing people alongside without the Spirit's leading – and it destroyed them. They just could not handle the visibility and the "success." So it is good if you do not get a call out of season to do ministry that the Holy Spirit is not initiating.

Jesus selected from those drawn to him by the Father through the Spirit

> All that the Father gives me will come to me…No one can come to me unless the Father who sent me draws him…No one can come to me unless the Father has enabled him…Have I not chosen you, the Twelve? Yet one of you is a devil! (John 6:44; 65; 70; cf. 15:16; 17:6; Matthew 4:19).

The Father still draws us to Jesus today, though of course our role is different from that of the apostles. So just as these verses in John provide information on the conversion process today, I believe there are contemporary lessons for leadership development that we can garner from Jesus' example.

Though I never equate the purpose for the kind of "drawing" that we read of in John with my own experience of developing leaders, from time to time I have had distinct impressions from the Lord where He speaks to my heart and says, "I am giving you this one." This leading doesn't mean literally, MINE. It means HIS – for HIS purposes in the Vineyard movement. However, we have a vested partnership together under the Lord's direction in the Vineyard. In that sense, the Lord says, "This one is yours." I learned to trust that voice; hundreds of leaders were developed that way. The ones drawn are the ones I choose. So far, in the nine years of my leadership in the Vineyard movement, I have only asked one person to come into the Vineyard. Of the 1400 or so "ordained" Vineyard pastors, I only invited one to leave what he was doing and come be with us. The Holy Spirit drew all the others who have come.

We must recognize that young leaders are drawn to pastors for a variety of reasons. Some are looking for father. Some seek mentors who can train them. Others are drawn with no well-thought-out reason at all; they simply want to hang out. Some with a particular nascent spiritual gift draw towards those who have that gift and were more mature in that area. In his helpful book, *The Making of a Leader*, Fuller professor Bobby Clinton calls this the "like-attracts-like-pattern." Older leaders should readily recognize when the Lord sends or "draws" a younger leader to them to mold: they *may* have a similar gifting that needs developing.

From crowd to core

Following Jesus' model, the lesson for leadership development is clear. Recruit those the Father is giving you. If they are not drawn to follow you, then you are not their leader. Furthermore, if you recruit through coercion and arm-twisting then you have to motivate them to perform the role for which you recruited them. As a rule, I never choose anyone for a leadership role who is not already tested, eager for more training, and drawn by the Father. I liken this to courtship: rarely does a man propose marriage to a woman not knowing what her answer will be. He expects – based on a growing relationship – an enthusiastic, "Yes!"

Jesus did kingdom ministry that attracted crowds: "News about him spread all over Syria…" (Matthew 4:24). From the crowds, he selected those the Father was giving him. They came on the basis of revelation – they saw (in part) who he was. He was then progressively revealed to His disciples. And He gave oral exams to test their progress! " Who do you say that I am?" (Matthew 16:13-20; Mark 8:27-29; Luke 9:18-20).

Recruiting foot soldiers who are leaders is always initiated by the Father, they are drawn by the Holy Spirit, chosen by Jesus. Jesus still asks recruits, "Who do you say I am?" And he still progressively reveals more of himself to them – and to us – each day.

JESUS TRAINED

Jesus modeled kingdom life and kingdom ministry in public

Jesus modeled kingdom life and kingdom ministry in public before His disciples:

> Jesus went throughout Galilee, teaching in their synagogues, preaching the good news of the kingdom, and healing every disease and sickness among the people. News about him spread all over Syria, and people brought to him all who were ill with various diseases, those suffering severe pain, the demon-possessed, those having seizures, and the paralyzed, and he healed them. Large crowds from Galilee, the Decapolis, Jerusalem, Judea and the region across the Jordan followed him (Matthew 4:23-25).

After modeling in public, Jesus clarified His purposes in private: "When he was alone, the Twelve and the others around him asked him about the parables. He told them, 'The secret of the kingdom of God has been given to you. But to those on the outside everything is said in parables'" (Mark 4:10-11). In this interaction with the disciples, we see a dynamic in which Jesus ministers and the disciples wonder, "Gee, what did he mean by that?" Jesus then pulls them aside and interacts with them privately.

Jesus observed the disciples in ministry and then debriefed privately

Jesus let his recruits "do the stuff" within proximity of Him and under His supervision. This, again, was followed by debriefing in private. The healing of the demonized boy in Matthew 17:14-21 illustrates this pattern. A man approached Jesus, knelt, and begged for mercy for his demonized son. He said,

> I brought him to your disciples, but they could not heal him… Jesus rebuked the demon and it came out of the boy and he was healed from that moment. Then the disciples came to Jesus in private and asked, "Why couldn't we drive it out?" He replied, "Because you have so little faith" (Matthew 17:16; 19-20). [In Mark's account, he adds, "…this kind only comes out with prayer." Some manuscripts add "and fasting" (Mark 9:29)].

The disciples were confused: "It was working the other day? We would say the right thing and the demons come out. How come it didn't work today?" My suspicion is that they relied on the anointing of the previous day or on same formulaic approach.

The kingdom ministry principle illustrated in this story is clear: you have to have fresh anointing every day. You cannot rely on past victories and you cannot turn ministering in the Spirit into a *charis-magic technique* where you say it the same way you did last time. You must rely on the Lord each time. We deepen our faith and reliance on Him through prayer and fasting.

Learning to rely on the Lord for each ministry situation comes through on-the-job training that is informal or non-formal and differs significantly from most schooling-based training models in use today. This is not to imply that formal education is unimportant - we need all the help we can get! However, for effective leadership development and ministry training we need to employ training models that resemble what we see in Jesus' life: Jesus observed the disciples minister and then he debriefed in private.

Jesus sent them on short-term trips alone and then they reported back

Take time to read Luke 10:1-24, where Jesus sends out the seventy-two. Notice that Jesus let the disciples "do the stuff" alone and then they reported the results back to him. Here we see another example of informal and non-formal training. You don't see Jesus sitting down with a primer and saying, "Let's memorize Isaiah 53 today and we'll discuss its theological significance in relationship to me." Jesus trained by example. And of course, He did explain the Scriptures as well, e.g., His interaction with the disciples on the Emmaus Road (Luke 24:13 ff.).

The point is this: Jesus trained through personal interaction – not a sterile classroom or schooling model. Jesus trained using dialogue, by questioning and administering what were in effect oral exams. He trained by observing His disciples doing kingdom ministry and then corrected them based on that observation. Jesus' disciples lived and ministered with their rabbi, observing His whole life.

JESUS DEPLOYED

Jesus modeled the kind of kingdom ministry that He wanted to impart and authorized His recruits with His power and authority.

> When Jesus had called the Twelve together, he gave them power and authority to drive out demons and to cure diseases, and he sent them out to preach the kingdom of God and to heal the sick (Luke 9:1-2; see also Matthew 28:19; Acts 1:8).

Jesus modeled kingdom ministry and sent them to a *specific people group:* "Do not go among the Gentiles or enter any town of the Samaritans. Go rather to the lost sheep of Israel" (Matthew 10:6).

Jesus modeled kingdom ministry and gave them a *specific message:* "As you go, preach *this* message: "The Kingdom of heaven is near." Heal the sick, raise the dead, cleanse those who have leprosy, drive out demons. Freely you have received, freely give" (Matthew 10:6-8).

I believe we're still to preach this message.

Jesus modeled kingdom ministry and told them how to *specifically finance outreach:*

> Do not take a purse or bag or sandals… Stay in that house, eating and drinking whatever they give you, for the worker deserves his wages. Do not move around from house to house. When you enter a town and are welcomed, eat what is set before you (Luke 10:4; 7-8).

Later on, He modified some of these guidelines. But for this particular ministry trip, there were certain policies extant. He gave them *specific guidance.* In Matthew's corollary account, we read that they were told not to go to the Samaritans and not to go, in effect, to the Gentiles, but to go home and minister among their own people.

When Jesus deploys us to do kingdom ministry, he not only gives authority and power to make and nature disciples, but specific instructions to obey.

JESUS MONITORED

Jesus monitored the disciples' heart attitudes, motivations and ambitions:

> Jesus called them together and said, "You know that the rulers of the Gentiles lord it over them, and their high officials exercise authority over them. Not so with you. Instead, whoever wants to become great among you must be your servant, and whoever wants to be first must be your slave – just as the Son of man did not come to be served but to serve, and to give his life as a ransom for many" (Matthew 20:25-28).

> But you are not to be called "rabbi" for you have only one master and you are all brothers. And do not call anyone on earth "father," for you have one father, and he is in heaven. Nor are you to be called "teacher", for you have one teacher, the Christ. The greatest among you will be your servant. (Matthew 23:8-11).

> Now that I, your lord and teacher, have washed your feet, you also should wash one another's feet. I have set you an example that you should do as I have done for you. I tell you the truth, no servant is greater than his master, nor is a messenger greater than the one who sent him. Now that you know these things, you will be blessed if you do them (John 13:14-17).

The contrast between the mentality of worldly leaders and Jesus shocks the mind. Jesus humbled himself and "made himself nothing, taking on the very nature of a servant" (Philippians 2:7). From the bosom of the Father and the splendor of heaven, Jesus stooped to a feed-trough cradle and an outlaw's execution. His goal was to serve – not to be served. In dark contrast, worldly leaders see co-workers as underlings, as chattel, as people to use who give service to them to get their aims accomplished. Jesus turns that upside down saying, "You've got to be a servant." He separates the model and mentality of the world of the Gentiles from what the Father wants.

He could just as easily apply this teaching to the Pharisees or the Sadducees because they adopted the Gentile mentality. But here he speaks to His own. If you are going to follow Him, then render humble service with an awareness that if the Lord exalts you it's the Lord's to give *and* the Lord's to take away. Like coins in His pocket, He can spend us any way he wants.

Jesus monitored, restored and nurtured the disciples when they failed. In His interaction with Thomas in a post-resurrection appearance we see Jesus' compassion towards a leader who wavered in his faith (John 20:24-29). In His tender interaction with Peter in another post-resurrection appearance, we see Jesus' heart of compassion for a leader who wavered in his commitment (John 21:15-23). Notice that He is not exasperated with either Thomas or Peter. He is willing to pardon lack of loyalty, unbelief, confusion and weakness. His restoring gentleness led them through shame to a deeper repentance and dependence. In the case of Thomas, we hear one of the most profound expressions of faith in the Bible: "My Lord and my God!" My hunch is that Thomas spoke these words from a broken heart and through quivering lips as he put his finger into the wounds of the Master.

In Revelation chapters two through three, we see Jesus monitoring local churches from the right hand of the Father. I believe he still monitors His disciples and His church today. Like Peter and Thomas and the seven churches in Revelation, we *all* fail in our devotion to Him: we can never love and loyally serve Jesus enough. We must trust that He will have compassion on us as well. If we are going to follow Jesus and make and nurture disciples and plant churches, then we must show compassion to co-workers in the kingdom who waver in their loyalty and commitment to Him.

JESUS NURTURED

When Jesus said, "Come and see – come and be with me" it was a permanent commitment, a covenant on His part to be beside the disciples. Jesus promised that he would continue to be present with His followers: "And surely I am with you *always*, to the very end of the age" (Matthew 28:20).

Jesus sent the Paraclete to continue to be alongside His followers. He is an Advisor – a Mentor – a Counselor who strengthens and encourages disciples by being an ever-present Advocate and Ally. The Holy Spirit thus gives ongoing guidance and empowers the preaching and teaching of the word so that it is alive. The Spirit reveals the truth and opens our heart to receive it: "I will ask the Father, and he will give you another Counselor to be with you forever…The Holy Spirit, who the Father will send in my name, will teach you all things and will remind you of everything I have said to you" (John 14:16; 25-26; cf. 15:26; 16:7-15).

The Holy Spirit impregnates and fills the church. He is the progenitor of the second birth (John 3:5-8) and the One who brings enlightenment to the soul (Ephesians 1:17-18). He makes us more and more like Jesus (2 Corinthians 3:18; Galatians 5:22-23; Romans 8:29). In all this work of saving and sanctifying and empowering, He brings great honor to the Father and the Son by revealing their glory.

Ultimately, we must encourage those foot soldiers we disciple into a deeper dependence on the Holy Spirit. That maddeningly desperate prayer of "Oh God! Oh God! Oh God!" is a good place to remain. Then the Holy Spirit can glorify the Son through the clay vessels of our lives and ministries. If we model this lifestyle of dependence on the Holy Spirit and "do only what the Father is doing," and if we make *His* name famous – not ours – then we will serve and develop young leaders well.

If the ability to love and nurture young leaders is like a jar of peanut butter, then my jar is usually empty! Since our own resource to nurture is so skimpy, we have no other choice but to bring them – again and again – to Jesus.

Jesus Will Reward According to One's Stewardship

Judgment and rewards have both a present reality and a dimension of deeper, future consummation.

Many leaders make a fundamental error of confusing the gift of encouragement with rewards for service rendered. If the people whom the Holy Spirit draws to us and whom we assemble do not understand the difference between encouragement and rewards, they will not stay motivated to serve for very long. Encouragement is a wonderful spiritual gift. God, however, postpones the ultimate reward for a life of servant-leadership until we see Him face to face.

Pastors "pay" their people in a variety of ways (attention, periodic recognition, retreats, parties, token gifts imbued with meaning) and this is a wise form of encouragement. We must also build up awareness in our people that service rendered *now* unto the King pays incredible "dividends" later in heaven. Thus, the encouragement we give today is like a token or a down payment of what is to come. Deferred "payment" is a difficult truth for baby boomers and young people to receive, because in our culture we swim in a sea of instant gratification.

When someone comes to me angry and upset and they say, "I've worked in the children's ministry for ten years and you've never recognized my service." I respond in the following way: "I know you work hard here for Jesus. I appreciate that a lot. Thanks for your humble service. Service to God is not a road easily traveled is it? If you think it is hard in the children's ministry you should see what some of your leaders go through. For that matter, you might consider what your brothers and sisters suffer in other countries for the service they render to Jesus. Jesus never promised to make it nice; His life wasn't very comfortable. Remember: it's Him you're serving – not me. And He will reward you. Now how can I make your time of service to Jesus in this life more fruitful and meaningful? Let's take the journey of service together."

A gentle and truthful answer like that will usually turn away wrath and focus them on whom they really serve when they change diapers in the children's ministry. For this to occur, you have to really believe it yourself, model it, and communicate this truth in love – without blinking.

His return is the greatest reward of all!

The best way to build a heart for service among leaders is to model it *and* teach it. I suggest that you periodically review these texts with the foot soldiers you want to develop.

The judgment seat of Christ [which may differ from the "great white throne" judgment of the unsaved dead (Revelation 20:5,7)] includes judgment of:

- All nations (Matthew 25:32).

- All Christians (Romans 14:10b-12; 2 Corinthians 5:10).

- All leaders (1 Corinthians 3:10-15).

- All angels (Jude 6; 2 Peter2:4).

His evaluation will include *rewards* for good stewards who are faithful and who persevere until the end:

- Train – and run – in such a way as to get the prize (1 Corinthians

9:24-27).

- Pour out your life like a drink offering, fight the good fight, finish the race, keep the faith – and then receive the crown of righteousness which the Lord, the righteous Judge, will award to you on that day (2 Timothy 4:6-8).

- To elders: "shepherd God's flock, serve as overseers – not because you must, but because you are willing; not greedy for money, but eager to serve; not lording it over those entrusted to you, but be examples. And when the Chief Shepherd appears, you will receive the crown of glory that will never fade away" (1 Peter 5:1-4).

Above all, remember that His return is the greatest reward of all!

HOW TO TRAIN FOOT SOLDIERS

In summary, Jesus is still training disciples to *be* like Him and *do* kingdom ministry. People hear about or see this ministry as God draws them towards Himself. Some come just for the food. Others just for miracles. Still others come to antagonize, like the Pharisees of old, because they find the whole thing suspect. But there are a group of people – disciples – who are truly drawn to Jesus through the clay vessels of our lives and ministries. We then must recognize what the Father is doing and cooperate with Him in His process of making and nurturing disciples.

This requires that we train through modeling. Often, they will not understand kingdom living, so we must pull them aside and clarify it privately. We may also need to confront bad attitudes and correct motivations and the ambition that flares up in their spirit and surfaces in unfruitful behavior. We must not only develop skilled and anointed foot soldiers but ones of sound character as well.

When God leads, we send them out with helpful directions on where to go and what to do. When they return, we use a feedback loop to bring deeper correction and training, reminding them to rejoice not in today's victories but in the consummation of our salvation on that Great Day that awaits all those who are found in Christ. There is usually testing and sifting – but God forgives and restores.

Finally, we continue to nurture. With some who are leaders of leaders, there comes a time when we send them out with blessing. And the cycle of leadership development, of training and leading foot soldiers, goes on. Our promise is that He is always with us – and with them – and our hope is in the reward of seeing God's glory fill the earth.

THE VINEYARD MOVEMENT

Steering A Course Between Chaos & Traditional Denomination-alism

October/November 1993 Volume 1, Issue 4

SUMMARY

The Association of Vineyard Churches – for better or worse – is a denomination. We see this primarily in the area of relational structure that provides accountability, cohesion, and encouragement.

I want to use this space to accomplish several things. I want to provide some definition of what we're trying to build in terms of AVC. Why we're trying to build it, and what are the guiding organization values that are guiding us as we build.

Admittedly, talk of the Vineyard as a denomination causes distress for some because the idea of denomination carries with it two negative pieces of baggage: sectarianism and institutionalism. These two "isms" are real threats to the vitality and effectiveness of the Vineyard movement. The antidote to sectarianism is to exalt Christ above all human structures. The antidote to institutionalization is to constantly seek renewal within the structures we create.

For the past thirty years, serving Jesus has been the primary goal of my life. Forming a new denomination has never been a goal. After all there's already at least 23,000 denominations in the world.

If asked whether the Vineyard has become a denomination, I would have to answer: If you mean do the churches across North America and over a dozen foreign countries called "Vineyard" have more *structure* than they did a decade ago, the answer is yes; there is more organizational and relational structure.

Again, I didn't set out to create a new denomination. God put the Vineyard in my hand. Kenn Gulliksen started this movement, handed it to me, and God told me he was right in doing it. So, I'm trying to make the best of what was handed to me.

By 1984, the number of Vineyards was growing rapidly. We made the decision to formalize the structure that had evolved. Until then, we really worked under Vineyard Ministries International. But VMI was a renewal organization, so we formed AVC for church planting and to provide oversight. Historically, we probably became a denomination when we incorporated AVC, appointed Regional Overseers, called a board of directors, and began ordaining ministers.

And because 99 percent of the churches in the Association of Vineyard Churches have the word "Vineyard" in their name, then because of the unified identity, yes, we've become a denomination.

Admittedly I still have mixed feelings about that.

Interestingly, there wasn't much criticism of what we did in 1984 until 1992. The criticisms reflected certain assumptions:

- Denominations are evil.

- God will lift his hand.

- We will be controlled.

But reading the New Testament, and church history, I can't find any alternative, since I see structure as necessary to growth and survival. Yes, there is some control with organization. But remember, we're in spiritual warfare. Would you rather be a lone soldier battalion? By being in the Army, you trade some personal freedom for the protection and encouragement of comrades in arms. Most pastors I've talked to recognize the wisdom in having some accountability structure. When I joined the movement, I had to yield some control to others.

Ten years ago I talked about explorers and homesteaders in the Vineyard. I said at that time that explorers are radicals and they usually spin out, because they can't stand the containment of an organization. Explorers seek adventure. Homesteaders, on the other hand, build community, leaving a heritage for future generations. Homesteaders use, need, and create structure; by the way, they also create wealth!

A few "explorers" who started out with the movement have not stayed with it, because as they saw encroachment of more structure, they resisted control.

THE ROLE OF ORGANIZATION

Some believe organization inhibits the work of the Holy Spirit. Less organization makes more room for the Spirit's leading. Yet even in the primitive church of Acts, the leadership recognized a need for organization. Therefore, deacons were appointed to deal with certain practical matters of benevolence, while the Twelve chose to "give [their] attention to prayer and the ministry of the word" (Acts 6:4).

Structure was undoubtedly important to the effectiveness of the New Testament ministry. In Paul's Pastoral letters, we read of church officers called "overseer" and "deacon" (1 Timothy 3:1,2,12; Titus 1:7). Paul obviously recognized the role of authority figures in each community (1 Corinthians 16:15-17; Galatians 6:6; 1 Thessalonians 5:12).

As Johnson points out in *The Writings of the New Testament,*

> sociological studies of intentional communities in every era suggest that they do not survive for decades without strong structures for decision making and social control; ...structure and charism, in fact, often coexist rather than follow each other. [7]

I slightly disagree with Johnson on the latter part of this statement, in that I have said for years that structure follows life. As an *organism,* the Vineyard needs *organization.* Compare two life forms: an amoeba and a human body. Which can accomplish more? Certainly, the more highly structured human body, if it is alive. The key: life and relationship with God, not organization or lack thereof.

---

[7]Luke T. Johnson, *The Writings of the New Testament: An Interpretation,* Philadelphia: Fortress Press, 1986, 385.

To father children, and not take responsibility for raising them is considered uncivilized. To make new converts, and not set them into a church, is unthinkable. Likewise, to plant new churches, and not band them together and mature them is irresponsible.

That's why I'm for structured relationship among churches with a shared sense of calling. I'm proposing we introduce structures carefully, always aware that the *organization is subservient to the organism.* We must make alterations whenever the organization thwarts the growth of the organism.

AVC ORGANIZATIONAL VALUES

Beginning in the 1960s as a result of the hippie movement, many young people were challenging the notion of formal marriage contracts to find something more pure in the way of relationship. It was interesting doing weddings in those days. I would sit down with young people and ask "What is it you want?" Often what they wanted reflected God's design for marriage, but they thought that having a ceremony and a license would somehow restrict the possibility of that. I think that describes the feeling of some Vineyard pastors as they've watched the development of organizational structure.

No one wants to join something they must be subservient to. We want to join something that will help us realize our potential. In the past, when pastors have asked "What are we building here? What am I signing up for?" I would talk about the Vineyard as something that would help leaders do more *together* than they could do independently.

Basically, we have tried to build an organization that will give people latitude and freedom, yet also give them the security that comes from the appropriate amount of structure and authority.

This organization ought to be propelled by an honest desire to serve God the best we can in this lifetime. I believe that desire can be expressed in five organizational values I hope will guide us in the future.

Minimal bureaucracy
Whatever organizational structure we build should be built on people who remain in pastoral positions. At present, only Bob Fulton gives full-time

governance as the national coordinator. Once you begin freeing large numbers of people whose only role is to govern a movement, that seems to set up a situation where bureaucrats become less focused on the original mission and become more devoted to self-preservation. A hardening of the structure is inevitable. Hopefully by maintaining a system where those giving governance are themselves on the front lines, we can avoid losing the vision in the process of carrying it out.

This approach has been burdensome for all of us, even me. I serve AVC in addition to serving a local church. I suppose in time we will probably release others to serve full-time as needed, but if we remain committed to the value of minimal bureaucracy, I think we will have a more viable structure.

The importance of relationship

Developing relationships among leaders who like to be together, work together, and get things done is primary to maintaining a highly relational movement. If we do that, we have the pleasure of serving God with our peers, equals, friends, and colleagues. That ought to satisfy all of us long-term.

Holding these friendships together are the kingdom values, goals, theology, and practices we share in common. Though we are not all equally gifted in any area of ministry, we *value* one another's distinctive contributions.

Local church autonomy

If the Vineyard is a denomination, some might worry that Anaheim will begin issuing edicts that prescribe what a Vineyard church should be like to create uniformity. That's not what I want. I want the local church to freely express itself within the constraints of the values, theology, and genetic code of the Vineyard. If a Vineyard in Valparaiso, Indiana has the genetic code, values, and theology, in a general sense, it doesn't have to be a clone of a Vineyard in Venice, California. In some ways the Indiana Vineyard will reflect a Midwestern cultural setting, and that's okay. We have to be careful about making judgments ("That's not Vineyard") because future Vineyards – especially those in a cross-cultural context – may have little *outward* similarity to Vineyards as we know them in say,

Southern California.

But it's also fair to say that wherever I went and started a church, certain kinds of things would be characteristic of that church. And I think that those who have been trained under me and by me would have very recognizable churches. They would have a "Vineyard" resemblance, without necessarily having an identical personality.

I've said in the past, they ought to be healing the sick, casting out demons, worshipping God, and teaching the bible. As long as the genetic code is intact, I don't care if they wear doilies on their head, or uniforms to church. I would prefer they do not do that, but if they want to that's their business.

AVC wants each Vineyard to have local autonomy. We want them to own their own property and have their own polity. We've given guidelines, of what we think works best, but we want them to be free to do what they need to do, to express their individuality. So, if they want a board of deacons, let them have a board of deacons. We do not want and have not set up a bureaucratic system that controls the local church.

Spiritual versus Legal Authority

We've not put structure together that gives us legal jurisdiction in the local church. We've assumed that if we have spiritual authority, we don't need legal authority. And if we don't have spiritual authority, we don't want legal authority. I don't want to govern people who don't want governance from me. I don't want to bring correction or direction to people who don't recognize my spiritual authority to do so.

If a local church or pastor won't take counsel from us, then they're not under our authority, and they need to change their name, and become identified with someone they can submit to. I assume people will come and go in the Vineyard. Maybe they'll "outgrow" the Vineyard. Maybe they'll see new horizons and want to get into other things. That's okay with me. That doesn't mean we're superior, and they're inferior. It means we're different. It should be no harder for a church to extricate itself as it was to enter the Vineyard. We're not going to try and keep people in the Vineyard who don't want to be. Therefore, I'm not looking for a polity structure that would give me or anyone else legal control over a local church.

Decentralization

Decentralization wasn't a guiding principle as the movement began to organize, but it is now. As the movement grew in maturity, I realized I needed to change the way I did business with the leadership and treat them in a more collegiate fashion by giving them a greater voice in decision-making.

When children are small, a parent will be much more directive than when the kids are in their 20s and 30s. And that's been true in the Vineyard's life. When I used to sit on board meetings where everyone was in their early 30s with babies in their lap, I was in a different place as a leader than I am now when some board members are grandpas like me. They have a little gray hair in their beards, and they've learned a few things. So, with the maturation of the Vineyard leadership, I'm recognizing and giving them greater voice in everything we do.

THE THREAT OF SECTARIANISM

Calling the Vineyard a denomination sends up red flags for some of our brethren. The word "denomination" denotes sectarianism, separatism, and factionalism, and a distorted view of the unity of the Body of Christ. Therefore, it's valuable to remind ourselves that the unity of the church is an important theme in the bible, beginning in the Old Testament.

Unity

Old Testament

Genesis records God creating by his will the world as an ordered unity, in which all creatures satisfy the Creator's purposes. "God saw all that he had made, and it was very good" (Genesis 1:31). When Adam and Eve sinned and alienated themselves from God and from one another, God acted to bring about mankind's reconciliation. God ordained a covenant with the Hebrew people and united the various tribes into one religious nation, Israel, bridging the alienation between God and humans and reconciling his people. Ancient Judaism, therefore, stood on the truth of the one people of God. Their faith in the oneness of God (Yahweh) expressed itself in their unity. Psalm 133:1 states: "How good and pleasant it is when brothers live together in unity!" Their mission was to preserve the faithfulness and unity of all God's people and to prepare them for the fulfillment of the kingdom of God.

New Testament

The concept of unity is pivotal to the gospel of Jesus Christ and the teachings of his Apostles. All who confess Jesus as Lord and Savior come together in a new community: the church. All New Testament writers presume that to be "in Christ" is to belong to one fellowship (Greek: *koinonia*). Jesus mandated this unity when at the Last Supper he interceded for his disciples and all those who believe in him "that all of them may be one, Father, just as you are in me and I am in you. May they also be in us so that the world may believe that you have sent me" (John 17:21). This unity manifested itself in the miracle of Pentecost (Acts 2) and the historic Council of Jerusalem (Acts 15), that worked out conflicts between Jewish and Gentile Christians.

The early church however was not entirely free from many tensions and conflicts that threatened unity. For example, tensions arose between Jewish Christian churches, and between Paul and the Judaizers.

Even with diversity and conflicts historian Paul A. Crow notes

> the early Christians remained of "one accord", visibly sharing the one Eucharist, accepting the ministries of the whole church, reaching out beyond their local situation in faith and witness with a sense of the universal community that held all Christians together.

As Paul taught the Ephesians, God's supreme purpose is "to unite all things in him [Christ], things in heaven and things on earth" (Ephesians 1:10).

Through centuries of sectarianism and fracturing, most Christians today allow differences to divide rather than appreciating and celebrating our distinctives and diversity. Our relations as an extended family are typically clouded by distrust, and disrespect.

I want to relate to the whole body of Christ. Biblical unity to me flows from learning to love what Jesus loves - learning to love the whole body of Christ. When I cross paths with a brother or sister in a group or denomination different from my own, I want to fellowship based on our shared allegiance to the Lord Jesus Christ. I want to see the Vineyard work through this question: "How can brethren major on the things we agree on, ignore the things we disagree on, and move forward together?" In my opinion, this applies inside and outside the Vineyard.

Last year, the Anaheim Vineyard hosted a fund-raising concert for Victory Outreach. Victory Outreach is a dynamic movement that has had a tremendous amount of success starting community-based drug rehab programs and planting churches among Latino communities. They reflect a Pentecostal heritage, but we were delighted to work *with* them, even though we aren't totally *like* them. Yet we agree on one thing: the world needs Jesus. And I must say Victory Outreach is effectively sharing Jesus with its part of the world.

DEFINITIONS

Are denominations in conflict with unity? Before I answer that, let's define some terms.

A *denomination*, according to Webster, is a class or society of individuals called by the same name: especially a religious group or a community of believers called by the same name. For example, the Presbyterian Church in America represents one denomination of Christians.

In an ideal world, there would be no denominations. But we can't turn the clock back on five hundred years of history. In contrast to denomination, *denominationalism* is the emphasizing of denominational differences to the point of being narrowly exclusive. A synonym is *sectarianism.* Denominationalism promotes one denomination over the rest of the Church and asserts that "our group is better than any other group."

I can make my peace with the reality of different denominations, but I totally reject the idea of *denominationalism.*

Recently I met with a group of Baptist pastors from Scandinavia. I'm not a Baptist, but I love them, because they're my brothers. We have relationship, fraternity, and fellowship. I am a Christian, and so are they, but I don't have to express it in the mode they do.

That's not separation. Separation is when I declare your "brand" of Christianity is inferior to mine because of what you belong to and what you avow or are committed to.

A denomination devoted to sectarianism can have correct theology and have wrong attitudes towards the rest of the body of Christ, which is an emphasis on "do it our way or take the highway".

We must remember that we can become so enamored of who we are and what we do…and that's a mistake in my opinion. It's reminiscent of the Tower of Babel in Genesis 11:4: "so that we may make a name for ourselves" which when emphasized produces divisiveness.

This divisiveness results from leaders cultivating sinful attitudes toward other members of the body of Christ. However, you don't have to be a denomination to take on this attitude. I have asserted that many groups, individual churches, and leaders who do not regard themselves as denominations are quite divisive. What I am saying is that division is not so much a structural problem, as a attitudinal one. It can affect an individual Christian as much as a group.

If twenty years from now, the leaders of the Vineyard turn inward, and become self-serving, shame on them. They need to take risks and continue to grow in the same way we took risks and continued to grow. If they don't, God will hopefully raise up some other renewal movement, and they will be seen as irresponsible radicals, in much the same way some parts of the institutional church regard the Vineyard today.

Remember, church history reveals a cycle in which the homesteaders of one renewal movement persecutes the "pioneers" of the most recent move.

The Methodist movement began as a sectarian protest against the worldliness of the Church of England; its success stimulated it to become a church which in turn spawned various sectarian protests, including charismatic communities. The Catholic Charismatic renewal was persecuted by the Pentecostals, because the Pentecostals couldn't believe the Catholics were Christians. If we're not diligently humbling ourselves before the Lord, the Vineyard will do the same thing to someone else eventually.

This sinful attitude is often the result of fear. This is because new and different group leaders frighten us, so we attack them, thereby sowing discord, perpetuating the practice of judging people and practices without properly examining. In this situation, slanderous reports that confirm our prejudices are often gladly accepted and passed off as fact to others. May the Vineyard never be accused of contributing to that ugliness.

The antidote for this sectarian spirit is exalting the name of Jesus. Even in the first century church, the apostle Paul had to plead the case for unity. In Philippians 2, he writes:

> If you have any encouragement from being united with Christ, if any comfort from his love, if any fellowship with the Spirit, if any tenderness and compassion, then make my joy complete by being like-minded, having the same love, being one in spirit and purpose.

> Do nothing out of selfish ambition or vain conceit, but in humility consider others better than yourselves. Each of you should look not only to your own interests, but also to the interests of others (2:1-4).

This applies both locally and globally. The essence of learning to love the rest of the church is learning how to love one another. We can't do one without the other.

I don't want to make a name for ourselves. The Vineyard is not the issue. We need organization to exist – God called us, and I'm not ashamed of us – but the issue is the body of Christ. We must lift up no other name but the hallowed name of Jesus. God is passionate for the glory of his own name and will not yield to any man or group.

If we don't keep buttressing and encouraging relationship with God first, and each other second, we will indeed evolve into a sectarian organization.

Diversity in unity

One illustration of diversity within unity is the twelve tribes of Israel. Each tribe had a different name, and a different identity. Jacob's prophetic blessings in Genesis chapter 49 describe different destinies for each tribe descending from his sons. Each tribe was unique.

However, in unity, the twelve tribes formed one nation, without losing their identity. As long as the tribes were united in purpose: e.g., serving Yahweh, things went well. But in time, as the spiritual vitality of the nation waned, individual tribes sought advantage for themselves rather than the welfare of the nation. Eventually northern tribes (Israel) were enemies of the southern tribes (Judah).

Without trying to justify denominations from Scripture, I see denominations as different tribes. The challenge of denominations is to strike a balance between the unity of the whole body, and their individual distinctiveness. Our differences may cause us pain, but they needn't polarize and alienate us. I may not agree with everything about Catholic doctrine, but there's a lot about individual Catholics I love. Our understanding of Scripture may prevent us from endorsing certain doctrines without causing us to despise other traditions in the body of Christ.

All separation of the body of Christ is unbiblical, whether denominational, or nondenominational. We need to be careful not to think more highly of the Vineyard that we ought "...but rather think of yourself with sober judgment, in accordance with the measure of faith God has given you" (Romans 12:3). The Vineyard is simply another experiment – in a long line of experiments – to live out pure Christianity within the larger church.

We need to cultivate an attitude that rejoices in the unique contributions various denominations, movements, and traditions have made and currently make to the cause of Christ. We can learn from one another. I rejoice when I read about how the Southern Baptist Convention, or the Assemblies of God are planting new churches. Many of our people here at the Anaheim Vineyard gladly participated with the Southern California Calvary Chapels for Greg Laurie's Summer Harvest Crusade. And I'm sure our people benefited from it.

I thank God for the diversity of so many groups, because I know our society needs to have many thousands of new and *different* churches. Not everyone who needs to find Christ is going to want to do so through a Vineyard. The Victory Outreach folks I mentioned earlier reach a strata of society the Vineyard may never touch. An attitude of Christian unity says "Who cares how many people the Presbyterians win, or the Methodists! I bless what I see God blessing".

Would our culture really be impressed if every Christian church was identical, and had the same name? Probably not. But they *would* be impressed if Christians refrained from bad-mouthing one another long enough to do the works of Jesus.

THE THREAT OF INSTITUTIONALIZATION

Becoming a denomination runs parallel to the process of institutionalization. The Vineyard movement in some ways reflects the classical Protestant model of new beginnings. In this model, as described by Paul Hiebert of Trinity Evangelical Divinity School, those tired of living in a "dead" church decide to leave and create a new church that's more alive and warm. They hope they can create one that will never fossilize.

The Vineyard, like any other human organization, is experiencing institutionalization. That means we are experiencing more structure as time goes on. This has both benefits and drawbacks for a church planting movement. Professor Paul Hiebert has adroitly reviewed both:

One benefit of increased structured relationship is *efficiency*. The men and women who work in the various offices of the Anaheim Vineyard are all my brothers and sisters in Christ. On Sunday we worship together, and once a month we take communion together. As individuals we are each pursuing closer and more intimate relationships with Jesus Christ. But on Monday through Friday, at 8:30 a.m. something changes. A new relationship figures in. I'm the boss. We have a structure that enables us to work efficiently toward the same overall objectives. The structured relationships make the accomplishment of certain goals possible. But the structure doesn't enhance or detract from the fact that we're just brothers and sisters in Christ.

Denominations, in their best light, do several things:

They attempt to bring good government – pastoral oversight and accountability – that cares for leaders and protects God's people from abuse in the following areas:

- Theological (heresy)

- Ecclesiological (abuse of power)

- Moral (ethical failures)

Structure provides oversight, and training (1 Timothy 2:2). As a movement we've needed those things; without them, it becomes chaos. Pastors left un-pastored often do things according to the dictates of their hearts, and sometimes those dictates aren't too healthy.

A second benefit according to Hiebert "is the ability to mobilize large numbers of people and resources to carry out an otherwise impossible program of missions and ministry."

Common theology, vision, values, and strategy make denominations more effective than individual churches in missions and church planting. Since like begets like, denominations can be more effective than parachurch organizations in missions. Why? Parachurch organizations normally do not plant churches (if they did, they would become denominations and cease to be parachurch organizations). Parachurch organizations are outside God's ordained means of government and oversight.

Furthermore, I think we need to organize and coordinate for continued growth. In 1992, I mandated a fresh emphasis of church planting, evangelism, and world missions to the semi-annual conference of the AVC Board and Council. Since that time, we've grown at an unprecedented rate, planting approximately 170 churches, which almost matches what we'd done in the preceding eight years. That was a sovereign move of God, but I believe

God worked through the organizational structures that had been put in place. So, if organization is detrimental, it's working well for us now.

A final benefit is the theological maturation of the Vineyard movement. New converts, particularly in new churches, often have little understanding of the bible or of a biblical worldview. We recognize the need to deepen the knowledge of the bible among our leaders and laity. This is why the Vineyard Bible Institute has expanded over the past few years, giving access through the correspondence course excellent biblical scholars (like Don Williams and Wayne Grudem) who reflect the Vineyard's kingdom values. The long-range survival of the Vineyard – and its remaining true to the Christian faith – depends upon cultivating leaders rooted in a deep understanding of the Scriptures. If I was starting all over in ministry, one thing I would do differently is give more time to the study of Scripture.

Dangers

There are also some dangers with institutionalization. Hiebert lists the following.

The vision is often lost in the process of carrying it out. That is why events such as training conferences, worship celebrations, and retreats are important. These events must have both the teaching as well as the modeling of the teaching to be effective in informing as well as transforming the attendees. These "rites of transformation" have the potential of renewing commitment and vision.

Another danger is that the focus on goals gives way to a concern for self-maintenance. Churches are initially started to evangelize and minister to peoples among which no previous churches exist. But as time passes, more of their resources and efforts are spent on simply maintaining the institutional structures. Many Vineyard plants initially make do with modest rented facilities like schools and office buildings. In time, some more established Vineyards may spend more on sanctuaries and parking lots. Larger and more elaborate facilities are not necessarily bad...unless they dilute the mission of the church.

Yet another danger of institutionalization is that flexibility gives way to inflexibility. Finally, the fourth danger is the shift in focus from people to programs. Young institutions are generally more people oriented. There is a strong emphasis on fellowship, trust, and meeting human needs. As an institution grows, more and more emphasis is often placed on building programs and maintaining institutional structures.

INEVITABLE TRAGEDY?

Does this spell tragedy for the Vineyard as the processes of institutionalization takes hold? True, there are some benefits, but to many the evils seem to outweigh the benefits in the long run.

Some people holding this view look at history and see an inevitable slide of all denominations into sin. The following analysis, coming from Harnack, sounds something like this:

- God raises up a Man with a vision: e.g. Luther, Calvin, Wesley.

- Men and women with leadership gifting are attracted to the Man and vision and come alongside: e.g. Luther's Wittenberg School; Calvin's Geneva; Wesley's Class meetings (i.e. small groups).

- Soon more men and women – the masses – join, and the need for greater organization arises. At this point growth is swift; we witness a classic Movement.

- Finally, the movement eventually ossifies under the weight of organization and new leaders who have forgotten (or rejected) the founder's vision. Frequently the Man himself is kicked out (e.g. St. Francis, Calvin), and the whole thing becomes an organizational Monument (e.g. much of Lutheranism, the Reformed Church, the Methodist Church). This can happen swiftly, or it can take generations.

How do we prevent the "Man, Men, Movement, Monument" scenario? Some say simply, reject "denominations". This comes in two forms: (1) Reject organization, and simply be a local church. [Problem: limited impact in reaching out and fulfilling vision]; (2) Organize anyway, then deny you are a denomination [e.g. "The Christian Church" is a classic illustration of a non-denominational denomination].

The other option – the one I endorse – is to say we cannot be held responsible for what the next generation will do with its inheritance, but we will serve God today in the most effective, efficient, and responsible way possible. Therefore, we can organize to beat today's devil, and trust God for the future.

Some say the only hope is for the Vineyard to avoid any semblance of becoming a denomination. Our only hope is to resist the formation of more organizational structures, and return to the "good ol' days" when there was less bureaucracy, fewer "rules", and things were done less by planning, and more by letting it happen. But, as Peter Berger points out,[8] anti-structural movements have never been successful. For one, they're unable to build stable enduring societies or organize people into communities of common purpose and mutual support.

The Vineyard as a burgeoning denomination can avoid the hardening effects of institutionalization by a commitment to *institutional renewal.* Periodic regeneration can enhance our ministries.

Spiritual renewal can neither be programmed, nor reduced to a "formula". But as Edwin Orr points out (1975), God responds to sincere prayers, and he uses individuals, human experiences, sermons, song, books, sacred places, sacred times, and other cultural symbols to move in the lives of people. Hiebert counsels that when we seek renewal, we need to understand the human processes that can make us open to the possibility of renewal. One way renewal can be an ongoing part of our experience is by emphasizing worship as our first priority and value. And most importantly, we must listen when God speaks.

RENEWAL STRUCTURES

Howard Snyder, in his book *The Radical Wesley*[9] contributes a model for a renewing structure which "brings new life to the larger church without either compromising its own vitality or causing a split".

Snyder believes this model can include renewal movements within the institutional church (like early Methodism) and other groups that become independent sects. The Vineyard movement can learn much from Snyder's model even though the Vineyard doesn't perfectly fit the model.

- The renewal movement exists as a smaller, more intimate expression of the church within the universal church. It sees itself not as a true church in an exclusive sense, but as a form of the church that is necessary to the life of the larger church, and which in turn needs

---

[8] Peter Berger, *The Homeless Mind: Modernization and Consciousness,* New York, Random House, 1973.

[9] Howard Snyder, *The Radical Wesley,* Downers Grove IL: Intervarsity Press, 1985.

the larger church to be complete.

- The renewing movement uses some form of small group structure within the local congregation. While the size and structure of these small groups may vary, they generally have a dozen or fewer persons and meet once a week.

- The renewal movement has some structural link with the institutional church. This is crucial if the renewal structure is to exercise a revitalizing impact without bringing division. Some kind of tie between the two structures is mutually sought and agreed upon.

- Because it sees itself not as the total church but as a necessary part of the church, the renewal structure is committed to the unity, vitality and wholeness of the larger church.

- The renewal structure is mission oriented. It senses keenly its specific purpose and mission, which is conceived in part as the renewal of the church and in part as witness to the world. It will stress practical ethics, attempting to combine faith and love, belief with everyday life.

  In an article titled "Missions and the Renewal of the Church" Paul Hiebert helpfully points out that "church planting and church renewal are the two central tasks of missions. The first without the second leads to widespread nominal Christianity; the second without the first leads to life without mission." In fact, the two go together. An effective mission to the world often revives the home church, and renewal at home often leads to a new missionary vision.

- *The renewal movement is especially conscious of being a distinct, covenant-based community.* It knows it is not the whole church; it senses its own incompleteness. But it sees itself as a visible form of the true church. Based on a well-understood covenant, it can exercise discipline, even to the point of exclusion, among its members.

  As a community the renewal movement prizes face-to-face relationships, mutuality and interdependence. It especially stresses Scriptures that speak of *koinonia*, mutual encouragement and admonition within the body, and sees itself as a primary structure for experiencing these aspects of the church.

- *The renewal movement provides the context for the rise, training, and exercise of new forms of ministry and leadership.* Out of its experience of community comes a practical emphasis on the gifts of the Spirit and the priesthood of believers. This consciousness generates new forms of ministry and new leaders who arise through the channels of practical experience and the shared life of the group.

The renewal group also provides a natural environment for training new leaders. Partly for this reason, a disproportionately high number of future church leaders often comes from the ranks of a renewal movement if it is not cut off from the established church.

- Finally, *the renewal structure maintains an emphasis on the Spirit and the Word as the basis of authority.* It is both Christological and pneumatological. It stresses the norm of Scripture and the life of the Spirit. If it veers to the right or the left at this point, it will become either a highly legalistic sect or an enthusiastic cult liable to extreme or heretical beliefs. In the case of Methodism, Wesley maintained a balance that prevented either extreme.

The renewal movement stresses the Spirit and the Word as the ultimate ground of authority, but within limits also recognizes the authority and traditions of the institutional church.

MOSAIC

Mosaic is the art of embedding small pieces of cut stone or pigmented glass in a plaster bed to decorate a floor or wall. Developed principally in ancient Greece, mosaic reached its greatest heights in Early Christian art and architecture. The beauty of a mosaic is enhanced by its complexity. The classical mosaic artists would use cubes of diverse size, shape, varieties, and color intensities.

In the small 11th Century monastery church at Daphni, near Athens, there is an example of Byzantine mosaic art that is unsurpassed. In the church's dome, the symbol of heaven, is a huge image of Christ, Lord of the Universe; circling the drum are sixteen Old Testament prophets. As your eyes move down the shimmering surface, the impression of flickering images and of movement renders a lively and otherworldly effect. On the wall areas in and around the nave are scenes from Christ's earthly life. Below these scenes are images of saints and martyrs.

Can you imagine anyone looking at this work of art, and bemoaning that the individual cubes are not identical in size, color, and position? Of course not, because diversity of the individual cubes only enhances the beauty, and unity of the whole, symbolizing as it does a microcosm of God's kingdom.

So too, we need not necessarily decry the diversity of the church of Jesus Christ. Denominations inasmuch as they isolate Christians from one another are tragic, but they can also be seen as pieces of a grand mosaic, some different only in degrees, others with very little surface similarity.

> Now to him who is able to do immeasurably more than all we ask or imagine, according to his power that is at work within us, to him be glory *in the church* and in Christ Jesus throughout all generations, for ever and ever! Amen (Ephesians 3:20.21 NIV).

A LEADERSHIP SHOPPING LIST

A biblical model for recruiting, training and deploying potential leaders for ministry

January/February 1994, Volume 2, Issue 1

Before the Anaheim Vineyard started, when I was a consultant to churches around America, one of the most common questions I would get from pastors was "How do you identify potential leaders?" Over a number of years, I had trained pastors in five western states on how to identify, recruit and deploy leaders for small groups. So I wrote up a list of things I looked for in potential leaders.

I occasionally dust off that list and use it to encourage pastors as the primary ministry recruiters in their churches. Imagine you're sitting down with a couple in your church who would like to work in some crucial area of the ministry. You recognize leadership potential in their lives. Nevertheless, to avoid being "...hasty in the laying on of hands..." (1 Timothy 5:22a), I suggest keeping the following "shopping list" of leadership values in mind.

This isn't a fail-safe method. Even with these criteria, I've managed to select poorly at times. But here at the Anaheim Vineyard, we have approximately 1,400 people working every week doing something. So, these values and principles have served us well over the years, both for managing professional staff, and mobilizing and recruiting volunteers from the congregation. I believe they can serve you as well.

SERVICE AND SELF-SACRIFICE

We conceive in our philosophy, leadership not as a position, a title, power, authority, respect, or privilege...but an obligation to service and self-sacrifice. There's a difference between structural authority (in which one has all the aforementioned) and spiritual authority based on attitude, character, gifting and anointing.

Without agreement here, you've got a problem from the outset. I'm not talking about false humility and putting yourself down. I'm talking about a willingness to render unassuming service.

That's what Jesus called for in Luke 17 when he told the story of the servant who went out into the field and came in that night. All he had done at the end of the day was to render humble service. All any of us will have done by the end of the day is render humble service. It doesn't matter whether you have to plough five hundred acres or one that day; you've just rendered humble service. You're the Master's and the Master can employ you any way he desires.

Some people equate leadership with position. The apostles had a little to learn about this business of humble service.

> And they said to him, "Grant that we may sit in your glory, one on your right, and one on your left…" And calling them to Himself, Jesus said to them, "You know that those who are recognized as the rulers of the Gentiles lord it over them; and their great men exercise authority over them. But it is not so among you, but whoever wishes to become great among you shall be your servant and whoever wishes to be first among you shall be slave of all. For even the Son of Man did not come to be served, but to serve, and to give His life as a ransom for many." (Mark 10:37, 42-45)

The disciples were already grousing over who was going to get the best spot. They were looking for rewards.

I don't care if you're recruiting a drummer, an usher or a nursery worker…if he or she doesn't understand that we humbly render our service *to the Lord,* then they'll constantly look for rewards. As a leader, you can certainly show appreciation in some appropriate way to those who are serving. Paul instructed the church in Philippi to welcome Epaphroditus "…and honor men like him, because he almost died for the work of Christ" (Philippians 2:29b-30a). But ultimately the servant must satisfy himself in Jesus, and the opportunity to serve Him.

FULLNESS OF THE HOLY SPIRIT, FAITH AND WISDOM

Along with people who provide humble service, you want to look for those who understand that service continually requires an unction and an anointing by the Spirit.

> But select from among you, brethren, seven men of good reputation, full of the Spirit and of wisdom, whom we may put in charge of this task…and they chose Stephen, a man full of faith and of the Holy Spirit. (Acts 6:3,5)

In our book *Power Points* Kevin Springer and I tried to clarify the different ways Luke uses the concept of "filling," "filled," and "being full." Luke employs three Greek words for filling, and they all give a slightly different twist to its meaning.

Acts 6:5 describes filling more like a *character quality* or disposition in which a person is habitually controlled by God's Spirit. Stephen was full [*pleres*] of faith and the Holy Spirit (see also Luke 4:1; 11:24). In the Acts 6 passage above, to be "full of the Holy Spirit" is synonymous with possessing mature character.

It doesn't really matter whether they're parking cars, changing diapers, or teaching 4th grade Sunday School, it's all the same stuff and at the end of the day we get the same pay for it (Matthew 20: 1-16).

LOYALTY

We're looking also for people who through exposure to and intimacy with the leader respond in loyalty.

For years I had people approach me and say, "I don't feel called to the movement. I feel called to *you*." I now know this is a bad sign. Usually it meant they had little consideration for their peers, and sometimes held their peers in disdain. What they were looking for was some kind of privileged place next to me. When I look back over the years, some of the recruits who have been the most unfruitful have approached me with that kind of language. So now, that rings a big alarm when I hear it. I respond, "Man, you're called to the wrong person. It's Jesus we're serving around here. You ought to go serve him for a while."

Yes, I want loyalty, but at this point of my life, I'm trying to carefully take tentacles off *me*, and put them *on the Lord*. I see this as essential if there's going to be a Vineyard after John Wimber.

> And He appointed twelve – designating them apostles – that they might be with him and that He might send them out to preach and to have authority to cast out the demons. (Mark 3:14-15)

Notice the phrase, *"that they might be with him"*. You're called to Jesus. Jesus was, and is, the only disciple-maker. We make disciples in the sense that we work with the people who are being called to be *His* disciples, but the ultimate loyalty and commitment belongs to Him.

That doesn't impugn an appropriate consideration and loyalty to the "family" that they've been united with. But there ought to be a balance. I'm not looking for people who are looking over their shoulder or looking at this church as a stepping-stone. "Let me sit under your ministry for a few years because I'm going to go do thus and so." I don't have any problem with training someone short-term; who is on his was to do something. But I want to make sure he's not *using* us in the process. I want some assurance they really are a part of the family. Then we can happily send them out as family.

Loyalty doesn't mean a person can't speak his or her mind from time to time. Anyone who knows my wife Carol and me, knows that Carol speaks her mind; but at the same time she's a submissive wife. I believe loyalty expresses itself in speaking one's mind. And then at the point that you've spoken your mind, being willing to continue to walk in the situation even though you don't agree.

At a very pivotal point a few years ago in our engagement with the prophetic ministers, John McClure wrote me a rather lengthy letter, and came and confronted me on three different occasions regarding his concerns. His loyalty compelled him to wave a flag of warning. As far as I know, he never shared that with any other human being other than possibly his wife, Margie. That's loyalty! He was working with me, but he was pointing out some problems, and he was right to do so.

Carl Tuttle, my associate is for me, but he'll confront hard if he feels there's a need. That's still loyalty. So, we're not looking for automatons, or people who always seem to agree, but who are inwardly seething with resentment, or talk behind your back. That's disloyalty.

People who won't stand up and be counted, how can you work with that? We all need a few people who can say, "I love you; I think you're wrong in this area; here are my reasons why."

Loyalty isn't tested by agreement or disagreement. But it can be reinforced by willingness to let things lie until such a time as they can be dealt with. I don't require people who work with me to sign or verbalize a "loyalty oath." I've never said to a colleague: "I want you to be loyal to me." Rather I encourage people many times to be loyal to one another, because that's a vital Christian characteristic.

TRUSTWORTHINESS

This implies the ability to resist being bribed or bought. It doesn't always relate to money. It comes sometimes with visibility, opportunity. I've seen some guys leave one staff and go to another simply for a more prominent position. And it never produces much in the realm of the Spirit; it usually was disastrous for everybody.

So, look for people who really have the same heart for what you're doing that you have. "Furthermore, you shall select out of all the people able men who fear God, men of truth, those who hate dishonest gain…" (Exodus 18:21). Ministry should be given away… but you don't give it away to just anyone.

Years ago, I had a staff member who, in the process if coming to me, cut some corners with the people he was working with. I confronted him about it. He said he had taken care of it. Later on, I found out from the people that he hadn't. Before long the pattern started showing in everything he did around us. Cutting corners had become a way of life. I realized he was gifted, but corrupted in an area of his character, so we had to confront him again. He didn't respond well, so we had to let him go. It became painfully clear I couldn't entrust anything in the way of ministry responsibility to him.

Now it's different for a parking lot attendant as opposed to an associate pastor, but the value is valid at any level. As a fisher of men, you want a net made up of people who are trustworthy, so the unsaved are caught in something healthy, whole, and righteous.

PROVEN MINISTRY ABILITY

When recruiting people for the weightier positions of leadership, look for those who are capable and respected, mature in the faith, and with proven ministry ability.

> An overseer, then, must be above reproach, the husband of one wife, temperate, prudent, respectable, hospitable, able to teach, not addicted to wine or pugnacious, but gentle, uncontentious, free from the love of money. He must be one who manages his own household well, keeping his children under control with all dignity…not a new convert…and he must have a good reputation with those outside the church…(1 Timothy 3:2-7).

I see this passage as *prescriptive,* as opposed to *descriptive.* Most of us fail in some way at some of these points. But we're all working toward this standard. We're all playing with the same rulebook. We're all measuring ourselves against what Scripture calls us to be.

Someone once told me, "I don't trust leaders who don't walk with a limp." Give me a leader who has wrestled with God and been shown the limitations in his character or makeup.

ACCOUNTABILITY

"Let not many of you become teachers, my brethren, knowing that as such we shall incur a stricter judgment" (James 3:1). That applies to teachers because of the multiplication of influence through teaching. But it's valid wherever one ministers, or whatever one does. There ought to be standards, with penalties extracted when you don't live by those standards.

Many times I've seen guys wearing themselves out to get their church off the ground, and at the same time, they undermine their ministry week after week by the way they treat their wives, handle their money, or brag over things that have gone on in the church. Someone coming alongside with a fatherly hug and saying, "Have you thought about this?" can help. Pointing out connections between lack of success and lifestyle issues, if done lovingly, can help greatly.

1 Peter 3:7 makes a connection between the effectiveness of our prayers, and the way we treat our wives. Ministries can be undermined, and the

confidence of the people eroded if we are not functioning well in our household and rearing our children. That doesn't mean we have unbroken success. All of us have had some tough moments – or even years – with our kids. But the issue in the 1 Timothy 3 text above is that we are trying. We are not ignoring or denying or running away from the problem. We're dealing with it the best we know how.

But we've been called to build a body of people, and we need accountable people and people who are willing to accept reproof. Many folks come to me and say, "You're my pastor." Carl Tuttle has a great comeback to that one: "We'll see if I'm your pastor after the first time I have to say 'no'." People say, "I'm with you!" Then when I have to correct them, I find out they're not with me. They were with me as long as I never crossed their path with any correction.

People who willingly accept reproof are people who can be built together in a body. You get 40 people together like that in a church, and you can take care of 500 people comfortably. You have this inner core of team players who want to do this thing together.

LOVE FOR GOD'S PEOPLE

> He said to him the third time, "Simon, son of John, do you love me? …And he said to him, "Lord, you know all things; You know that I love you." Jesus said to him, "Tend my sheep." (John 21:17).

Peter had avoided the crucible of identifying with Christ by denying him three times. Now the resurrected Jesus probes the very core of Peter's motivations. Before Jesus was going to turn the keys to the kingdom over to this impetuous Galilean fisherman, he wanted to fortify him with the essential motive: if you really love me, then tend my sheep. Love my people.

There's a terrible price to be paid for such commitment. It cost Peter and the rest of the Apostles their lives. Vineyard leaders have paid an awful price for the privilege of tending the sheep. I've spoken elsewhere about the dynamic of attack and counterattack. This past year has been a grim reminder of that reality, but by God's grace we're still here. And as a movement we're a stronger, tougher crew as a result of the fiery trials that have come our way, especially since we rededicated ourselves to evangelism, church planting, and missions.

Years ago I consulted with a young man (not in the Vineyard) during a conference in the Midwest. He had been an evangelist in a certain denomination for several years, and had wearied of that, and wanted to pastor. His denominational leader had said to him, "Why don't you go up to this community here. We have a little church that hasn't done too well. Go up there and see what you can get stirred up, and if you do well, then I'll give you a more choice position later on in a bigger church."

We met at a restaurant and he brashly told me what he was going to do. He wanted my advice on how to "jump start" the church.

I said, "I can't do that."

"Why"

"Because there's no integrity in what you're doing. You're going up to that little community like a gigolo, pretending you love this part of the bride of Christ. You're going to have intercourse with her in hopes of having children, but you have no intention of raising them. No intention of loving, protecting or caring for her. You just want to have a few babies with her so you can get a chance to have some other babies somewhere else. I can't bless that, and I don't want any part of what you're about to do."

This really angered him. He swore at me, then got up and left. He called me at my hotel around eleven o'clock that night. "I'm sorry I swore at you, but you made me really angry."

"It was calculated to do that. I was trying to show you the bottom line."

"Well, you're right. That's exactly my motivation for going there. And that's exactly what I was told to do. Who was wrong here? Me or my supervisor?"

"I don't know about your supervisor, but you were the one who was going to do it. So, you have to take the responsibility."

"Well, I talked to my wife, and we both agreed that if we can't go there with the intentions of staying there permanently, I'm not going to take the assignment."

"If you do that," I said, "there'll be integrity, and I'll be glad to help you."

There's got to be some integrity and sincerity in all of this. We can't just do something to advance our career, or position. We need to recruit people who love God's people. I know it's always a love-hate thing, but if you don't love the church most of the time, get out of the ministry. Let's raise up people who love the church. That's true with your team in the church. If they don't love the church, why do they want a position other than to make something out of it, or use it? You don't want to give position to someone who doesn't love the church.

A TEAM PLAYER

Look for willingness to be a "team player" and to help one's co-workers succeed.

> Do nothing from selfishness or empty conceit, but with humility of mind let each of you regard one another as more important than himself; do not merely look out for your own personal interests, but also for the interests of others (Philippians2: 3-4).

That doesn't mean that we live constantly in touch with this feeling, but whenever the issue presents itself, we defer to that. This attitude manifests itself in ministry situations by praying not only for my portion of the work, but also praying for other areas of the ministry. We will be confronted with our own selfishness in this arena, but when you see that, like anything else in the way of sin, you just confess it ("Oh God, I've let up on this again…Forgive me.")

BOTH HUSBAND AND WIFE SENSE THE CALL

If the wife resents the guy being the Sunday School leader or director or taking over all the house groups, and being out a couple of nights a week extra because of that, you're in trouble. If you're going to ask someone to give a ten hour a week commitment, on top of going to church and all the other things they have to do, you better sit down with both of them and find out. And if she doesn't say it with her mouth, she'll say it with her body whether she's happy or not. So, watch what's going on when you're talking. Sometimes the roles are reversed. You don't want a husband who is dragging his feet either while the wife is getting more involved.

CONCLUSION

If these values I've listed are shared, taught and rigorously adhered to, over a period of time, it will build a culture of commitment among your lay leaders.

I would hold scrupulously to these values in recruiting whether I had 50 people in my church or 500. In fact, when you're building a church from the bottom up, it's even more important to set these values in place at the beginning and make them intrinsic to everything you do.

Several months before Germany surrendered to the Allies, Franklin Roosevelt had expressed hopes that the Yalta conference would not last more than five or six days. Sir Winston Churchill had a more patient outlook: "I do not see any way of realizing our hopes about a world organization in five or six days. Even the Almighty took seven." Take your time and listen to the Spirit as you recruit and deploy leaders. There's no hurry when you're building something lasting.

LIBERATING WOMEN FOR MINISTRY AND LEADERSHIP

Is there any reason why women, created in God's image, should not enjoy the same freedom – and responsibility – as men enjoy?

March/April 1994, Volume 2, Issue 2

When Anne Watson lost her husband (one of the U.K.'s great church leaders) she still had a lot of life to live. She still knew how to teach the bible. She still knew how to lead people to Jesus, still knew how to lay hands on the sick and nurture. She still knew how to sit down with someone and say, "Walk in all the way that the Lord your God has commanded you, so that you may live ..." (Deuteronomy 5:33). Her life wasn't over. Since the death of her husband, she has been a tireless worker in the Vineyard movement in England. I wish I had a hundred church planting leaders with her wisdom, vision, and heart for the lost.

Some may question her role, but we must learn to recognize the work and the hand of God. To relegate a gifted believer to a desolate place in the body of Christ because of gender would be an injustice in my opinion. When God's hand is on someone, we need to bless what God is doing.

Let me say at the outset that I believe God has established a gender-based eldership of the church. I endorse the traditional (and what I consider the *scriptural*) view of a unique leadership role for men in marriage, family, and in the church. This ultimately reflects the hierarchy of the Trinity: "For this reason I kneel before the Father, from whom his whole family in heaven and on earth derives its name" (Ephesians 3:14,15). Consequently I personally do not favor ordaining women as elders in the local church.

I have articulated in the past that I see the act of "elding" as a function in the church that is for both male and female to perform. Whereas I see eldership as an office that is reserved for male leadership only (and I would add that my personal conviction is that it is for ordained men only.) This ought not to create a problem in that the function is for everyone and the office for a few.

Nevertheless something has been happening the last few years in the Vineyard about women. In watching the flow of things in the Vineyard movement, I've detected – in the Spirit, and in the natural – a certain hesitation from our women. I've seen them back off.

Certain cultural tendencies within society, and particularly the church, have truncated somewhat the wonderful freedom for ministry God intends for women. Surely the Lord would have us achieve some balance in this area.

During the AVC Pastor's Conference last summer, my wife Carol and I felt compelled to give a blessing to the women present, and by extension to all our women that God might lead them in doing great things for him.

I encourage our women to participate in any ministry, except church governance. A woman can preach, teach, evangelize, heal, prophesy, counsel, nurture, administrate, and build up the flock of God. There are women in some of our congregations who are evangelizing and building churches because it's the peculiar call of God on their lives. I don't think they have to confine their ministry to women. They, in my opinion, can freely minister to men also, but only under authority. As I understand the biblical texts that apparently proscribe the activity of women in ministry (especially in a speaking mode) I believe we're dealing with the misuse of authority. We all have to come under the authority of the word of God, and those overseers the Lord has placed in the flock. This can be done easily with joy and pleasure.

Of course, we should use restraint and wisdom, looking at every situation and circumstance with the utmost care and discernment. Ultimately, we must recognize God's hand among us.

HEADSHIP NOT DOMINANCE

Certain sectors of the church in the past have created absolute regulations based on some New Testament passages like 1 Corinthians 14:34: "Women should remain silent in the churches" and 1 Timothy 2:12: "I do not permit a woman to teach or to have authority over a man." These scriptures may have been intended for specific situations. This has confused the subject of women in ministry. The position accorded to women in the church has often been a sign of the church's worldliness, rather than faithfulness to scripture.

Charles Finney, in one of his Revival Lectures, commented on how revivals usually are accompanied by certain innovations in ministry that invariably raise the ire of those in control of the institutional structures. Writing in the nineteenth century, one of these innovations that was bitterly criticized was of all things, women's prayer meetings!

> Within the last few years women's prayer-meetings have been extensively opposed. What dreadful things! A minister said that when he first attempted to establish these meetings, he had all the clergy around opposed to him. "Set women to pray? Why, the next thing, I suppose, will be set them to preach!" Serious apprehensions were entertained for the safety of Zion if women should be allowed to get together to pray, and even now it is not tolerated in some churches.

It could be said that restricted rights of ministry to men may be one of Satan's slickest tricks to undermine the church's proclamation of freedom.

Some foundational truths serve as a plumb line for answering questions concerning women ministering and leading in the church. First, man and woman were created in the image of God. This is referenced in Genesis 1:26-27:

> Let us make man in our image and in our likeness and let them rule over the fish of the sea and the birds of the air, over the livestock, over all the creatures that move along the ground. So God created man in his own image and in the image of God he created him; male and female he created them.

Both man and woman were given dominion over the earth. Since woman was created *from* man, one aspect of her identity includes that of a suitable helper to man. This doesn't diminish her identity as an equal bearer of God's image. Thus we don't have man ruling and woman ruling. We have woman helping man rule. Raymond Ortlund, Jr. writes:

> We see neither the words "male-female equality" nor "male headship" here or anywhere in Genesis 1-3. What Moses does provide is a series of more or less obvious hints as to his doctrine of manhood and womanhood. The burden of Genesis 1:26-28 is male-female equality. That seems obvious – wonderfully obvious! But God's

naming of the race "man" whispers male headship, which Moses will bring forward boldly in chapter two [of Genesis].

Male headship is not the same as male dominance. Male dominance, in this fallen world, leads to victimization of women. The answer is not to reject the doctrine of godly male headship (which results in female fulfillment) but to clarify its biblical meaning, and to live it out in our families, and in our churches.

From the time of the Fall and throughout the history of civilization, mankind has had to deal with the problem of people enslaving one another. We have all been incarcerated and enslaved in various levels of our lives. We need to be freed of those things that keep us from becoming all that we're supposed to be in this life. Only in Scripture can we find the basis of our personal significance.

EQUALITY

Paul gives one of the clearest proclamations of a woman's spiritual position in God's economy in Galatians 3:28: "There is neither Jew nor Greek, slave nor free, male nor female, for you are all one in Christ Jesus."

Martin Luther (1483-1546), the great German Reformer, in his commentary on Galatians sees the text as meaning that all believers have the same status in Christ. But in other spheres – such as the family – a biblical submission of women to the godly headship of men harmonizes with that equality.

John Calvin (1509-1564) pointed out in his *Institutes*, that the liberty of all in Christ has its limits, for "the same apostle who bids us stand and not submit to the 'yoke of bondage' (Galatians 5:1) elsewhere forbids slaves to be anxious about their state" (1 Corinthians 7:21). In other words, freedom truly exists within limits and restrictions of a different order.

John Piper and Wayne Grudem point out that Paul is affirming the equality of men and women in Christ, without abolishing "gender-based roles established by God and redeemed by Christ." What does this equality entail? By looking at the context of verse 28 we discover men and women are:

- Equally justified by faith (v. 24)
- Equally free from bondage of legalism (v. 25)

- Equally children of God (v. 26)
- Equally clothed with Christ (v. 27)
- Equally possessed by Christ (v. 29)
- Equally heirs of the promises to Abraham (v. 29).

In my view the "neither-male-nor-female" principle regarding our inheritance doesn't conflict with the headship-submission principle regarding our roles found elsewhere in the New Testament; Piper and Grudem point out that in 1 Peter 3:1-8, the blessing of being joint heirs "of the gracious gift of life" is connected with the exhortation for women to submit to their husbands (v.1) and for their husbands to treat their wives "with respect as the weaker partner."

SUBORDINATION

Now let's look at the issue of subordination. This area has been the greatest source of contention in the past thirty years concerning women and their relationship in the church. In 1 Corinthians 11:3-16, Paul speaks of three headships: Christ to man, man to women and God to Christ.

> Now I want you to realize that the head of every man is Christ, and the head of the woman is man, and the head of Christ is God. Every man who prophesies with head covered dishonors his head. And every woman who prays with her head uncovered dishonors her head – it is just as though her head were shaved. If a woman does not cover her head, she should have her hair cut off. It is a disgrace for a woman to have her hair cut off or shaved off, she should cover her head. A man ought not to cover his head, since he is the image and the glory of God; but woman is the glory of man. For man did not come from woman, woman from man; neither was man created for woman, but woman for man. For this reason, and because of the angels, the woman ought to have a sign of authority on her head. In the Lord, however, woman is not independent of man, nor is man independent of woman. For as woman came from man, so also man is born of woman. But everything comes from God.

There also appears this contrasting statement of complementarity in verse 11. Both man and woman owe their existence to each other and cannot do without each other. Here there is equality of life, while there is differentiation of function.

Another important passage is Ephesians 5:21 ff.

> Submit to one another out of reverence for Christ. Wives, submit to your husbands as to the Lord. For the husband is the head of the wife as Christ is the head of the church, his body, of which he is the Savior. Now as the church submits to Christ, so also wives should submit to their husbands in everything. Husbands, love your wives, just as Christ loved the church and gave himself up for her …

Paul reminds us that the relationship between Christ and the church is the pattern for the relationship between husband and wife. The wife is to treat the husband as the church treats Jesus, while the husband is to treat his wife as Jesus treats the church.

Christ submitted himself to the church, by laying down his life on the cross for the church, not by yielding to the authority of the church. However, the church submits to Christ *in a different way* by affirming his rule and following his lead.

Piper and Grudem help us by stating that "mutual submission" between husband and wife does not mean they submit to each other in the same ways. So Paul's exhortation of mutual submission doesn't soften either the headship of a godly husband or Christ's headship over the church.

SILENT WOMEN?

Paul allows for women to pray and prophesy in the church (1 Corinthians 11:5). Then he tells them to be silent (1 Corinthians 14:34). Is he contradicting himself? I agree with Piper and Grudem that Paul did not desire the total silence of Corinthian women but an appropriate involvement that affirmed the leadership of the men God had called to be the guardians and overseers of the flock.

What do we do about the issue of teaching? In 1 Timothy 2:12, Paul wrote, "I do not permit a woman to teach or to have authority over a man; she must be silent." In my view Paul wasn't barring all teaching by women. Piper and Grudem have listed various ways women teach within the church according to the New Testament: Paul enjoins the older women to "teach what is good. Then they can train the younger women" (Titus 2:3-

4). And he commends the teaching that Eunice and Lois gave to their son and grandson Timothy (2 Timothy 1:5; 3:14). Proverbs praises the ideal wife because she speaks with wisdom, and "faithful instruction is on her tongue" (Proverbs 31:26). Paul endorses women prophesying in church (1 Corinthians 11:5) and says that men "learn" by such prophesying (1 Corinthians 14:31) and that the members (presumably men and women) should "teach and admonish one another with all wisdom, as you sing psalms, hymns and spiritual songs" (Colossians 3:16). Teaching happens in a wonderful variety of ways, and women can appropriately be used to bless both men and women.

So what did Paul mean in 1 Timothy 2:15? Piper and Grudem believe

> the best clue is the coupling of "teaching" with "having authority over men." We would say that the teaching inappropriate for a woman is the teaching of men in settings or ways that dishonor the calling of men to bear the primary responsibility for teaching and leadership. This primary responsibility is to be carried by the pastors or elders.[10]

On numerous occasions in the past I have asked my wife to teach portions of messages I was giving as well as messages on her own. I have always felt that those messages were well received by the congregation and were entirely in biblical order.

SHOULDER TO SHOULDER

With the coming of Jesus Christ, we see a major turnover in the interaction with women. (See *How To Treat A Lady* by Susan Foh.) Jesus himself interacted with women on a whole different plane than we see anywhere else in the Bible. Women ought to be operating shoulder to shoulder with the men in every sense. They ought to be ministering with all the freedom that the men enjoy.

We have a number of New Testament examples of women who ministered effectively. The husband and wife team of Priscilla and Aquila seem

---

[10]For a thorough theological and biblical discussion of the basis for male eldership, I heartily recommend John Piper and Wayne Grudem, editors *Recovering Biblical Manhood & Womanhood Womanhood: A Response to Evangelical Feminism,* Wheaton, Ill., Crossway Books, 1991.

to minister side by side. They certainly had a strategic effect vis-à-vis the discipling of Apollos (Acts 18:26). If you've ever had the privilege of hearing Ray and Anne Ortlund minister together, you know there's a special blessing on this modern Priscilla and Aquila. When they speak on marriage, or worship, after a while, it's hard to tell where one stops and the other picks up. It's almost like listening to "Ranne" Ortlund. There's a beautiful complementarity that honors Ray's headship while giving voice to the wisdom and insight of Anne.

Paul expresses gratitude to numerous women for their involvement and service in blessing and strengthening the church. They were functional in hospitality (Acts12:12), they ministered in acts of charity (Acts 9:36-41). Women were active in evangelism (Philippians 4:3). Then we have the role of deacon. In Romans 16:1-2 Paul says about Phoebe, "I commend her to you. She is a servant in the church. You should receive her. Help her in what she may require from you or have need from you."

In summary we should consider the risk of liberating the women in our fellowships to minister and to lead as God directs them and ordains.

The largest church in the world today is pastored by Paul Yonggi Cho in Seoul, South Korea. It is growing as such an incredible rate that soon it will go over 750, 000 in attendance. Cho attributes most of the church's growth to thousands of cell groups where believers receive teaching and nurture. It may interest you to know that most of those small groups are led by women who minister under the pastoral authority of Cho.

How to Treat a Lady by Susan T. Foh[11]

Jesus' treatment of women was a radical break with the status quo. In the first century Palestine, the men, especially rabbis, did not speak to women in public. Jesus not only talked with women, he healed them (Matthew 15:21-28), he taught them (John 4:7ff), and he called on them to witness to their faith in him (Mark 5:25-34).

Jesus taught women individually as well as in mixed groups, and he revealed some of the most important truths to them. He told the Samaritan woman that God is spirit and must be worshipped in spirit and truth (John 11:25). After he had risen from the dead Jesus told Mary Magdalene about

---

[11]Susan T. Foh, a graduate of Westminster Theological Seminary, is the author of *Women and the Word of God, a response to Biblical Feminism,* Phillipsburg, N.J., Presbyterian & Reformed, 1979.

his ascension to God the Father (John 20:17) and she was sent to tell his disciples about his resurrection (Matthew 28:7; Mark 16:7; John 20:17-18).

In Luke 10:38-42 (involving Mary and Martha,), Jesus defended a woman's right to learn about the gospel against any who would deny her religious education, even against another woman who placed too great a value on maintaining and managing the home. The first priority, the only needful, for men and women, is to hear and obey Jesus' word.

In his parables, (Jesus) included illustrations from women's experience: the woman leavening bread to depict the growth of God's kingdom (Matthew 13:33); and the woman rejoicing because she had found her one lost coin (Luke 15:8-10).

Perhaps the most startling aspect of Jesus' relationship with women is the band of women who followed him wherever he went, and it happened in a day when women only appeared in public when absolutely necessary. The women, several of whom are mentioned by name (Matthew 27:55-56; Luke 8:1-4), traveled with him from the beginning of his earthly ministry in Galilee to the end in Jerusalem. They, unlike the male disciples, did not flee Jerusalem when Christ was crucified.

In short, Jesus related to women as human beings of worth. Women were active workers for his kingdom and valued disciples but the specifics of their activity are not recorded in the Gospels.

DAUGHTERS OF THE CROSS

Catherine of Genoa (1447 – 1510) - Italian noblewoman, mystic, and humanitarian[12]

For diplomatic purposes, her marriage to the nobleman Guiliano Adorni was arranged. Adorni proved a wayward and self-indulgent husband. Catherine was converted in 1473, and at the same time her husband's financial reverses brought about his conversion. They became affiliated with benevolent orders, caring for the sick and poor in Genoa. She was the administrative director of the St. Lazarus hospital from 1490 – 1496.

---

[12]Adapted from J.D. Douglas, editor *Who's Who in Christian History,* Tyndale 1992.

Elizabeth Fry (1780 – 1845) - English Quaker who initiated many social reform ministries

Elizabeth Fry received strong support from her husband as she began ministering to the needs of others. She gave medicine and clothes to the needy, encouraged parents to send their children to school, advocated bible reading, and organized libraries in more than five hundred coastguard stations around Britain. She also established the "Nursing Sisters of Devonshire Square," a pioneer English institution for training nurses. Fry also found time to raise her eleven children.

Fanny Crosby (1821 – 1915) - American hymn writer

Fanny Crosby was blinded through a physician's negligence at the age of six weeks. Under her own name, as well as under a curious assortment of initials and pen names, she wrote over two thousand hymns, including "Jesus Keep Me Near the Cross," and "To God Be the Glory." Her hymns speak of the gospel of Jesus Christ in a way that has been meaningful to millions of people.

Hanna Whitall Smith (1832 – 1911) - Spokesperson for inner piety and author of the spiritual classic [13]

Hanna was raised in a strict Quaker home and was married to Robert Piersall Smith in 1851. They were converted under Plymouth Brethren influence in 1858 and in 1867 had a new experience of faith that propelled them on a speaking tour of the United States and Europe. Their "Higher Christian Life" meetings in England were exceedingly popular, partly because of D.L. Moody's success there. They observed the founding of the Keswick Convention in 1874, an outgrowth of their conferences.

Amy Charmichael (1867 - 1951) - Missionary to India

Amy Charmichael arrived in India in 1895 under the Church of England Zenana Missionary Society. She served in India for fifty-six years without a furlough. The children of India, especially those who were to be dedicated as temple prostitutes, became the focus of her efforts. From it arose in 1901 the Dohnavur Fellowship, with more than one thousand children in three homes, a hospital, and evangelistic work.

---

[13]*The Christian's Secret of a Happy Life,* London, Nisbet, 1875.

Mildred Cable (1877 – 1952) - Missionary in central Asia

Mildred Cable went to China as a worker with the China Inland Mission in 1900. With two other female missionaries, she developed a model girls' school in Hwochou, graded from kindergarten to a teachers' training department. In 1923 the women set out to be pioneer missionaries among the polyglot peoples of the Gobi Desert (Mongolia). For fifteen years they led "a free, untrammeled missionary life," itinerating among the Gobi oases, "gossiping the gospel."

Valuable Ministries of Women, by Thomas Schreiner[14]

There is so much to do to advance the gospel of Christ that no woman should fear that there is no place for her ministry.

One of the most significant ministries for women (and men too!) is prayer. Without prayer, God's kingdom work on earth will not advance. If in practice we put prayer low on the list of our priorities, then we are actually saying that it is not crucial.

Titus 2:3-5 indicates that mature women have the responsibility of instructing younger women regarding a life of godliness. How the church needs godly women who will instruct younger women in the Christian life! Any woman who has a gift for teaching will find great fulfillment in instructing other women in this way.

It is appropriate for women … to address a mixed audience as articulate and thoughtful representatives of a feminine perspective on many experiences of life. One thinks here of the ministry of Elisabeth Elliot, whom God has used significantly. Moreover, women can exercise their creative gifts through writing, including the writing of curriculum, fiction, nonfiction, scholarly writing about Scripture, and editing.

There are so many ministries today in which a woman can advance the cause of Christ and righteousness: engaging in personal witnessing and joining campus organizations committed to spreading the gospel, ministering to the sick and elderly, fighting against abortion, fighting against pornography, helping with literacy, writing to government leaders to support the cause of righteousness, helping the disabled, aiding the poor,

---

[14]Thomas R. Schreiner is Associate Professor New Testament at Bethel Theological Seminary. Taken from Piper and Grudem, *Recovering Biblical Manhood and Womanhood,* Crossway Books, 1991.

ministering in prisons, counseling and praying with the troubled and confused, supporting missionaries and the church financially, visiting newcomers to the church, extending hospitality to the lonely, using artistic gifts by ministering in music, the visual arts, drama, and theater, helping in youth ministry, etc.

Probably one of the most significant ministry roles for women, although it is not their only role, is their roles as wives and mothers. Paul says that mature women are to "train the younger women to love their husbands and children" (Titus 2:4). One thinks of the godly mothers in Scripture like Sarah, Hannah, Ruth, and Mary. What a significant role they played in the history of redemption as wives and mothers! Countless unknown wives and mothers have had a tremendous impact on their husbands and children, and the influence of these women will only be revealed on the day of redemption.

SEASON OF NEW BEGINNINGS

What many people in our churches are experiencing is NOT revival. But it is the only thing that becomes revival.

May/June 1994 Volume 2, Issue 3

In recent months the Holy Spirit has been falling in meetings throughout the Vineyard. The season of visitation began about the same time in Toronto, Canada at the airport Vineyard and in Anaheim, California, then rippled out across America, Canada, United Kingdom, Australia, New Zealand, and to other parts of the world by now.

As the leader of the Vineyard, many ask me "Is this revival?" My answer is, in my opinion, not yet. But it is the only thing that becomes revival. We're seeing the early stages of an outpouring of the Spirit of God. Some have estimated that as many as 80,000 individuals have been significantly touched and revived to date. It has not yet evolved into what most church historians define as revival: an outpouring of the Holy Spirit in the church and then in the aftermath, through the church into the community resulting in the conversion of thousands.

What is revival? I like John White's definition: "an action of God whereby he pours out his Holy Spirit, initially upon the church, and it comes as an alternative to his judgment which is about to fall on the church and on the secular world."[15] True revival is marked by widespread repentance both within the church, and among unbelievers. Although as many as four thousand have been converted to date (in various Vineyard churches) we've not yet seen the dynamic of thousands and thousands of people coming to Christ rapidly. Of course, that is our prayer and I thought that it would be helpful to review some basic things concerning revival to get us focused.

---

[15]John White, "Prayer and Renewal" course, Canadian Theological Seminary, 7/1/91.

VINEYARD HISTORY

During the last approximately seventeen years God has poured out his Spirit, beginning in what is now called the Vineyard Christian Fellowship in Anaheim and extending through us to churches all over the United States, Canada and Europe, as well as to other places in the world.

Beginning at some time in September of '76, Bob Fulton, Carol Wimber, Carl Tuttle, along with others, began assembling at the home of Carl Tuttle's sister. The agenda was simple: praying, worshipping and seeking the Lord. By the time I came several months later, the Spirit of God was already moving powerfully. There was a great brokenness and responsiveness in the hearts of many. This evolved into what became our church on Mother's Day in 1977.

Soon God began dealing with me about the work of the Spirit related to healing. I began teaching in this area. Over the next year and a half God began visiting in various and sundry ways. There were words of knowledge, healing, casting out of demons, and conversions.

Later we saw an intensification of this when Lonnie Frisbee came and ministered. Lonnie had been a Calvary Chapel pastor and evangelist, being used mightily in the Jesus People Movement. After our Sunday morning service on Mothers' Day 1979, I was walking out the door behind Lonnie, and the Lord told me "Ask that young man to give his testimony tonight." I hadn't even met him, though I knew who he was and how the Lord had used him in the past. That night, after he gave his testimony, Lonnie asked the Holy Spirit to come and the repercussions were incredible. The Spirit of God literally knocked people to the floor and shook them silly. Many people spoke in tongues, prophesied or had visions.

Then over the next few months, hundreds and hundreds of people came to Christ as the result of the witness of the individuals who were touched that night, and in the aftermath. The church saw approximately 1,700 converted to Christ in a period of about three months.

This evolved into a series of opportunities, beginning in 1980, to minister around the world. Thus, the Vineyard renewal ministry and the Vineyard movement were birthed.

EBBS AND FLOWS

By July 1993, VCF Anaheim had an ongoing interaction with the Holy Spirit in which we'd had ebbs and flows. There were times when we had a great sense of nearness and times in which there seemed to be a withdrawal to some degree. But there was never a time in which God was not willing to bless, heal, deliver and touch people. It just wasn't with the same intensity that we'd had early on. Sometimes your family may have a filet mignon for dinner, and sometimes you have leftovers. But you still eat, and you're thankful for whatever it is you have to eat. Many of the folks who were present at the beginning would look back to those early extravagant days when we met "in the gymnasium" as "the good ol' days."

Most of you know about the discovery of my cancer in April of 1993 and the ensuing treatment. In July of 1993, right before the International Vineyard Pastor's Conference began, the Holy Spirit spoke to Carol, my wife. He told her I was to go to the nations. We understood then it meant go to the church in the nations, as against go to evangelize the lost of the world. This in my mind meant a ministry of renewal and revival.

Carol responded, "Lord, my husband is sleeping 20-22 hours a day. He has no voice. Tomorrow pastors from all over the world are going to be here and he won't even be able to participate. If this is indeed your will, touch him tonight. Please give him his voice back so that he may minister."

That's exactly what he did the next morning. I woke up able to speak and with just barely enough energy to go and participate in the conference. It was a very blessed event for me as well as for those that love me in the Vineyard.

By October of 1993 God had spoken 27 times confirming that I should go the nations. Seventeen times he spoke in the same context and said that this would be a "season of new beginnings." The Lord was saying, "I'm going to start it all over again. I'm going to pour out my Spirit in your midst like I did in the beginning."

Last fall, I was sitting in my usual spot in the sanctuary, praying during the worship in song. In my spirit, I felt like Abraham might have felt when he was waiting for the fulfillment of God's promises. The New Testament credits Abraham with not wavering in his faith. He had faith that God was going to do it, but I'm sure Abraham and Sarah had a few moments when they wondered *how* it was going to come together. (That's how Ishmael came about.) Anyway, I was looking at my age – 59, going on 90. I was coming through an incredibly tough year with the cancer. The church had endured the season of adversity coming through it with a new sturdiness and strength. I saw a new strength in our movement. I knew God was moving.

But I looked at myself, and thought, *I'm out of energy.* In my spirit I was just murmuring "Oh God, oh God." And at that point (mid- January) the Lord gave me a word. I heard myself say: *Shall I have this pleasure in my old age?* The very words of Sarah laughingly said to herself when she overheard the Lord say she was going to have a son from her 90-year-old womb by her 100-year-old husband (Genesis 18:10). This was a word of life from the Lord, and it touched me deeply.

I had brought this message of new beginnings to our AVC National Board and Council meeting in November of 1993 at Palm Springs. Then the Lord confirmed this word in the hearts and minds of our national leadership. They laid hands on Bob Fulton and me and they blessed us to go, and stir up the church.

At the same meeting, John Arnott, an APC of the Vineyards in Ontario, Canada, learned from Happy Leman, Midwest RO, how the Holy Spirit had recently powerfully renewed and refreshed Randy Clark (VCF St. Louis) in a meeting conducted by evangelist Rodney Howard-Browne in Tulsa, Oklahoma. How the Lord got Randy to Tulsa for a meeting conducted by a South African Pentecostal is a story in itself. Nevertheless Randy began seeing similar outpourings of the Spirit in his home church and elsewhere as he had occasion to minister. It was as if the "times of refreshing" had begun.

So John Arnott, knowing that a season of new beginnings in the Vineyard was near at hand, and hearing about Randy Clark's transformed ministry, invited Randy to come to Toronto to minister in his church, as well as those folks from the surrounding area that would like to attend. This occurred on January 20, 1994. Four days of meetings turned into five months of almost nightly meetings in numerous locations in Ontario. It has since poured out through those who have visited there into similar renewal meetings all over the United States, Canada, the United Kingdom, and even Europe.

ANAHEIM

Meanwhile at the Anaheim Vineyard beginning on Sunday, December 5, 1993, the Holy Spirit told me to stir up the gifts of the Spirit that our people may have a greater hunger for the Giver, Jesus. Throughout the month of December and early January, we set aside Sunday nights for that with an ever-increasing sense of the Lord's presence and willingness to bless.

On the afternoon of Sunday, January 16, 1994, the Holy Spirit gave me the word "Pentecost." I spent the rest of the afternoon asking the Lord what he meant by it. No answer. At that evening's church service, the Lord gave me a vision of young people in a certain set and order. During the ministry time, from the pulpit I asked the young people to come forward. They did and the Lord came, consuming them in a beautiful and powerful way. It began a significant increase of the outflowing of power at Anaheim that has continued until this writing.

TERMINOLOGY

In interaction with leaders and workers across both the United States and Canada, I have encouraged the Arnott's, as well as Randy Clark and others that have been touched by the Spirit and are being used to share with others, to refer to this present visitation of the Spirit in our churches as a "refreshing" or "renewal" rather than a revival. I have no problem with the notion that people are being revived. I just have a problem with our using a term, that most evangelicals at least, reserve for that *phase* of revival that is an outpouring, not only *on* the church but through the church and *into* the community. The result is the salvation of thousands.

WHERE IN HISTORY?

I recently received an unpublished manuscript by Jerry Steingard, pastor of the Jubilee Vineyard in Stratford, Ontario. Jerry writes, "Throughout biblical history and church history, the hearts of God's people perpetually cool off and harden towards him, creating the need for revival. The Bible records at least a dozen revivals within its history."[16]

In modern history, many movements of renewal and revival have taken place before the Protestant Reformation of the sixteenth century. And don't forget the Puritan and Pietist movements of the seventeenth century. Space doesn't allow me to give much historical detail, but in the past 250 years we've seen many revivals. The intensity of a revival may last only a few years, but the effects reverberate in the church and society for decades to come. Following are some recognized revivals with the approximate time spans.

The First Awakening	1727-80
Second Awakening	1792-1842
The Prayer Meeting Revival or "Businessman's Revival"	1857-9
Welsh Revival	1904
The Pentecostal Revival	1905
The Charismatic Renewal	1960s and 70s

One of the clearest evidences of the efficacy of the English Revival is seen in an article published in a secular magazine called *Gentlemen's Magazine*. The magazine had previously criticized John Wesley, but this is what it had to say about him after his death in 1791:

> The great point in which his name and mission will be honored is this: he directed his labors towards those who had no instructor; to the highways and hedges; to the miners in Cornwall and the colliers in Kingswood ... By the humane and active endeavors of him and his brother Charles, a sense of decency, morals, and religion was introduced into the lowest classes of mankind; the ignorant were instructed; the wretched relieved; and the abandoned reclaimed...

WHAT ABOUT THE PHENOMENA?

Nearly everything we've seen (falling, weeping, laughing, shaking) has been seen before, not only in our memory, but in revivals all over the world. One of my colleagues on the AVC staff, Steve Holt has compiled an

---

[16] Walter C. Kaiser, Jr. *Quest for Renewal.*

extremely helpful summary of Jonathan Edward's thoughts on the place of physical manifestations and phenomena in the midst of revival. During the first Great Awakening in America, Edwards was right in the middle of it all. Not only was he a thoughtful participant, and observer, but he applied his keen theological mind to the "problem" of religious enthusiasms, which were the object of much scorn and criticism among the religious establishment. Edwards's perspective on revival can be very helpful to us as we evaluate some of the manifestations of the Spirit that we see in our meetings. Edwards saw them too, and he developed a very wise counsel regarding it.

Edwards attempted to answer the question, "How do we judge whether these phenomena are from God or the Devil?" Edwards' logic is lucid and spiritual, but after 250 years, some of his language is a challenge. Following are his main points in outline form. For further detail on the writings of Jonathan Edwards, I refer you to his *Complete Works.*

- *We do not judge by a part:* the way it began, the instruments emphasized, the means used, the methods that have been taken. We judge by the effects upon the people (Isaiah 40:13, 14, Jn 3:8; Isaiah 2:17). Edwards reminds us that God often uses the most foolish things to confound the wise.

- We should judge by *the whole of Scripture*, not our own personal rules and measures, nor some portion of Scripture. Furthermore, Edwards enjoins us not to judge phenomena negatively just because we have not personally had such an experience.

- We should *distinguish the good from the bad*, and not judge the whole by the parts. Summation: We can become so paranoid of extremism that we actually sin by grieving the Holy Spirit and stopping his work. To accomplish his work, God seems more willing at times to tolerate extreme behavior (that is not clearly sinful) than we are.

- We should *judge by the fruit of the work in general*. Edwards could justify in his own mind the extravagance of some in the revival because of the revival's impact in New England. The bible was more greatly esteemed; multitudes had been brought to conviction of truth and certainty of the gospel; and the Indians were more open to the gospel than ever before.

- We should *judge by the fruit of the work in particular instances.*

Edwards wrote of many examples of people who had been transported into the glories of the heavenlies for hours at a time. Great rejoicing, transports (visions and dreams), and trembling have produced an increase in humility, holiness, and purity. Answered prayers became the norm.

- *We should judge by the glory of the work.* Edwards passionately called for the church to be seized by the rapture, glory, and enthusiasm of God. In his view, the Great Awakening (with all its various manifestations) was exceedingly glorious in extraordinary degrees of light, love, and spiritual joy that God had bestowed on great multitudes.

RESTORATION AND REVIVAL

There's a time of restoration coming. There's a time of revival coming. There's an outpouring of the Spirit that's preparing the hearts and lives of men and women across our country, and around the world. We saw it recently in New Zealand, and in Australia. The Lord poured out his Spirit mightily. We've seen it in the Anaheim Vineyard this past Spring. We've seen it across the country. It's not just happening in the Vineyard. It's happening wherever there is receptivity.

Remember, as long as people keep hearing about this, and as long as people keep coming, the Spirit will be poured out. The laughter will bubble forth. So don't be afraid of it. It indicates the ongoing truth of God's word. It's another verification that God is among us. It's another standard if you will, being lifted up and exalted unto the Lord. It's his work. It's not craziness. It's not people acting weird. (Not that they don't look crazy and seem strange.) But it's appropriate. The Lord is being exalted by his own means. Remember, the Lord says, "My thoughts are not your thoughts, neither are your ways my ways" (Isaiah 55:8). And God just goes about doing things differently than you or I would.

WHAT DO THE PHENOMENA MEAN?

Our theology and experience of revival must be tempered by our understanding of sanctification. Sanctification is the necessary counterpart to justification, or the forgiveness of sins.

I view sanctification as that work of the Holy Spirit which takes place both as "a one-time act, valid for all time, imputing and imparting holiness, and as an ongoing, progressive work."[17] In the sense that it's ongoing, we co-operate with the Holy Spirit.

All Christians need to be cleansed, and dedicated to the service of God (Romans 12:1,2) and thereby make practical our prayer "Your kingdom come, your will be done on earth (and in my life) as it is in heaven."

Let us not allow ourselves to equate the experience of various manifestations of the Spirit with sanctification. Such experience may accompany, accent, or provide a milestone on the journey of sanctification, but they are not necessarily the agents of sanctification.

HANDLING THE FIRE

In my interaction with Vineyard pastors and leaders across the country, as well as the principles in the early stages of this refreshing, I've given the following counsel.

First I've encouraged the smaller churches to do things a little differently than the mid-sized and larger churches. Keep in mind that the smaller church work force can be quickly consumed and as a consequence burned out when a move of the Spirit comes. They simply do not have the work force and the resources to handle daily meetings in their church. I encourage them not to have daily meetings, but weekly or bi-weekly meetings dedicated to allowing the Spirit to come. I've called these *seeker meetings*. By that I'm simply referring to Christians who are seeking more of the presence and work of God in their lives. Those meetings ought to be characterized by messages that are Christ-centered and altar calls that are Christ-centered, as over against phenomena-centered. In my opinion, it is not valid to invite people forward simply to shake, fall, laugh or cry, or any of the phenomena that we've referenced in this particular event. The phenomena are not at issue. The issue is the impact of the presence of God on the individual's life and the growth of godly character in the aftermath.

For the mid-sized and larger churches, I've encouraged them to have meetings, perhaps one or two or three a week for "seekers". I've also

---

[17]*New Dictionary of Theology*, 615.

encouraged weekly inquiry meetings where people can come and ask questions about the phenomena because it is so disturbing to some and significantly interesting to others. I believe there ought to be room for interaction and that's why I've written this *Reflections* newsletter as well as encourage the writing of a position paper with a number of people in the Vineyard. That paper will soon be available to all the pastors so that they can have a basic understanding of the phenomena in ministry.

In summary, what I'm saying is this. Let's keep the message Christ-centered. Let's keep the meetings to a minimum. Make room for the work of the Spirit, but do not allow the ongoing program of the church to be depleted by it unless the Holy Spirit specifically speaks and is corroborated by those who have oversight of the local church, as well as the Area and the Region.

One last point concerning the ministry. As a result of the influence of both Benny Hinn and Rodney Howard-Browne, some of the churches that have been influenced by the move of the Spirit in Toronto have picked up the habit of providing catchers for the people who have come forward in the meetings. In my interaction with both John and Carol Arnott and Randy Clark, I've expressed my concern that this creates somewhat of a difficult problem for me in that it focuses the phenomena of the Spirit primarily on the issue of falling and whatever would occur in the aftermath. I believe that will, long term, prove to be a negative as over against a positive.

Second, it produces first and second class people. Those who are ministering, are looked on as the powerful ones and those who are catching are just playing, as it were, accompaniment to the powerful ministry of others. On the other hand, those who are leading in ministry, can seek to train "catchers" so that they don't remain in a passive role. This multiplies ministry, and harmonizes with the historical Vineyard practice of encouraging everyone with the thought – and I believe biblical teaching – that we can all minister in the power of the Spirit. In other words, there are no superstars.

Consequently I am encouraging Vineyard pastors at these meetings to have people stand where they're seated and pray over them, instead of having them come forward. Then if they fall, they'll fall back into their seats. If you have any kind of a loose seating arrangement, give it an additional three or four inches between rows so that people can get into them and pray for them, as well as those people surrounding them. This would be consistent with our ministry pattern in the past and I think it'll readily serve the affect that we're looking for and the people we're ministering to.

This advice, of course doesn't disallow altar calls or catchers if you feel led to do so. I'm simply encouraging a consistency with our prayer models.

In discussing all of this with John Arnott, he has encouraged me to remind you of the issues of faith and vulnerability. It's been their experience to date that many people don't receive readily and need to be encouraged to give a protracted period of time over the seeking of the Lord. This is consistent with our experience over the years as well.

Last of all, I would encourage the continuing prayer for the individual in that I do believe there is benefit, at least in some cases, for protracted periods of prayer over people that the Spirit of God is resting on. Pray as the Holy Spirit leads you so that they will get the best benefit.

SUMMARY

In summary I believe that this could readily become the revival we've all longed for and prayed for. I do not believe that it has reached its full stature yet, but I believe it may be around the corner. People have asked me what I think the next step may be. I've said that I know that at some point in time we must give a call to full scale repentance under-girded by deep and heart felt contrition. Changed lives and the fruit of true repentance will result.

The Best Effects, by Jonathan Edwards[18]

> Whatever imprudences there have been, and whatever sinful irregularities; whatever vehemence of the passions, and heats of the imagination, transports, and ecstasies; whatever error in judgment, indiscreet zeal; and whatever outcries, faintings, and agitations of body; yet, it is manifest and notorious, that there has been of late a very uncommon influence upon the minds of a very great part of the inhabitants of New England, attended with the best effects.

> There has been a great increase of seriousness, and sober consideration of eternal things; a disposition to hearken to what is said of such things, with attention and affection; a disposition to treat

---

[18]From *Some Thoughts Concerning the Present Revival,* 1743.

matters of religion with solemnity, and as of great importance; to make these things the subject of conversation; to hear the word of God preached, and to take all opportunities in order to …

97

REFRESHING, RENEWAL, AND REVIVAL

If you then, though you are evil, know how to give good gifts to your children, how much more will your Father in heaven give the Holy Spirit to those who ask him! (Luke 11:13)

July/August 1994, Volume 2, Issue 4

In the last edition of *Reflections,* I wrote about the recent move of the Spirit in many of our churches, calling it a season of new beginnings. The Holy Spirit has recently touched many of you in powerful – and extraordinary – ways.

Approximately 5,000 different people came to Anaheim for the "Let the Fire Fall" meetings in July. Many – including myself – were ministered to profoundly. Since "Fire Fall" over a thousand people have responded with phone calls, interaction in the hallways, letters and notes. That's the largest response to any meeting or conference we've ever had.

As this move of the Spirit has increased and spread, we've had both positive and negative responses. In this article I want to address some of the ways we look at these things, and respond to them.

Most people love babies, but they don't necessarily like the details of the birthing process. The birthing of a child is a messy experience at best. Not many people want to hear about that part. The same thing applies to revival. We love to read and hear about revival. But going through the birthing process of revival, is very much like the birthing of a child: messy. And it can bring all kinds of reactions, some of which are positive, and some of which are negative.

In my opinion, it's not necessary to explain everything connected with revival any more than a young mother needs to share in detail the travail of the birthing process. All she has to do is hold the baby up and everyone shares in the joy.

TESTING THE FRUIT

First, I think it's too soon to evaluate this move of the Spirit in its entirety. We have the challenge of evaluating something that we are participating in as well as observing. Nevertheless, we assess this from both biblical criteria and from an objective understanding of our experience. That doesn't mean experience carries the same weight as the word of God, but experience, church history (and tradition to a certain degree) are undoubtedly lenses through which we view life. Church history helps illustrate how other godly people have interacted with the scriptures while trying to discern the activity of the Holy Spirit around them. As we relate as Christians, there are things we've learned, and that understanding acts as a foundation for evaluating what happens to us.

Scripture uses the idea of fruit as a way of evaluating spiritual teaching. Jesus told how to recognize false prophets in Matthew 7:16: "By their fruit you will recognize them. Do people pick grapes from thorn bushes, or figs from thistles?" Jesus was teaching that any evaluation must go beyond initial impressions, or outward appearances. Look for the fruit. Fruit takes time to grow, and time to see what something will become over time. In Southern California you can find apples on the tree in July, but they won't be ready to eat until around October.

So we must not react too quickly or in some way unjustly, merely because what we're seeing doesn't fit our particular understanding. Gamaliel used the same "wait and see" approach in the fifth chapter of Acts when debating the Sanhedrin over what to do with the apostles who had disregarded the gag order to stop teaching in the name of Jesus. The Sanhedrin was on the verge of killing Peter and the other apostles. Gamaliel stepped in to offer his wise advice: "Leave these men alone! Let them go! For if their purpose or activity is of human origin, it will fail. But if it is from God, you will not be able to stop these men; you will only find yourselves fighting against God" (Acts 5:38,39).

We find another illustration of a balanced attitude towards unusual spiritual reality in Acts 11:17. In Acts chapter 10, Peter preached the gospel of Christ in the house of Cornelius, a Gentile. Remember, it took an angelic visit, a vision, and the voice of the Holy Spirit to get Peter to this divine appointment. Peter, a Jew, was way beyond his comfort zone just being in the house of a Roman centurion. When he found a large gathering of people there, he began preaching the gospel of Christ. Before Peter could finish his sermon, "the Holy Spirit came on all who heard the message" (Acts 10:44). God shook things up. They began speaking in tongues and praising God, in essence a repeat of what happened in Jerusalem on the Day of Pentecost. Peter made the connection between what he saw and something Jesus said: "John baptized with water, but you will be baptized with the Holy Spirit" (Acts 11:16; Acts 1:5).

How was the news of this mighty visitation of God's Spirit received by the apostles and other believers in Judea? With criticism! The church hadn't yet developed a theological grid for understanding what had happened at Cornelius' house. Hadn't the prophecy of Joel said God would pour out his Sprit on all people? Even though he may not have fully understood it – even though he may not have even liked it - Peter defused the anti-Gentile prejudice in Jerusalem by saying: "So if God gave them the same gift as he gave us, who believe in the Lord Jesus Christ, who was I to think I could oppose God?" (v.17).

God sometimes offends our intellect, and our sense of propriety (John 6:53ff. esp. v. 61). But that's all right, because he's God. Peter in effect is saying, "Guys, I know this isn't the way we would have done this. But we're not in charge, God is. He filled these people with the Spirit. He touched them in the same way that he touched us. Let's see what God wants to do next, and by all means let's not condemn this. Let's not let our prejudices blind us to God's work. Let's wait and see what the fruit will be."

As we evaluate this season of renewal, let's realize that little happens in and through the church that's not some sort of mixture of humanity and the Holy Spirit. And we can't rule out the possibility of demonic activity either, or else why do we read in the epistles "Test everything. Hold on to the good" (1 Thessalonians 5:21). So some may say "Oh that's the flesh" or "That's a demon." Or "That's just people acting up." Or "That's God." All those analyses might be accurate at any given time. Our role, as pastoral leaders, is to exercise discernment, and bring correction when it's needed.

Unfortunately, revival and refreshing sometimes stimulate responses that are less than 100 percent godly. Revival and refreshing come because the church is at a low ebb. The church, in spite of its avowal of biblical truth, is not experiencing that reality. God doesn't revive people who have it all together. He revives people who are hungry, thirsty, weak, naked, blind, and less that spotless.

Regarding the current season of renewal, yes, some people are reacting, or overreacting, and resisting. But it's too soon to know what it's all going to become. So based on the New Testament perspective of fruit, we must wait and look for the fruit of what happens.

Yes, there have been some negative responses. By comparison, they are in the minority, but it's nonetheless true. Some who attended the "Fire Fall" were confused by what they saw and heard. Other felt left out because of an unspoken assumption that unless something outwardly dramatic happens to you, then you haven't received anything beneficial. In the afterglow of a glorious meeting, one lady approached Lance Pittluck with a worried look on her face. "The only thing that happened to me," she said, "is that I have this incredible inner sense of peace and joy." Lance reassured her that she shouldn't feel left out if the only immediate by-product is a sense of peace and joy. That's the fruit of the Spirit.

A few other participants felt used or abused by overzealous ministry on the part of some. This obviously needs correction because we want people to receive ministry in a loving, affirming, biblically sound way. Nonetheless, it's the way some people are when they are excited, touched and moved.

In the excitement of the infilling and empowering, and moving of the Spirit, some people momentarily do things that they really ought not to do. They say or do things that they think are in vogue, like "Fall, fall, fall…" or "Roar, roar, roar…". Frankly, that zeal is excusable – for now – but the methodology of the ministry to one another needs correction.

We have pastoral obligation to bring correction to our teams and to those that minister, but we also have responsibility to interact with those who have has for one reason or another, a negative experience.

Some pastors present were concerned by the experiences they were witnessing. Some of the explanations seemed inadequate, and frankly some of them were. And they were concerned about the administration of the meetings. I want to address the issue of pastoral administration of renewal meetings.

ADMINISTRATION

Some of the pastors were bothered by having people make noises or falling or doing other unusual things during preaching. They felt that the ministry of preaching ought not to be mixed with phenomena, or at least not interrupted. (During "Fire Fall", some speakers used their pastoral authority to restrain outbreaks of laughter during their talks without quenching the work of the Spirit.)

From nearly 2,000 years of church history we've inherited a biblical framework within which to work. We've developed and refined orthodoxy – right belief. And we've defined orthopraxy, right practice. As a church movement the Vineyard is theologically congruent with historical orthodoxy. But with practice, I admit we're bumping against the borders. So whatever we endorse, in the way of teaching or experience must have a solid grounding in the word of God.

Most of what we've been experiencing in our meetings has been of God. But it's God in humans. I trust God entirely - its human beings that concern me. That doesn't mean we have to expel every little thing that doesn't have a proof text. For the time being, we can leave a few things in the file folder labeled "I don't know."

Nevertheless, let's focus on the "fruit" that we can clearly demonstrate in the Scripture, like devotional life, witnessing, healing the sick, casting out demons, and feeding the poor.

EDIFICATION AS THE GOAL

First Corinthians 11.18 through 14.40 deals with the abuses of the gifts and spiritual phenomena in the church at Corinth. Beginning at 11.18, Paul addresses the issue of divisions among them. In Corinth, people were polarized along lines of personal allegiance (1 Corinthians 1:12), along economic lines (1 Corinthians 11:22), and apparently along lines of spiritual gifting.

In the twelfth chapter, the first eleven verses he deals with the ignorance concerning spiritual gifts. Paul uses the "body metaphor" to explain the exquisite interaction of the spiritual gifts. He talks about the eye, the ear, the nose, and the foot, and how we all need each other as a body. When we gather, there ought to be a functioning together for the edification and benefit of all. He hammers the theme of respecting, honoring, blessing, deferring, loving, edifying, and building up one another. We use our spiritual gifts to edify and build the whole church, not to lift up ourselves.

Using that criterion alone, the overall effect of this visitation has been overwhelmingly positive. There was some excessive enthusiasm going on at Corinth, and we see it from time to time in contemporary settings. But we can deal with it in a positive way that will encourage the ongoing dynamic of God's visitation among us. I've seen people strengthened, and encouraged. I see a greater willingness for the saints to roll up their sleeves and work in various avenues on ministry. It's a lovely thing to see people hungry for and excited about God. That reality however has to be weighed against the various and sundry instances of emotion excess.

Paul goes on in the thirteenth chapter to deal with the issue of love. Paul diagnoses the problem in Corinth as disunity, disrespect, distorting of gifts, and divisions. But it's also a lack of love. Paul wants the Corinthian church to love each other with the love of Christ in a more manifest, and demonstrable way.

In the fourteenth chapter, he prescribes three earmarks of ministry in corporate gathering of the church:

- Intelligibility – vv. 4,5,7,9,11,23.

- Order – vv. 26-33, and then summarizes in v. 40.

- Edification – vv. 12,17,19, and 23.

When the Spirit is moving in a church – made up of fallible human beings – there's potential for abuse. The answer is love, order, clarity and edification. He gives a summary text in v. 40 of the fourteenth chapter that says: "But everything should be done in a fitting and orderly way."

We don't need to legislate what goes on in our renewal meetings as long as the brethren are being built up and edified. But we do need to administrate our meetings based on biblical discernment. Some people have more openness and ease in the presence of the "chaos" of the Spirit. Some have little tolerance for this activity. Fine. We must learn, as pastors, to minister to people at both ends of the spectrum…and everyone in between.

Some will insist on a "right and wrong" approach to this situation, but it isn't that way. As pastors we have to keep everybody balanced to encourage the growth and nurture of the body of Christ. Therefore meetings ought to have some sort of order and blessing. Yet, the idea of order is largely defined within a culture. A worship service that would be considered orderly in Brazil might be seen as anything but orderly by someone in Scotland.

We don't have a New Testament text that prescribes what elements a New Testament worship service must have, but many scriptures give us enough to form an outline. For example we find scriptures that talk about worshipping God through song: Colossians 3:16, Acts 16:25; Ephesians

5:19. These and many other scriptures formed the building blocks for our theology of worship, helping us to understand worship as our first priority.

Other elements of the church gathered can be found: preaching; (1 Timothy 4:13, 5:17); fellowship (Acts 2:42); breaking bread (Acts 2:42); prayer (Acts 2:42; 16:25); reading of Scripture (1 Tim 4:13); collecting tithes, offerings, and alms for the poor (Romans 15:25-27; 2 Corinthians 9:7ff; 1 Timothy 5:8).

Then there's what we would call the gifts or ministry area of gathering (1 Corinthians 12:8-11): revelation; knowledge; prophecy; prophecy/interpretation; healing; deliverance, etc. All these things, in my opinion are normative activities in the church.

Do Paul's prescriptions in First Corinthians regarding the exercise of gifts in a public setting apply to any and every situation in which the body of Christ meets? I don't think so.

Different kinds of situation utilize different kinds of "order." The church can meet for a variety of purposes: prayer, funerals, weddings. We meet for the purpose of evangelism. The church in Jerusalem met for the distribution of food to the widows. The church carries out its mission in a variety of settings, each with its own proper sense of order. "Order" in one type of meeting will mean something different than order in another type. We have funerals in our church. And we have baptisms in swimming pools. Both gatherings are for important reasons, but what serves as order for one would be inappropriate for the other.

Therefore, the expectation of what constitutes order in a meeting devoted to renewal may differ from a typical Sunday morning worship service that is open to the public. On certain occasions in Scripture God demonstrates a different understanding of order that we have within our culture. Within the Western rational mind-set which most of us in the US have inherited, we have some naturalistic assumptions. We usually think of everything in terms of cause and effect. Well, not everything we read about in Scripture fits within that framework. There are things where we can't see the cause and/or effect. Some things happen that cannot be explained by natural means.

For instance, chapter 5 of 2 Chronicles related how the Ark of the Covenant was installed in the new Temple. In the midst of resounding worship, with musicians and singers, the text says that "… the house of the Lord was filled with a cloud, so that the priests could not continue ministering (lit. stand to minister) because of the cloud; for the glory of the Lord filled the house of God" (2 Chronicles 5:13, 14).

How would that fit into our culturally viewed understanding of "order"? We like things in a certain sequence, without surprises. We like things dished up in a certain way. And I don't have any problem with that. But neither do I have a problem with having less order *for short periods of time or a specific focus.* But I probably have more tolerance for that than many people.

EXPERIENCES

Neither the bible nor I equate phenomena such as falling, shaking, crying out, laughing or making animal noises as an experience with God. However, you can have an experience with God that may result in some of those responses. So when I pray for someone I don't say "shake" "fall" or "roar". I've never prayed for anybody to do anything except get closer to God, get filled with the Spirit, get touched by God, get blessed, come into greater belief – things that are clearly defined in Scripture.

I want the experience of God's blessing to be as sovereign as it possibly can be, with the proviso that God is using human instruments. Most of us have had encounters with God at the hands of other people. Someone told me about Jesus. Someone prayed for me to receive Christ. Someone else laid hands on me at a given time to be baptized with the Spirit.

One of the problems with human instruments is that quite often the human explanation is inadequate to the experience. In my case I was converted at one point, and I was baptized in the Spirit at another point. Later someone tried to explain it to me. So for a time I saw these works if God as sequential. But when I started studying the New Testament, I saw individuals getting it all at once. In time, my understanding of Scripture tempered the explanations I had been given. Not every experience will yield and explanation. Some things are a mystery, because there is much about God that we don't understand (Isaiah 55:8).

I see these unusual experiences as one of many means to get where we want to go in our walk with Christ. For Peter, James, and John seeing Jesus transfigured on the mountain into his glorified state was an awesome experience with few parallels. Their natural tendency was to build some monuments to the experience. God interjected: "This is my Son, whom I love; with him I am well pleased. Listen to him!" (Matthew 15:5b). That's the test of all these renewal experiences – they need to direct our eyes and ears, to God's Son, Jesus.

So if someone comes to me after they've shaken, fallen down, or made a noise, my question is "Do you love Jesus more? Do you believe in him more? Are you more committed to Him?" If the answer is "Yes!" then praise the Lord! I hope that from this day forward she will walk closer to God in a more accountable, more mature, and more godly way that she ever has before.

EXPLAINING THE UNEXPLAINABLE

I'm comfortable with the fact that people, under the excitement of a visitation, do some far out things. Some things do occur because of over zealousness, emotional disorder, or the devil. And some occur because of God. Most of us come to God with all that in place anyway. That's why we need sanctification. That's why the word of God has to be worked in us and out of us in a daily way.

We spend a lifetime sorting out the fleshly, and devilish influences in our lives from the things of the Spirit, so that those things that are wrought of God, and of the Spirit will be built into our lives. As the Westminster Shorter Catechism describes, through "God's free grace…we are renewed in the whole man after the image of God, and are enabled more and more to die to sin and live unto righteousness."

So I discourage trying to pry an explanation out of the Bible for the more exotic, and extra biblical experiences of some. You won't find any scripture that says "pogo your way to Jesus." But it does happen to people from time to time. We've seen various vocal expressions of roaring, moaning, crying out or screaming. We've also seen an increase in what we might call the emotional responses: laughing, crying, the screaming again. Whereas many bible characters responded emotionally to God from time to time, I don't see any place where the Scripture endorses or recommends that activity, other than it might relate to repentance. These are just some to the varied ways human beings respond to an encounter with God, so therefore they can be allowed.

TRADITIONAL SIGNS OF REVIVAL

During this season of renewal, I've been looking for some of the historic signs of revival. Until fairly recently in the Toronto meetings, they were seeing a few conversion every week. Recently John Arnott told me that in the last month they've gone from just a handful, to averaging about 50-100 new converts a week in their renewal meetings.

That's what we've been looking for, a quickened response to the gospel, and seeing more and more people saved. You say, "Well does that mean this other part is not important?" No! It's the warming of the church. It's the blessing of the church. We need to be blessed so we can go out. We don't get revival without the church being blessed out of its mind, and touched by the Spirit of God.

FUTURE DIRECTION

After an exhaustive study of the Scriptures relating to these issues I prayed, "Lord, what do you want me to bring in the way of direction to this whole thing? As the leader of the movement, what do you want me to say to our people?" The Lord gave me an extremely vivid open vision.

In the picture he showed me a magnificent mountain lake. Beautiful sunshine reflected off the water that was so fresh and inviting. The water of the lake spilled over a dam and cascaded into a river and come down the sides of a mountain into a large plain. In the plain, there were thousands and thousands of acres of vineyards. I saw men working in the fields, digging irrigation ditches. Then the vision ended.

So I said, "Lord, what does it mean?" In my mind, he gave me "The lake is the blessing I'm pouring out. Isn't it beautiful? Isn't it fresh?" I was so touched, I began crying. He then said, "The cascading stream is the church. I'm pouring it first into the church." And I wept more. I just thought, "Oh thank you Lord. Thank you for the blessing on the church."

Then I saw again how the water came down to the bottom of the mountain in to the plain, where the workers were tending the irrigation ditches. I recognized these irrigation ditches as "Ministry to the poor, ministry to the weak, sick, broken and lost." There were different kinds of vineyards with different kinds of fruit growing on the vines. Then he said, "That's my people. This blessing can either stay in the church, with great meetings that eventually end. Or we can pull the gates up and let the water begin flowing. If you want, you can direct the water, the blessing into the fields."

I got the clear impression of a co-laboring. God was pouring out his blessing. But if we don't dig the channels, if we don't go out into the highways and by-ways, if we don't put evangelism forward, if we didn't do the things God called us to do, revival won't spread.

When I recently shared that with some other pastors, some began weeping. John Arnott said, "That's it. And that's the whole issue." In Arnott's church people are showing up nightly from all over the world wanting a touch from God. The Anaheim Vineyard has also seen an increase in visitors. With so many people coming from so many places, I would like to see us mobilize ourselves so that when the phone rings in the church office, the receptionist answers this way: "Yes, we are having renewal meetings, you're welcome to come. We'll also be going out into the community during the day to give it away."

What if each day of the week there was a different opportunity for the newly revived people to immediately take the water into the fields? Today we're going to package food and take it to the poor. Tomorrow we're going to give out tracts and witness and minister in the streets. The next day we're going to go to all the hospitals and the old age homes.

In other words let's begin organizing ourselves to give this blessing away. Then the person who comes to a renewal meeting will not only get a touch from God, but he'll also be touching others for God. They'll go home with the whole story. They won't go home and talk about how they shook for three hours. They'll go home and talk about the 87-year-old lady they led to the Lord, or the 56-year-old man who was sick in the hospital and got up and went home after they prayed for him. They'll talk about the evidences that are clear and well-articulated in the Scripture. God has called us to the *doing* of the gospel.

Those of you who have received and are continuing to receive, need to give some of it away? The next step, I believe, is into the community, among the people.

Let's not get distracted with the overzealous activity of some, but keep our focus on the main and plain things of Scripture. Jesus Christ has chosen to bless us. We've now had over 100,000 people in all our combined churches touched by the Spirit. God is moving.

One of our Vineyard pastors called to say they were having a thousand people a day in meetings in Atlanta this last week. They were having 300 pastors a day. He said, "God is pouring out His Spirit. What do we do?"

"Do more of it! Just do it with everything you've got in you, as hard as you can, and as fast as you can and for as long as you can. Do it in a way that will be a blessing to everybody that you have opportunity to bless."

A number of years ago I pasted in the front of my bible a quote from John Wesley that's been a delight to me. In 1791, he wrote, "Do all the good you can, by all the means you can, and in all the ways you can, and in all the places you can, and at all the times you can, and to all the people you can, as long as you ever can."

Let the fire fall, but remember the fire is for others, as well as for us. If we miss that, we've missed the whole point of the blessing.

In the next edition of *Reflections* I will share some of the conclusions of a recent AVC Board meeting held here in Anaheim. The agenda of that meeting dealt with many issues surrounding the season of renewal, including how the Vineyard model of ministry relates to how we in the Vineyard are experiencing God's breath of renewal today.

AN UNCHANGING DESTINATION

As a movement where can we find a moral, spiritual, and intellectual grid for evaluating the current renewal activity in the Vineyard? The Word of God.

September/October 1994, Volume 2, Issue 5

In recent days Todd Hunter and I have had the privilege of interacting with the ideas of three world-wide Pentecostal leaders. These exchanges have helped solidify our thinking on the current renewal in the Vineyard. In this edition of *Reflections,* I want to share these convictions with you.

Many people have asked me how I interpret the current move of the Spirit. It is important to understand the context and presuppositions from which I draw my conclusions. Our earliest commission as a group of churches was to be a church planting movement for the sake of winning the lost. In this sense, being true to our young traditions and ideals will serve us well. For me, our historic identity provides a moral, spiritual and intellectual grid for evaluating the current renewal activity in the Vineyard.

My chief concern as overseer of the Vineyard is whether the renewal activity will contribute to or hinder our ability to achieve our goals of evangelism through church planting. Esteemed missiologist Donald McGavran describes revival as revitalizing a pre-existing church which was made up of people who professed to already being converted. A "revived" church then produces new converts: this is a measuring rod, and a destination. I liken it to a rocket ship launched with a pre-determined flight plan and enough fuel to arrive. If the Vineyard has run out of fuel, and needs a booster rocket (similar to the ones I will cite from Acts) and the current renewal will provide additional fuel to reach our destination, then I welcome it and humbly and gratefully receive it.

If, however, the renewal is merely a flashy explosion in the sky, or if it causes a change in the trajectory of the rocket, then I must - out of obedience to God - bring correction to it so we do not go off course.

POWER FOR MISSION

According to historian Vinson Synan, few revivals since the time of Wesley did not include such phenomena as laughing, falling, shaking, loud cries, etc. What has not been as common, however, is a judicious understanding of, or a strategy for dealing with the phenomena.

Along with Dr. Synan and my friend Jack Hayford, I see the current phenomena taking place in some of our meetings as signs. A sign points to something beyond itself; it is not the main focus. They're signs God is moving in our midst. That doesn't mean that when no one is shaking or falling, God it not with us. God is omnipresent. He is present in the Word, in the sacraments, and in the common fellowship of the saints. However, in the phenomena we see signs of his "manifest" presence.

Logically we might ask: What do the signs mean? Where do they point us? In my judgment, they are analogous to marching orders. Here again, my friends' confirmations to me were helpful: Phenomena are not the essence of revival. The essence of revival in the usual historical sense of the word consists of:

- Mass conversions

- Changed lives (i.e. sanctification and increased personal piety)

- Measurable impact on society

- Christians have a spiritual breakthrough whereby they are given a great commission, the power for service, and the spiritual giftedness to carry out their commission as ambassadors of Christ's kingdom.

These elements describe the focus of historic, mainstream Pentecostalism that has always targeted world evangelization, using church planting as its main vehicle to achieve its end. According to Dr Synan, at this time over one million churches (one-quarter of all the churches worldwide and three-quarters of evangelicalism) trace their spiritual lineage to the Azusa Street Revival.

One historian described early Pentecostal missionaries as "...a breed of men and women unlike any before them".

They carried a burden for lost souls and were marked by the sacrificial self-giving of their predecessors. But they were also the recipients of a new move of God in their time. They saw Pentecostal baptism with its resulting supernatural signs as evidence that...God's hour of reaping was at hand.[19]

This emphasis of course has biblical precedent. Michael Green in his book *I Believe in the Holy Spirit* clarifies when he writes, "the Spirit of God comes upon Christian individuals in order to create in them a quality of life that would otherwise be beyond their powers." He adds, "There can be no doubt from a candid examination of the New Testament accounts that the prime purpose of the coming of the Spirit of God upon the disciples was to equip them for mission."[20] Finally, Green rightly says, "it is the Spirit who energizes the evangelism of the church and drives its often unwilling members in the task for which God laid His hand on them; Mission."[21]

A surprising illustration is found in the life of D.L. Moody. Surprising because he was not a Pentecostal or charismatic evangelist. Yet this is Moody's testimony after many years of preaching:

> ...two women would say to him regularly, "You need the power of the Holy Spirit". Moody reflected thereafter: "I need the power! Why, I thought I had the power (because) I had the largest congregation in Chicago and there were many conversions. I was in a sense satisfied." Soon, though, the two godly women were praying with Moody, and "they poured out their hearts in prayer that I might receive the filling of the Holy Spirit. There came a great hunger into my soul...I began to cry out as I never did before. I really felt that I did not want to live if I could not have this power for service." Sometime later Moody related this: "One day, in the city of New York - oh, what a day! - I cannot describe it, I seldom refer to it; it is almost too sacred an experience to name. Paul had an experience of which he never spoke for fourteen years. I can only say that God revealed Himself to me, and I had such an experience of His love that I had

---

[19]L. Grant McClung, Jr., Editor, *Azusa Street and Beyond: Pentecostal Missions and Church Growth in the Twentieth Century,* South Plainfield, N.J., Bridge, 1986, 32, explanation added.

[20]Michael Green, *I Believe in the Holy Spirit,* London, Hodder & Stoughton, 1975, 68.

[21]*I Believe in the Holy Spirit,* 77.

to ask Him to stay His hand. I went to preaching again. The sermons were not different; I did not present any new truths, and yet hundreds were converted. I would not now be placed back before that blessed experience if you should give me all the world."[22]

Moody's associate R.A. Torrey, put it this way:

If I may be baptized with the Spirit, I must be...If I am not willing to pay the price of this baptism, and therefore am not so baptized, I am responsible before God for all the souls that might have been saved but were not saved through me because I was not baptized with the Holy Spirit.[23]

PERSPECTIVE

It is of utmost importance to me for every Vineyard leader to realize that phenomena are not central to church life. The vital aspects of our roles as pastors who direct church life are:

- Teaching the Word of God; not merely teaching from the bible or about the bible, but communicating the word of God as contained in the scripture. Noted missiologist Donald McGavran, writing on the relationship between God's word and revival says, "Knowledge of the Bible is...necessary. It does not invariably lead to revival; but unless it is there, revival in the classic sense does not usually occur."24

- Administering the ordinances of communion for all the believers, and baptism following conversion. In so doing we continually lift up the essence of Christianity: Christ's substitutionary death on the cross, and our subsequent new life as publicly expressed in baptism.

- Pastoring our people through the normal ups-and-downs of everyday living; training them in the basic skills needed to be effective

---

[22]W. R. Moody, *The Life of Dwight L Moody, by his son W.R. Moody,* London: Morgan & Scott, 19, 146-47, 149.
[23]E. W. Blumhofer, *The Assemblies of God: A Popular History,* Springfield, Mo: Radiant Books, 1985, 11 (emphasis hers).
[24]Donald McGavran, *Understanding Church Growth, 3rd Edition,* Grand Rapids Michigan: Eerdmans, 1990, 135.

spouses, parents, workers, business leaders, etc.

- Equipping the saints for ministry so they have a solid biblical and practical basis for launching out with their newly experienced renewal.

- Leading our people in worship - Worship that is honest about where we are, and honoring of who God is.

- Finally, we all need to "do the work of an evangelist" (1 Timothy 4:5). We are not all equally gifted in evangelism, but we all are equally called to do the work of evangelism.

This list of six characteristics is not exhaustive, but it does cover the basic, vital issues. If you think of a six cylinder car, how happy would you be if it were operating on only five cylinders? How about four? Three? We cannot neglect even one of the above and hope to have truly healthy churches, much less revived ones! In my opinion, any Vineyard pastor who neglects the above to pursue or give too great a place to phenomena long-term is making a potentially fatal mistake, as far as that local congregation is concerned.

Many people are discussing Jonathan Edwards in our current context, and I want to share my views as well. The phenomena that sometimes accompanied his preaching ministry were in his word "surprising." Based on my understanding, Edwards would have never thought to employ techniques to insure the continuance of phenomena. He saw them as spontaneous. And like us, as having to do with the unity of man, meaning sometimes the presence of the Spirit produces intellectual, spiritual, physical, and emotional reactions.

Edwards would say we cannot discern what is really happening to someone based solely on what is happening to their body. This being the case, bodily reactions were not the end or the goal for Edwards; conversions were.

The long and wooden (to modern ears) title of this treatise says it all: "A Humble Attempt to Promote Explicit Agreement and Visible Union of God's People in Extraordinary Prayer for the Revival of Religion and the Advancement of Christ's Kingdom on Earth."

As you can see, Edwards was concerned with:

- The spiritually sick state of the church,

- The moral collapse of Britain and America,

- And most importantly, that men and women would be converted.

Conversion was the most important manifestation to Jonathan Edwards!

In short, it seems to me he conceived of it propositionally, this way: if we will humbly and sincerely pray, God will send His power. This is spiritual power to do God's will in all the spheres of Christian life: worshipping, learning, working, playing, holy living and evangelizing, but especially power to proclaim the Gospel. Christians endued with this power and working in obedience to the Spirit will advance God's kingdom, and then, in God's sovereign timing, the end shall come (Matthew24:14).

THE SPIRIT'S FIRE

First Thessalonians 5:19 contains an important imperative that rings constantly in my ears: "Do not put out the Spirit's fire" (NIV). Using the rule of thumb for understanding the Greek construction of this sentence, one could also properly translate it, "Stop quenching the Spirit." Paul could be saying to not do something in the future; or he may be saying to stop what is already going on. The latter interpretation fits the larger context of the Thessalonian letters. If we assume, as most scholars do, that these two letters are linked thematically, and were written very close chronologically, then 2 Thessalonians 2:2 may shed some light here. In that passage Paul addresses the Thessalonian confusion and fear about missing the second coming of Christ. Evidently prophecy (literally "a spirit") was causing some of their discomfiture and may have provided the background for a negative predisposition concerning prophecy and the work of the Spirit.

Come closer to home, here in the Vineyard many of us have had some negative experiences with prophecy and various manifestations of the Holy Spirit. These disappointments can easily result in "putting out the Spirit's fire." With all that is within us, we leaders will strive to not make that mistake. But neither will we let the Spirit's fire be used in destructive ways. Following all the relevant biblical mandates will help us "keep the fire in the fireplace" where it is productive and not on the carpet where it could spread and burn down the house! We'll endeavor to strike this balance by following the remaining verses in the passage from I Thessalonians: "Do not treat prophecies with contempt. Test everything. Hold on to the good" (I Thessalonians5:20-21 NIV).

One way for us to keep the fire in the fireplace in our context has to do with the objective of and the way we conduct ministry times. One sure sign of renewal in our midst is the obvious hunger of people who come forward for ministry. We have an important responsibility before God to handle these people and their hunger in godly and biblical ways.

Our objective when the Spirit begins to move on people seeking renewal is three-fold:

1. To insure that they have had the initiating (for service) experience of the baptism of the Holy Spirit.

2. To facilitate the actualizing of the gifts of the Spirit in their lives.

3. And finally, to secure in them a "great commission consciousness" that will thrust them into mission; at work or school, in their neighborhood or on the foreign mission field.

BIBLICAL MANIFESTATION

A review of six times the Spirit fell upon people in Acts (chapters 2, 4, 8, 9, 10, 19) demonstrates the kinds of manifestations we can be sure are godly and biblical.

Acts 2

- The church is empowered to witness.
- They spoke in tongues.
- Peter was transformed from a man who denied Christ to a simple, direct, effective and powerful preacher (Acts 2:37, 41; 1 Peter 1:12).
- 3,000 listeners were converted.

Acts 4

- The church is persecuted.
- The church prayed.
- The church is empowered (with boldness).

Acts 8

- Simon "saw" something (presumably tongues or prophecy) that demonstrated to him that the Spirit was given at the laying on of the apostle's hands.

- The gospel was extended "from Jerusalem to Samaria" through Philip who was "full of the Spirit and wisdom" (Acts 9:20 [NIV]).

Acts 9

- The Spirit falls upon Saul (Paul) and empowers him. He "at once began to preach that Jesus is the Son of God" (Acts 9:20 [NIV]).

- Paul's entire apostolic ministry is empowered by this event (Acts 9:15, 31; 22:15; 26:16).

- Thus, the Gospel is spread to the Gentiles.

Acts 10

- The Spirit is "poured out": on the Gentiles (a still further missions thrust).

- The Gospel is now spread not only to the Gentiles, but will be spread through them as well to the uttermost parts of the earth!

Acts 19

- The Holy Spirit falls on some disciples in Ephesus and they spoke in tongues and prophesied.

- Paul taught (and modeled kingdom ministry) for almost three years. One of the most explosive expansions of Christianity in the New Testament breaks out in the process.

In summary, the primary biblical manifestations of the Spirit's falling (popularly spoken of as the "baptism of the Holy Spirit") are:

- Speaking in tongues,

- prophesying in boldness, and

- power for service/world evangelization.

In addition to these six passages in Acts that are usually used to describe "being baptized in the Holy Spirit", there are also instances of: visions, power encounters, people being raised from the dead, miracles, healings, laying on of hands, sense phenomena (i.e. sounds like wind, tongues like fire, etc.), signs and wonders, and angelic visitations.

It is clear from Luke/Acts that Luke took every opportunity to emphasize the Spirit's role in the advancement of the gospel, the kingdom, and the church. Note the obvious links between the disciples going out and preaching the gospel, and the Lord working with them and confirming his word by the accompanying signs (cf. Also Mark 16:20).

- *Visions:* Paul has a vision of a man in Macedonia that leads to the establishment of churches in Europe (Acts 16:6-10).

- *Power Encounters:* Acts 13:4ff records the power encounter between Paul and Alamos that results in the proconsul believing.

- *Raised from the dead:* In Acts 9:36 the raising of Dorcas from the dead leads to many people believing (9:42).

- *Miracles:* The Spirit transports Philip from Samaria to Azotus (8:39) that leads to the mission expansion Jesus spoke of (1:8 NASB) as "...Samaria, and even to the remotest part of the earth."

- *Healing:* The healing of the lame man at the Gate Beautiful (3:1) causes the man to cling to Peter and John. The people in the temple area run over to see what is happening. This gives Peter an opportunity to preach to a large crowd. As a result, thousands more are converted (4:4). See also Acts 9:32-35 that records the healing of Aeneas: "...all those who lived in Lydda and Sharon saw him (Aeneas) and turned to the Lord"(v.35).

- *Nature Phenomena:* The sovereign rescue of Paul and Silas from the Philippian jail by means of an earthquake (16:25ff) results in the conversion of the jailer and his household (16:34).

- *Signs and wonders:* Acts 5:12 says that "the Apostles performed many sign and wonders among the people" (NIV) and that as a result "more and more men and women believed in the Lord and were added to their number" (Acts 5:14 NIV).

Surely this is a clear and powerful argument for the biblical and historic effect of the Spirit's work, and provides a clear vision for the future we hope for in the Vineyard.

THE SPIRIT'S FIRE

The famous evangelical missionary of a generation ago, Jim Elliot, captured the essence of what it means to have "the Spirit's fire" in a well-known quote from his journal. Responding to Psalm 104:4/Hebrews 1:7 ("he makes his minister a flame of fire" [KJV]), Jim wrote:

> Am I ignitable? God deliver me from the dread asbestos of "other things"! Saturate me with the oil of the Spirit that I may be aflame. But flame is transient, often short-lived. Canst thou bear this, my soul-short life? In me there dwells the Spirit of the Great Short-Lived, whose zeal for God's house consumed Him. And he has promised baptism with the Spirit and with fire. Make me Thy fuel, flame of God.[25]

Jim Elliot had "the Spirit's fire." My heart's cry for the Vineyard is that in my life time, thousands of young people like Jim Elliot would be saturated by the Holy Spirit and become the fuel of God for the planting of thousands of churches worldwide. Whatever the accompanying phenomena, power to witness (Acts 1:8) along with a powerful new love for the world (1 Corinthians13) have always been central to expressing the Spirit's fire.

CONCLUSION: A MODEL TO FOLLOW

Like most of you, as a young man, I looked for role models in the history of the church. I wanted to find a person who was effective, who had a similar call on their life, and who followed closely the example of Jesus and the mandates of scripture. After many years of searching and analyzing, I settled on John Wesley. Though I in no way equate myself with Wesley (nor am I a "Wesleyan") he has been a good model for me, and remains a good model for young pastors today.

As I talk to our pastors, I find many of them are discouraged, tired, and looking for something to "get them over the hump" so they can be effective in America today. Many feel impotent in the face of rising drug use, divorce, homosexuality, business and political corruption, abortion and the decline of the influence of religion in America today.

---

[25]Elisabeth Elliot, *Shadow of the Almighty*, San Francisco: Harper & Row, 1958, 58.

Wesley may have faced an even harsher reality. In Wesley's day,

> Great Britain was marked by moral disorder; in fact, some believed the nation was on the verge of moral disintegration. Contemporary vices were open and notorious. The theater was lewd, the staple of the novel market was despicable beyond imagination. The nation found itself enmeshed in the twin snares of drink and gambling. Violent crime soared alarmingly; gangs of young hooligans roamed the city streets professing to be emissaries of the devil, addressed blasphemous prayers to him and drank to his health. In short, morality and religion had collapsed to a degree which was never known in a Christian country.[26]

This is the England into which God thrust forth John Wesley. Wesley was a man committed to possessing the Spirit's fire for the purpose of winning people to Christ. In his sermons Wesley often spoke of the Spirit's activity at every stage of a person's experience with God; He called the Spirit "the fountain of all spiritual life."[27]

Wesley, as a man full of the Spirit, did not merely deplore the evils of his day; he attacked them by preaching repentance and conversion; by trying to renew his Anglican church and by starting new groups (classes bands, societies, churches, etc.) for the development of Christian character and service. At his death at eighty-three, Wesley had founded over 12,000 new groups/churches and had been a true social reformer. God changed the face of England through this determined, Spirit-filled man who was brilliant at organization. Wesley was "ignitable" and found a way to keep the Spirit's fire burning hot in very biblical and productive ways. My prayer is that historians will be able to say similar things about us when our lives are over.

In his final words (Luke 24:49; Acts 1:4,5,8) Jesus told his disciples to wait in Jerusalem for the promised outpouring of the Spirit for power for service. Many of us have received an outpouring of the Spirit this past year. Now we need to take aim again at the target of church planting and evangelism.

There is nothing to wait for. The lost world awaits those who will be

---

[26]A Skevington Wood, *The Burning Heart, John Wesley: Evangelist*, Bethany House, 1967, 9-16.

[27]*The Works of John Wesley, Vol. III*, Oxford: Clarendon Press, 1975-1983, 49.

givers of what they have received.

LEARNING FROM OUR ELDERS

Back in the mid-1970's before I had any inkling of leading our movement, I had already been introduced to the rapid growth of the Pentecostal church (primarily in the Third World). This introduction occurred in the midst of my association with Fuller Evangelistic Association and the School of World Mission. In various lectures that I gave at the School I would draw the following graph:

	Theology	Experience
Conservative Evangelicals	The Vineyard	
Pentecostal Evangelicals		The Vineyard

At the time, I had resisted the Pentecostal experience, because I was only aware of the Pentecostal extremes (and their usually negative examples). In the ensuring years I have become aware of mainstream Pentecostalism that has produced so much fruit for the kingdom. Early on in the development of the Vineyard, I decided I wanted to be part of a church that embraced the best of conservative evangelical theology along with the Pentecostal experience. Thus the birth of the Vineyard.

David Barrett, the foremost statistician of the Christian church, has estimated that if current growth rates continue, by the end of this century over 600 million Christians will be able to trace their spiritual lineage back to the Azuza Street Revival of 1906. This 600 million represents 29.1 percent of the whole world's Christians. That includes Pentecostals, charismatics, and what Peter Wagner refers to as the "Third Wave". "Their contribution to Christianity," writes Dr Barrett, "is a new awareness of spiritual gifts as a ministry to the life of the church."

In our ethos, the Vineyard also identifies with what occurred on an obscure street in a tiny church, in Los Angeles. We love the work of renewal the Holy Spirit is bringing to the church. We want more. But we must take counsel both from Scriptures, and from men and women who have gone ahead of us in this century, and who have faced many of the issues we're facing.

Therefore, we've given a large portion of this edition of *Vineyard Reflections* to an article by a man named Guy Duffield. We were so impressed with the clarity and relevance of Mr. Duffield's thinking as it relates to the current season of renewal within the Vineyard movement, (and the larger church) that we've shared an excerpt from his out-of-print book, *Pentecostal Preaching*. Duffield was a pastor with the International Church of the Foursquare Gospel. His message was originally delivered in lecture form at L.I.F.E. Bible College in Los Angeles, in the mid-1950's. Even though Mr. Duffield penned these words approximately 40 years ago, and though he was addressing his remarks to the "Full Gospel" movements, his pastoral wisdom is worth heeding - even in 1995.

The Greatest of all Callings, By Guy P. Duffield[28]

Some within our Full Gospel ranks seem to believe God is only really having his way in the service when the preacher does not have the opportunity to preach. How often we have heard a minister say: "We surely had a wonderful service yesterday. The Lord certainly had his way ... I didn't even get to preach." We believe in those precious times when the Spirit supersedes our plans and moves in power upon the hearts of men. We should keep ourselves in that place where the Spirit of God can sweetly move upon us and set aside what we have planned for something greater he may have in mind. Yet I feel there is a distinct danger in any attitude that minimizes the ministry of preaching. It is the greatest of all callings.

A man may have a gifted ministry in other ways, but in the long run the fruitful and abiding ministry is based primarily on strong Holy Ghost preaching. There may be a flurry here, and what seems to be a great stir over there, but the lasting, the solid, stable work in Full Gospel circles today is accomplished through strong Spirit filled preaching of the Word of God. Here is the point in which our great Full Gospel movement is the weakest. If you are going to be a minister of the Gospel of Jesus Christ,

---

[28]Guy P. Duffield, excerpted and adapted with the author's permission from *Pentecostal Preaching: Lectures from the L.I.F.E. Alumni Preaching Lectureship*, published 1956.

major in preaching. There are many other phases to the ministry, but the man who is a strong, able preacher of the Word will succeed where others, who are strong in other points but weak in preaching, will fail.

BALANCE

We must preach the Word [because] we need it as a stabilizing force in our particular type of ministry. If any church needs the Bible, we do. We believe in and practice an inspirational ministry. But inspiration can run away with itself if it does not have some balance. The written Word of God is that. It is surprising to find that other churches have emphasized the Word so much, in Bible study and Bible conferences and Bible reading, while we have emphasized it so little. Our people are more interested in coming to a prayer meeting than a bible study. We need both, but we especially need the Word of God.

We believe in a supernatural ministry – in the gifts of the Spirit, prophetic utterances, tongues and interpretations, miracles and gifts of healing. Let us not forget, however, that all these supernatural ministries are administered through very natural channels and agencies, and it is possible for the ministry to take some most unusual flights. An inspirational and supernatural ministry must be controlled, guided, and anchored. It must have some norm, some standard or court of appeal to make sure it is spiritually supernatural and not inspirationally imaginative and emotional. Without such a control or authority, anyone can tell us he had a vision or a revelation, and if he puts it over with enough gusto people will believe him. There is no telling where they will go. How gullible people are, especially if somebody says he had a revelation and God said something special to him.

Discernment

Let us not be the least bit afraid to judge anything anyone tells by the Word of God. If it is not according to the Word of God, it matters not how much inspiration he has, it is not true. The Holy Spirit does not anoint the Word of God at one time and then give someone something contrary to the Word at another time. The Holy Spirit is not confused, even if some people are. "To the law and to the testimony: if they speak not according to this word, it is because there is no light in them" (Isaiah 8: 20). If we disregard this principle how can we know what is true? Our people would be a prey to every deceiver. It is encouraging to see that many of our Full Gospel people are maturing to the point where they realize it is not unspiritual to follow the Word of God. The Holy Spirit moves only in keeping with the Word.

It is especially important that we discern between the soul and the spirit. Only the Word of God, which is "sharper than any two-edged sword" can do that. It pierces "even to the dividing asunder of soul and spirit ..." (Hebrews 4:12). The soul is the seat of the psychic nature, while the spirit is the base of the spiritual part of man's being. Sometimes these two can be so close together that only the Word of God can separate them. We want something more than just psychic results. There is no limit to what may be expected if we allow ourselves to be carried away into the realms of the psychic.

Donald Gee pointed out in one of his messages a number of years ago, a man may go into a great cathedral: the building is beautiful; he listens to the chanting of the choir in another language, and though he may not understand a word that is being said, it is so impressive. The candles are flickering in the dim light, and the incense is burning. The priest is there in his flowing robes, and everything is so ordered and arranged to appeal to the senses that those who are present receive a deep inspiration. They go out with a particular thrill in their being. But it is just psychic. It is not spiritual.

Another man goes into a beautiful, rich, liberal church. The ushers with their white gloves on lead the people to their seats down the thickly carpeted aisles. Everything is perfect in its appointments. The trained choir and the paid singers render their numbers with musical perfection. The minister, a polished and highly trained orator, gives a dissertation that stirs the hearts of those who hear. They go out and say, "Wasn't it wonderful! How I enjoyed that!" But the effect may be entirely psychic.

Then another person walks into a Full Gospel church. Some are playing guitars in a syncopated rhythm while the drum beats and the piano keeps time.

The song leader waves his arms like a windmill and calls on the folk to get into the spirit of the singing, and before long almost everyone is dancing all over the place. And they say, "Wasn't it a wonderful service!" It could be just psychic reaction, and not spiritual at all. We must be careful to discern between what is psychic and what is spiritual. And I say again, only the preaching of the Word of God can make that discernment.

Let us make sure our folk receive a sound, biblical, spiritual blessing as they come into our places of worship! The Word of God gives some definite instructions on how to accomplish this. Jesus said, concerning the Holy Spirit, "He shall glorify me ..." (John 16:14). Let us be very careful lest one should seek to exalt or magnify himself in the administration of spiritual gifts or ministries.

Signs following ... or leading?

Let us make sure that in our preaching we so emphasize the Word of God that people's faith will be based on it rather than on the results it produces! In Mark 16:20 we read, "And they went forth, and preached everywhere, the Lord working with them, and confirming the Word with signs following." Have we not often laid more emphasis on the signs than on the preaching of the Word? Have we not often rejoiced when the Word was not preached and the signs alone were manifested? I am calling for a great new devotion to the preaching of the Word that the signs may follow. Thank God for the signs, but let us keep them following instead of leading. If we follow the signs, instead of the signs following the Word, where will we go? They will most certainly follow when the Word is preached, for it is a living Word.

We are passing through an era when much attention is being called to, and much advertising is being done of, the extra-biblical manifestations of the Spirit. By extra-Biblical I mean those manifestations not mentioned in the Scriptures. I am not saying the Holy Spirit cannot and does not manifest himself in ways not mentioned specifically in the Bible. I realize it would have been difficult for Paul to have given any scriptural authority for the healings accomplished through the handkerchiefs and aprons (Acts 19:11, 12). It would have been impossible for Peter to have given chapter and verse for people's faith in his shadow falling upon them (Acts 5:15).

Yet apparently those things took place. *But neither Paul nor Peter ever preached on this particular experience. Neither of them made any mention of these events in their epistles.*

We may expect the unusual when the Spirit is moving upon men, for his ways are far above our ways. However, we should *not* cause people's faith to be centered in these things, but rather in the revealed Word of God. It is amazing how excited people will become over some unusual sign, but how little they are stirred by the wonderful promises of the Word of God. I wish we could get people more excited over what God says than over what happens to an individual.

Faith is based on the Word of God. Angels can speak to God's servants, and men may receive signs in some portion of their body. But if we train a congregation to place its faith in such things, we will have a very unstable people. These are the unusual things that a sovereign God has every right to do, but our faith cannot stand on the unusual. It must stand on the usual, the revealed, the avowed methods and purposes of God.

There is just too much attention being called today to the very unusual things, seeking to get people to raise their faith on that basis. That cannot be. Faith has to be based on the usual; on the thing you can depend on – what you know is going to work, not on something that may happen tomorrow and then never happen again. Let us get our people believing the Word of God, for it is forever "settled in heaven" and it will not be altered! Let us preach those promises and teach our people from the Word those great revealed purposes and methods by which our God works.

Definite promises

Let us be careful not to overdo our allegorical preaching. Allegorical preaching, particularly from the Old Testament, is a favorite method among Pentecostal preachers. There is a very fine place for this type. It is interesting and inspirational. But unless it is tied very closely to definite, positive New Testament doctrinal Scripture, it may become very fanciful. It may bless for the moment, but there is nothing like a positive truth, or promise, to uphold you when the trials begin to bear down upon you.

Which is more helpful in a time of temporal crises and need: the story of Elijah's need being met when the cruse of oil did not fail and the barrel of meal was not wasted, or such a promise as "My God shall supply all your need according to his riches in glory by Christ Jesus" (Philippians 4:18)? True the experience of the rugged Tishbite is very inspiring, and I personally love to think of it and be blessed by it. Yet in my hour of test I want more than the account of what happened to Elijah. I want a definite promise I can take to God and say, "Lord, your Word says 'My God shall supply all your need.'" I'm not a prophet of the stature of Elijah. I have not commanded the heavens to withhold their rain; I have not been up by the brook eating what the ravens brought me; and, as far as I know, there is no widow who is going to take care of my needs.

But when I read Paul's gracious words I can put myself right in there and make it my own very personal promise. Elijah's unusual experience illustrates one way in which Philippians 4:19 *might* be fulfilled, but I need to cling to the promise more that I need the illustration. Let us tie folk to the definite promise of God.

Romans 10.4 says, "for whatsoever things were written aforetime were written for our learning, that we through patience and comfort of the Scriptures might have hope." But these wonderful Old Testament stories must be anchored solidly to a definite promise in the New Testament writings that are addressed to the Church. If this is not done in our preaching, we are going to have a company of people whose Christian life is based on experience instead of the more sure word of Prophecy.

Peter teaches us this very plainly in 2 Peter 1:16-19. He is talking about the power and the coming again of Jesus. He declares that he was not following any cunningly devised fable, for he says we "…were eyewitnesses of his majesty." He was referring, of course, to his experience on the mount of transfiguration, when he and James and John saw Jesus in a little preview of his glory and power. His own personal experience was blessed indeed, but that is not the main basis of his authority. He emphatically declares, "We have a more sure word of Prophecy" and then magnifies the authority of the written Word of God.

We have been guilty of rearing a great host of spiritual children whose Christian life is based too much on experiences, and the result has been twofold. First, virtually every community has an all too large company of backsliders who were once members of Pentecostal churches but who never learned to stand on the Word of God for themselves when the storms come and the winds of testing and adversity blew. Second, our people have been entirely too open and gullible to every wind of doctrine and the cunning craftiness of men. You can find just about every brand of error in Pentecost. If someone lays claim to a great experience we seem to accept him or it without questioning its scripturalness or his spirituality.

If Paul had been like some preachers who are living today, he would have had an extra special sermon on "What I heard When I Was Caught Up Into the Third Heaven," and he would probably preach it on the last night of his campaign, when his extra love offering was going to be received. When are we going to learn to preach the Word and keep our visions and experiences pretty much to ourselves? People are not going to triumph in the time of their crucial tests by my great personal revelation. They need to be taught the Word of God.

Do not misunderstand me. God does give visions and revelations, but never apart from the teaching of His Word, and usually these are for our personal inspiration. Their value is usually in the effect they produce in the life and ministry of the one to whom they are given. Maybe you will get a bigger crowd if you announce you are going to tell folks all about your vision and revelation. But what you accomplish through that will not be one thousandth part as lasting as what you will accomplish if you preach the Word of God.

It is not what happens in your church that counts. It is what happens for eternity that is really important, in the long run. If you do not build for eternity, you will be wasting your time in the end. Preaching the Word is not as spectacular but it is more permanent. And when you stand around the throne of God, it will not be important how many people came to your meetings. But it will be important how many souls are there because you were faithful to the Word of God. It will be important how many Christians were sustained when the storms came because you sowed the Word of God into their lives.

Let us build for eternity.

One Message

There is only one message for any minister of the gospel. We are not raised up to preach the Holy Ghost. We are called to preach Jesus Christ. "He shall glorify me..." said Jesus of the promised Comforter (John 16:14). Much of the criticism leveled at the entire Full Gospel movement by sincere, biblical ministers who are not identified with us has been called forth because some in our ranks have in the past been guilty of exalting the Holy Ghost almost more than Jesus. Thus perhaps the greatest Bible expositor of the twentieth century has yet produced makes the statement that "the movement associated with the phrase, the gift of tongues, at the present time has upon it the hallmark of hell." He said this because he believed the scriptural way you can test a movement is as it exalts Christ. Our brother was wrong in his analysis of the Pentecostal movement. If there are any people who love, honor, and exalt the person and ministry of Christ Jesus, they are those who have received the baptism with the Holy Spirit.

But let us be careful! Our message is not the Holy Spirit and his gifts. It is Christ Jesus and his resurrection. The ministry of the Spirit, in all his operation and gifts, is to magnify the Lord Jesus. In all things he must have the pre-eminence (Colossians 1:18).

It is important that we emphasize the fact that the Spirit's ministry is to exalt Christ because in our particular type of ministry people easily get their eyes on the gifted and anointed minister. Where there are supernatural manifestations of the power of God, people will naturally look at the person through whom God is working. Thus it becomes the special, holy responsibility of the anointed minister to see that people's eyes are turned away from him to Christ who is doing the work.

Paul and Barnabas had such an experience at Lystra after the healing of the man who had been crippled since birth. The populace declared the gods had come down among them, and they called Barnabas "Zeus" and Paul "Hermes".

> But when the apostles Barnabas and Paul heard of this, they tore their clothes and rushed out into the crowd, shouting: "Men, why are you doing this? We too are only men, human like you. We are bringing you good news, telling you to turn from these worthless things to the living God, who made heaven and earth and sea and everything in them..." Even with these words, they had difficulty keeping the crowd from sacrificing to them (Acts 14:14-18).

Here is one of the sweetest and surest controls of the use of all spiritual gifts in our services. If they exalt the Lord they are of the Holy Spirit. If they exalt the individual so that attention is drawn to the person and not to Christ, then there is something wrong. It should ever be the desire of every Spirit-filled person that his life and ministry may always magnify the Lord Jesus.

BOARD REPORT

***Summary Report on the Current Renewal and the Phenomena
Surrounding It***

Association of Vineyard Churches September/October 1994

INTRODUCTION

The guidelines that follow represent the majority consensus of the board.
It is not possible in a brief document to adequately express all the discussion or all of the minority positions that are held by various board members. It is, therefore, important to remember that this statement is subject
to the autonomy of the local church and its pastor. All of this must be
worked through in a way that does not violate one's faith or conscience.

THE PASTORAL ADMINISTRATION OF PHENOMENA

- We are willing to allow "experiences" to happen without endorsing,
  encouraging or stimulating them; nor should we seek to "explain"
  them by inappropriate "proof-texting". Biblical metaphors (similar
  to those concerning a lion or a dove, etc.) do not justify or provide
  a proof-text for animal behavior.

  There are some manifestations, that while socially uncomfortable
  (i.e., they wouldn't seem "decent and in order" in most church con-
  texts today), have biblical precedent (cf. Daniel 8:16-18, 27; 10:8-10;
  Matthew 17:6-7; Revelation 1:17, etc.). The absence of a proof-text,
  however, does not necessarily disallow an experience. If so, none of
  us could go to Disneyland, use computers to write messages, or have
  worships bands. The point is, don't try to defend unusual manifestations from biblical texts that obviously lack a one-to-one

correspondence with a current experience.

We also need to be careful in our use of revival history and tradition to justify manifestation. People like Jonathan Edwards are helpful in that they give us examples of how godly men, who submitted themselves to the Scriptures as their final authority, sorted out similar issues. But in fairness to them, we don't know exactly what they would say about the current phenomena.

What we do know is that men like Edwards are shining examples of how to responsibly use Scripture.

We do not necessarily equate an "experience" as a manifestation of the Holy Spirit. For example, one person may have a genuine response to the presence of God which involves shaking and/or falling down. A person standing next to him or her, however, may do the exact same thing out of emotionalism or some other excess. While there has been some excess in our meetings, questionable manifestations have not been the major part of the renewal, but have attracted a disproportionate amount of attention.

- Although there was some particular concern about animal noises (some would discourage them; others would rule them our completely), the board was not prepared to make a blanket statement rejecting or "barring" any particular manifestation unless it is prohibited by Scripture. Each extra-biblical manifestation must be discerned individually. The ultimate test of manifestation should be the long-term fruit produced in a person's life, and the edification of the body of Christ (i.e., through prophecy, etc.).

- Rather than promoting, displaying or focusing on phenomena, we want to focus on the main/plain issues of Scripture. For instance, witnessing, healing, demon expulsion, ministering to the poor and widows, etc. This way people will find their identity in doing Scriptural work, not in experiencing phenomena. We would like people to be known as "evangelists" or "zealous Christian workers" rather than "roarers" or "shakers". We do not want manifestations to be a mark of spirituality. Rather, the fruit and gifts of the Spirit and a godly character should attest to true spirituality.

- When extra-biblical or exotic phenomena do occur, we want to avoid theologizing from them. *No doctrine should be based on a prophetic interpretation of a particular manifestation.* Admitting, "I don't know" about an occurrence of a phenomenon will promote more balance in the ongoing development of this renewal that focusing people on it by endorsing everything as a work of God.

Tentative "observations" can be made concerning patterns we witness in ministry; but they should never be catalogued as doctrine. For example, our "Five-Step Healing Model" is a useful tool to initiate people into praying for the sick; but it is not doctrinal in nature, it is methodological.

It has also proven unhelpful to describe vocal sounds as "animal noises" (lions, chickens, dogs, etc.). In most cases, the people making the sounds are, in fact, not intentionally imitating animals, and therefore, should not be labeled as such.

- We want to avoid linking the present work of the Spirit to any precise eschatological scenario (e.g. Hal Lindsay or the Latter Rain Movement, etc.). It would probably be wiser to maintain the loose pre-millennial views held by the vast majority, but not all – namely, that we have been in "the last days" since Pentecost and we don't know when the precise last moments of time are. Consequently, we don't know if this current renewal is the "last big one" or not.

- We want this renewal to motivate people to the obvious kingdom works of Scripture (cf. #3 above). People should go home from our meetings telling a well-rounded story: "I got it to give it away!" Those who are the most filled with the Spirit and a renewed love for Jesus naturally and easily express it by demonstrating His love for the lost, broken, sick and demonized.

- We want the ongoing lives of Vineyard churches to be governed by our previously stated values and priorities. Key values to remember in a renewal context are: simplicity, do nothing for effect's sake (i.e., hype or manipulate), always equip the saints, respect the privacy and dignity of individuals, etc. (cf. the current AVC Statement of Faith). We do not want to establish a new pattern of church life that revolves only around renewal meetings. We are encouraging pastors to maintain the basic infrastructure and program of their churches so as to meet all the needs of all the people.

- While we will listen to our critics and learn from them, we do not want to be governed by them. If they can prove to us by sound exegesis and logic that we are wrong, we will change. By the nature of our movement (renewal of the things of the Spirit) we have always had, and always will have critics; let's interact with them as godly men and women without becoming reactionary, bitter, unteachable, or controlled by them.

- We so not want to equate the experience of phenomena with instant healing unless there is clear evidence for such a claim. Because a person shakes or falls does not mean all his or her problems and temptations or testings are over.

CONCERNING THE APPLICATION OF 1 CORINTHIANS 14

Some people have been concerned that a proper understanding and application of 1 Corinthians 14 would rule out much of the current phenomena. Below are the board's thoughts on the matter.

- *The nature and purpose* of a meeting determines the context for its administration. 1 Corinthians 14 is the main guidelines we have in Scripture to govern Christian meetings. Because Paul was not writing with every imaginable modern context in view, we must seek to properly understand the principles he lays out and apply the same to our situation.

  The main questions that arise out of the text are "what should be limited?" (vv.27-29) and "what should be encouraged?" (v.39). Though some would see Paul's own application of his principles (vv.27-29) as completely ruling out extra-biblical phenomena (anything that could cause someone to say "you are out of your mind," I Corinthians 14:24 NIV), the majority of the board were content to judge each manifestation on its own merit.

- *The principles the emerge* from 1 Corinthians 14 are:

  a) For an experience, manifestation, phenomenon, or gift to be "decent and in order," it must edify the body of Christ. In order to edify, it must be intelligible. Therefore, someone in the group must make spiritual manifestations understandable to all (i.e., interpretation of tongues, etc.).

  Gordon Fee's commentary on 1 Corinthians is helpful here. Fee says, "the real issue is not tongues or prophecy per se, but the building up of the community, which can only be effected by understandable utterances, prophecy being the primary representative"[29] ... "edification controls the thought of the entire chapter."[30]

Edification in its verb and noun form is used seven times in this chapter, along with related words which seem to describe what Paul means by "edification." They are:

- v. 3   Encouragement/exhortation
- v. 6   Profit/benefit
- v. 19   Teach/instruct
- v. 25   Worship
- v. 31   Learn

b) Manifestations should have:

- Christ-exalting content (1 Corinthians 12:3; 1 John4:1-3; Revelation 19:10).

- Christ-resembling character (1 Corinthians 13, esp. vv. 4-7); "only when charisma is manifested as the expression of grace (i.e. humble, selfless love) will it benefit either the individual or the community."[31]

- Community-building consequences – Paul's argument with the Corinthians was not so much whether their manifestations were from God on not (1:17), but whether they were building up or tearing down the unity and spiritual growth of the body of Christ.

- Paul's criteria for community building are 1) a sense of unity amidst the diversity of gifts, 2) intelligibility, and 3) order – meaning corporate etiquette (vv. 26-27; 29-31) in consonance with God's character (v. 33).

- *If an extra-biblical or exotic* manifestation is thought to have some prophetic value to the group, and is helpful in the context of a

---

[29]Gordon Fee, *The First Epistle to the Corinthians, NICNT*, Grand Rapids: Eerdmans, 1987, 652.

[30]Fee, 657.

[31]James Dunn, *Jesus and the Spirit*, London: SCM, 1975, 294.

meeting, it is the responsibility of the leader to ensure that it is made intelligible to all (vv.16,17). If it is not prophetic or intelligible or is disrupting the preaching of the Word, it is to be controlled and kept from dominating the attention of the group.

- *There will always* be inherent tension as we seek to apply these principles to our meetings. The tension is between appropriately "controlling" a meeting using the principles of 1 Corinthians 14 versus "quenching" the Holy Spirit (1 Thessalonians 5:19-21). In 1 Corinthians 14 Paul is obviously not arguing that we should "quench" the Spirit. Rather, his concern is that as leaders or participants we should "control" ourselves so as to ensure our expressions of the Spirit build up the body of Christ.

THE MESSAGE AND THEMES OF THIS RENEWAL ARE:

Some have asked "What does all this mean?" "Where is this going?" "Is there any central thrust?" etc. Below are the themes the board would like to see emphasized.

- Passion for Christ
- Intimacy with God expressed in fervent worship
- Compassion for others
- A new reality of the love of the Father
- Refreshing, emboldening, and impartation of power for kingdom service
- Isaiah 55: "come and drink!"
- Renewal of godly character
- Final result of effective discipleship

CONCLUSION

You may ask, "in simple terms, what does all the above mean?" It means that it is our desire to embrace all that is good about this renewal while correcting that which is excessive, long-term hurtful or contrary to biblical mandates. We also want to interact with the renewal based on our historical and firmly held vision, mission and purpose. Namely, that we are committed to "power evangelism," not just "power"; we are committed to "signs and wonders and church growth," not just "signs and wonders." The Lord has clearly instructed us to direct these current blessings into practical activities that will minister to and bless those outside of our churches. It is our hope that every Vineyard pastor will do so through the grace and power of God.

Todd Hunter, for the AVC Board
Anaheim, California
October 1994

JOHN WIMBER RESPONDS TO PHE-NOMENA

The following is an excerpt taken from a letter by John Wimber respond-ing to questions regarding some of the phenomena experienced in recent Vineyard meetings.

My views as to the issue of "roaring" under the anointing

- I would say that there is no biblical or theological framework for such phenomena. I don't see anywhere in the New Testament where Jesus and/or the apostles encouraged such phenomena or encoun-tered such phenomena. Therefore, I think these kinds of things have to be put in a category of "non-biblical" and "exotic".

- However, there have been some revival reports in church tradition where people have made various and sundry "animal noises" (or noises that could be labeled as such, though I doubt making animal sounds was the intent of the people). For instance, at the Cane Ridge Revival in Kentucky during the Second Great Awakening, there were a number of people that did so.

  Furthermore, I understand that Charles Finney had some sort of ex-perience where he made a kind of "roaring noise", although I don't think he, in retrospect, equated it with a lion. He did equate it, how-ever, with an anointing from God that transformed his life and min-istry.

- I've had, to date, seven or eight testimonies from people who have "roared." Here are the conclusions they drew from the experience.
  - There was a sense of God's indignation at the state of the church and the impact of the enemy's presence in the church.

As a consequence, people responded with a "prophetic roar," which was a sort of an "announcement" of God's intention to take back territory.

- Furthermore, it seemed to affirm the issue of the Lord's authority in their lives and ministries, and as a consequence they've been very excited about the potential for more powerful ministry in the future.

- It seems to me that nearly all of them have equated this with some sort of prophetic experience, either personal anointing for prophecy and/or prophetic in the sense that God is saying to the church, "Rise up, and take back the land/people/things that the enemy has one way or another wrongfully usurped control of."

- However, having said that, I must point out that there is some disagreement in our circles here in the Vineyard.

    - There are those that are very enthusiastic endorsers of the experience and I think are, as a consequence, even encouraging others in this kind of experience. I strongly feel that it is excessive to do so, in that again I know of no biblical mandate for encouraging anyone to "roar".

      However, based on the rubric of "bless what the Father's doing," I suppose, if I were in a ministry context and somebody started "roaring," I would bless what I thought the Father was doing regardless of the "roaring" or any other manifestation. Keep in mind, however, we do not equate phenomena with God; we see these usually as human responses to God.

    - One the other hand, there are people who sharply disagree with the notion that anything such as this kind of phenomena could be perceived to be something of God, and would quickly point out that there's no biblical support for equating the experience with God, and I would have to agree that this, indeed, has to be viewed as an exotic and non-biblically endorsed experience.

      Having said that, I do not, personally, hold the opinion that this is "demonic" and/or necessarily "divine." I put this in the category of "pondering/I don't know." I am looking for, in the aftermath, the effects of the experience to see how it relates to the person's life. If we see fruit (i.e. Matthew 7:15ff, 1 Corinthians 14, Acts 5:33ff, 1 John 4:1-3), then I suppose I would accept the notion that, if the people who have had the experience are advancing, perhaps it was something from God.

In light of all the above, here are my views on "phenomena"

1. I cannot endorse or even encourage this experience in our movement and ministry, but at the same time I recognize that it is happening and I would just leave it in the same category as I have of people shaking, or falling or having other kinds of exotic phenomena that may have some limited biblical representation. Therefore this is not necessarily anything that we ought to equate as "always" something of God, or even "sometimes" something of God, though it may be a reaction to the Spirit's activity. I think that we ought to endorse and encourage the "main and plain things" of Scripture: i.e. salvation, sanctification, justification by faith and the consequent experiences of such, where people would have testimonies of how they are advancing in their initial relationship with God and then moving on in progression with God.

2. I feel that it's very important that we direct the "refreshing" and "enabling" move of the Spirit to the New Testament works of the church, that is to say, having been refreshed, we now must channel these people into work that would express that refreshing in solid, biblical context. That is to say that they should begin interceding, sharing their faith in an evangelistic context: they should be feeding the hungry, ministering to the poor, the widow, the divorcee, etc., etc. I believe that if we channel this energy away from a "bless me" kind of focus to a "bless them" kind of focus we will indeed be utilizing this fresh anointing in a biblically appropriate fashion.

    Finally, I want to close by saying this. I feel that the exuberant and initial response of many in this area is well taken, and I'm happy for their testimonies. I just don't want to make our meetings a focus on "phenomena". I would like to make our meetings focused on the Word and works of the Spirit.

Now, having said all that, I recognize that there are certain manifestations of the Spirit that have gone on in our meetings for fifteen years that we supposed were demonic in origin. And there have been times in the past where we've attempted to cast demons out of people who made "animal noises." On some occasions demons manifested and we did cast them out and on other occasions we were puzzled by the lack of deliverance.

Therefore, I think in the past we've had a simplistic view of all these kinds of things. These new phenomena and their apparent "fruit" have been a circumstance that has caused me to stop and think and review again, my presupposition as they relate to all this.

FACING THE FIRES OF FANATICISM – PART I

Calling the Church to a Loving & Accepting Attitude

March/April 1995, Volume 3, Issue 1

> When they came to the other disciples, they saw a large crowd around them and the teachers of the law arguing with them. As soon as all the people saw Jesus, they were overwhelmed with wonder and ran to greet him. "What are you arguing with them about?" he asked (Mark 9:14-16).

A number of years ago an angry young man accosted me at a local restaurant. His face was beet red and his eyes were bulging. For a moment I thought he was going to attack me. I prayed silently, *Lord, if it's your will that he attack me, let it happen. But, I don't intend to respond to him in anything but a loving manner.*

"You're in league with the anti-Christ!" he said

"I am?"

"Yes"

With God's grace, I gave him a "soft answer." As we talked, he calmed down. After a while, he finally quit trembling. Apparently something his pastor had said incited him. The pastor (whom I knew) might have said something *like* that, in the passion of the moment. Like many (but not all) Christian "fundamentalists" he'd been taught to make sweeping condemnations of things he didn't understand or people he couldn't relate to - even other Christians.

"Look," I said, "if your pastors believes that, he'll acknowledge it. Go and ask him if he believes I'm in league with the anti-Christ. If he does, then I would be glad for us to sit down and dialogue. But, I'm not going to argue with you about this." I never heard from the young man or saw him again. Hopefully his heart was touched with something other than the spirit of combat he had been steeped in.

SPIRIT OF RUDENESS

Our society at large has succumbed to a spirit of rudeness, vitriol, and put-down. Some destructive forces are running rampant, and the danger has to do with, in my opinion, intolerance and lack of acceptance projected in our culture.

We're rapidly becoming a society of fearful people, pitted against each other along racial, political, and economic lines. Politically, we have the radical "right" and "left". Both sides use pejorative language to paint with broad brush strokes the failings of the other side. Consider these appalling examples we've seen within the last year.

- A US Senator says the President better not visit his state without a body guard.

- A congressman ominously characterizes the prayer in school initiative as the beginning of a "new civil war".

- A radio talk show host advises listeners to shoot at the head if attacked by federal agents using bullet proof vests.

Our leaders wield words more as a bludgeon to injure, than a lamp to enlighten. I see that in political circles, talk shows, and in the pulpits.

The belligerent words and attitudes divide people be stressing difference, rather than creating common ground to understand legitimate differences. Harsh labels are pasted on the opposition, using caustic clichés and criticism resulting in barriers, misunderstanding and further mistrust. Few people today voice a moderate message of acceptance and love, a message of understanding.

The bible teaches a relationship between sowing and reaping. Sadly, we're reaping as a society the effects of an "In your face!" attitude, both in private discourse, and public debate. Our culture glorifies rudeness. Sarcasm has become our trade language. A free-for-all of name calling has polarized us, making true communication nearly impossible.

IN THE CHURCH

It's bad enough when this mentality saturates the political environment. But, when it infiltrates the church, it breaks my heart. So much of what's said today from the pulpits across the country is argumentative and judgmental.

For instance, we attack practices or teachings that differ from "our" group. It's a sad commentary on the state of the church when we must advance our cause by arguing against one another. This kind of attitude sometimes happens under the banner of protecting the truth! Scripture urges us "to contend for the faith that was once for all entrusted to the saints" (Jude 3). Tragically, we more often contend *with the saints*, rather than contend *for the faith*.

A particular group, with a particular spokesman, became the self-appointed conservator of orthodoxy for all time. They alone, through their golden mallet, have broken open the Scripture and they have grasped the essentials of all truth for all time. *Anybody*, who doesn't practice what they practice, and believe exactly as they do, is less of a Christian.

In the current evangelical mainstream literature, we're seeing more of this bickering attitude, and arguing for our cause and our position, our rights. I don't know what kind of gospel you received when you were converted, but I understood I gave up my rights when I came to the cross.

I cannot reconcile what the bible reveals to us about the nature and attitude of our Lord Jesus Christ with what has become so prevalent in the church: labelling, building walls, posturing attitudes that engender misunderstandings, and choosing sides. I can't see Jesus of Nazareth - if he was ministering on earth today - using sound bites, and yanking comments out of context and broadcasting them. Yet today some Christians do this - with a judgmental and harsh spirit - to advance their positions as "authorities" who supposedly speak for a major portion of the body of Christ.

Tragically, the momentum of this argumentative attitude is growing. Some teachers with large followings routinely use pejorative labels, characterizing somebody as heretical, or ascribing sinful motivations to their heart and life. Remember the Book of Revelation calls Satan the accuser of the brethren. Satan dances a jig every time the church gets up in arms at each other - shouting each other down, defiling one another with words, speaking ill of one another in an unloving manner, without respect for the body of Christ. When the people of God align themselves with the enemy and speak this way, it breaks the heart of God.

No one "wins" in these battles...except the devil.

PUGILISTIC SPIRITUALITY

The roots of the contentious atmosphere we see in the church today reach back to the rift between evangelical orthodoxy and Protestant liberalism of the early part of the century. We can applaud those who became known as "fundamentalists" for defending biblical infallibility and a supernatural faith. Unfortunately, their staunch resistance to the effects of liberalism begot an attitude known as "fundamentalism" in which one insists on a rigid doctrinal uniformity. Anybody who doesn't pass their test of doctrinal purity is somehow less godly or sub-Christian.

Carl F. H. Henry, when he was the editor of *Christianity Today* in the mid-fifties, wrote a series of essays decrying the effects of "pugilistic spirituality". He wrote in his second essay:

> The real bankruptcy of fundamentalism has resulted not so much from a reactionary spirit - lamentable as this was - as from a harsh temperament, a spirit of lovelessness and strife contributed by much of its leadership in the recent past. One of the ironies of contemporary church history is that the more fundamentalists stressed separation from apostasy as a theme in their churches, the more a spirit of lovelessness seemed to prevail. The theological conflict with liberalism deteriorated into an attack upon organizations and personalities.[32]

That quarrelsome spirit eventually turned on itself. Henry describes how this condemnation, in turn, grew to include conservative churchmen and churches not ready to align with separatist movements.

> More recently, the evangelistic ministry of Billy Graham and of other evangelical leaders, and efforts whose disapproval of liberalism and advocacy of conservative Christianity are beyond dispute, have become the target of bitter volubility.[33]

---

[32]Carl F. H. Henry, "Dare We Renew the Controversy Part II: The Fundamental Reduction" *Christianity Today,* June 24, 1957, 26.

[33]*Ibid.*

The church is still suffering from this rise of vitriolic polemics. It's like an unbridled animal voraciously devouring the church. One of my biggest concerns for the Vineyard is that we not engage in attack and counter-attack, and become tainted by it. Sometimes when you're being attacked, it's very difficult to not fire back. Antagonistic behaviour has a way of "hooking" our passions and drawing us into disputes that degenerate into a "macho" confrontation. These disputes are then perpetuated to save face. Unless we're careful, we can find ourselves passionately advocating things that, in our heart of hearts, we know are not right. The New Testament clearly prohibits the mature minister from being drawn into these "word-battles".

QUARRELS

When choosing leaders in the church Paul counselled Timothy to look for men who were "...not violent but gentle, *not quarrelsome*" (1 Timothy 3:4). A person might avoid coming to blows, but being quarrelsome, he would still lack a crucial character trait required of an overseer.

In his first letter to the Corinthians, Paul lamented the quarrelsome atmosphere marring the church in Corinth: "One of you says, 'I follow Paul'; another, 'I follow Apollos;' another, 'I follow Cephas'; still another, 'I follow Christ'" (1 Corinthians1:12).

In the second chapter of 2 Timothy, Paul charges Timothy: "Warn them (church leaders) before God against quarrelling about words; it is of no value, and only ruins those who listen" (v.14). William Hendriksen believes Paul was probably referring to quarrels about certain Jewish myths and genealogies. Timothy was to warn the Ephesian church leaders "not to wage thoroughly useless word-battles."[34]

The warning to Timothy and his leaders holds true for us today. Do not wage useless word-battles about eschatology, apocryphal material, angels, spiritual phenomena, or any other topic that creates an atmosphere of rancor and hostility. It ruins those who listen, so how can it be good for those who are talking? Let us avoid chasing down rabbit trails of vain arguments.

As ministers, we will from time to time have critics. In verse 24 of 2

---

[34]William Hendriksen, *New Testament Commentary: Exposition of the Pastoral Epistles,* Grand Rapids Michigan: Baker Book House, 1979, 261.

Timothy 2, Paul deals with the response of the Lord's servant, which applies to any minister:

> And the Lord's servant must not quarrel; instead, he must be kind to everyone, able to teach, not resentful. Those who oppose him he must gently instruct, in the hope that God will grant them repentance leading them to a knowledge of the truth, and that they will come to their senses and escape from the trap of the devil, who has taken them captive to do his will (2 Timothy 2:24-26).

Even born again Christians have prejudicial viewpoints and attitudes that can emerge given the right stimulus. What do we do about it?

I will not argue with brothers, even when they want to argue with me. That's not to say I will back down on my teachings. In fact, it infuriates our critics even further, because I don't respond, *and* I don't back down. That's because I'm sure of foot. I believe what we're doing and teaching is valid, helpful and godly. At any point where I have any questions, I review my assumptions and seek counsel from Scripture, and from godly persons.

We don't retaliate and argue. We ignore the behavior and accept the person. We teach, pray and show mercy. Love *is* greater than hate. God's word is true, no matter what satanically derived teaching emanates from our culture. We can never separate love and truth.

The underlying problem is that we have allowed an emphasis on truth to overshadow the values of acceptance and love. I'm not saying we compromise the truth. I'm saying we speak the truth in the appropriate and biblical framework, in ways God would bless and advocate (see Ephesians 4:15). Does that mean we never confront when clear truth is violated? No. There are times and ways to talk to a sinning brother to help and restore him. Accepting him does not mean overlooking sin. The bible clearly teaches us to go privately with a desire to restore. We're to go with two or three if that is not effective. Finally, after much exchange, if necessary, bring it before the church with a goal to fully restore both godly behavior and inter-personal relationships, out of love and humility.

Some, in an effort to be more loving, have de-emphasized truth. Either extreme position can weaken us. If you're not valuing truth, you could over-emphasize the importance of mercy, and somehow degrade it and bring it down from the mercy we see in Scripture, and in the heart of God. Some have turned mercy into some humanistic endeavor in which you choose to ignore the things God chooses not to ignore.

ACCEPTANCE

Many times after disciplining some leader in our flock, or in our movement, individuals will come to me and say. "Well, I'm going to remain accepting of this person, because you guys are persecuting him."

I've said, "We're not persecuting him. We're brokenhearted. But, the man (or woman) has sinned, and they're not repentant. There's a major difference between being 'sorry that you did it' and 'sorry that you're caught.'"

Sometimes under the banner of ministering mercy and grace to needy people, someone will say, "Well, I'm not going to be judgmental!" Neither am I, but we have to keep a balance between truth and mercy. That's why the Scriptures encourage us to go tenderly when we have to deal with a brother or sister that's caught up in sin (Galatians 6:1).

We could take either position, feel justified in it, and all the time subtly build walls between other brother and sisters in Christ. As fallible human beings we may understand more of one side than the other. I know, because I used to preach against people like me. I thought, "Surely, those folks who speak in tongues can't be right, because we're right - and we don't do that." When the Lord gave me the gift of tongues (without me even asking for it) I had a real problem. Thank goodness God showed me my sin - accusations, prejudices, slander, and bigotry. I'm still in process. It's a slow process - as my wife will tell you - but I am making progress.

WALK IN LOVE

How can we avoid the militant mindset against other believers, and embrace others with differing views? It comes down to Paul's admonition: "Accept one another, then, just as Christ accepted you..." (Romans 15:7). The church is called to a loving and accepting attitude. That's the ethos I desire for the Vineyard movement.

How are we, then, to accept one another in the body of Christ? Like Jesus did, with warts and all, differing viewpoints, argumentative attitudes.

How did Christ accept us? Did Christ wait until we were "acceptable" or "eligible" for fellowship before dying for us? No, he adopted us into the family, even before we knew we needed him. Actually he accepted us while we were still his spiritual enemies. "But God demonstrates his own love for us in this: While we were still sinners, Christ died for us" (Romans 5:8). That's the standard of love and acceptance we have as Christians.

You might say, "You mean I'm supposed to accept my 'brother' when he's out of line, and when he doesn't even seem to be trying to get along, and he's doing stuff I hate?"

It all comes down to this issue of truth and mercy. In truth Jesus accepted you at a time when you weren't ready to be accepted. Your life wasn't in line. You weren't in the place you should have been.

The way out of the dilemma is by learning to walk in maturity and love.

GRACE AND TRUTH

In the first chapter of his Gospel, John tries to describe in human language the indescribable glory of the Word made flesh: "The Word became flesh and made his dwelling among us. We have seen his glory, the glory of the One and Only, who came from the Father, full of grace and truth" (John 1:14). He uses two powerful words to capture the essence of the incarnate Word: grace and truth. It is the incarnate Word - Jesus - who is full of grace and truth.

Leon Morris in his commentary on John points out that the word grace in John 1:14 connotes "that which causes joy," and "winsomeness". It speaks of God's "good-will," and "kindness," towards mankind, although it's undeserved. For the Christian the highest expression of grace is God's provision for man's spiritual need by sending his Son to be man's savior. Grace speaks also of the good gifts God imparts to those he saves. Finally grace reminds us of the attitude of thankfulness we ought to have to God for all his goodness to us.[35]

With this John links "truth." Truth, for John, was more than simply the opposite of falsehood. When he speaks of the incarnate Word as full of grace and truth he underlines that truth and the complete reliability of God go hand in hand. Either one - truth or grace - taken by itself is not a complete picture. Truth cannot be known apart from God. The Word reveals truth as well as grace. Grace alone gives an unbalanced picture. God is the God of grace, but he is also the God who desires of men "truth in the

---

[35]Leon Morris, NICNT, *The Gospel according to John*, Grand Rapids, Michigan: Wm. B Eerdmans Publishing Co. 1971, 106.

inward parts" (Psalm 51:6).

One without the other is incomplete. We must have both. We must walk in truth, but we must walk in grace. If we are untempered in our attitudes about truth, we will become victimizers and harsh legalists, and begin criticizing people for not walking in the truth (or at least our view of the truth). If we overemphasize grace, it becomes something less than godly in its character and makeup, and becomes humanistic in its source, and we begin ignoring the very foundations of the issue of sin in people's lives.

I'm not saying we're to judge one another's sins. We're never called to judge. But, we are to go to brothers and sisters who are not walking in a godly manner and, in a loving way, hold them accountable, and help them walk out of the mess they are in. Nine times out of ten, they'll thank us for it later.

WHAT'S IMPORTANT

Leith Anderson, in his book, *Winning the Values War in a Changing Culture* reminds us of the need for balance in our attitudes between truth and mercy.

> Some truths are unimportant (like the ancient debate over how many angels could sit on the head of a pin). Some truths are important. Some truths are very important. Some truths are extremely important. Some truths are infinitely important.

> Family feuds have lasted for generations over differences about truths that really didn't matter. The same can be said about fellowship within the family of God. Some Christians have refused to fellowship with others because of truths as relatively unimportant as the angel count on a pinhead.

> We should balance our wholehearted commitment to God's absolute truth with our love for our neighbors as ourselves and our application of God given wisdom on what is more important and what is less important.[36]

---

[36]Leith Anderson, *Winning the Values War in a Changing Culture,* Minneapolis: Bethany House Publishers, 1994, 66.

Let us be conciliatory towards those Christians with whom we agree on the cardinal doctrines. At the same time, let us avoid a belligerent spirit towards Christians who may differ with us on some relatively minor issue. Let us continue to love what Christ loves: his whole church.

FACING THE FIRES OF FANATICISM – PART 2

Calling the Church to a Loving & Accepting Attitude

May/June 1995, Volume 3, Issue 2

"In things essential unity; in doubtful liberty; in all things, charity" *(Anonymous)*.

This past summer, another church movement with which we've had relationship in the past sponsored their national pastors' conference. One of the workshops was apparently dedicated to explaining why the Vineyard movement was off the wall theologically. At least one of their keynote speakers has become notorious for his denunciations of the "Toronto blessing," and the Vineyard movement. After the conference, one of their zealous pastors made copies of the anti-Vineyard tapes and distributed them to all the pastors in his city of over one million people.

I'm not going to rebut or respond to anything that might have been charged in the forum. I just want to illustrate that my thoughts about calling the Vineyard (and the church at large) to a loving and accepting attitude are relevant and timely. It's really hard not to push back when someone pushes you. I bring these things up because we've always had our detractors…and we probably always will.

BALANCE GRACE AND TRUTH

In the last issue of *Vineyard Reflections* I discussed how Jesus presents in himself the necessary balance between grace and truth. "For the law was given through Moses; *grace and truth came through Jesus Christ*" (John 1:17 emphasis mine).

God has lovingly and kindly blessed us in the person of the Lord Jesus

Christ with all the provision that we need. Jesus was full of *both* grace and truth. That's why whenever he's been preached, wherever he's been made known across the world, he has, for the most part, an excellent reputation. People, by and large, don't attack Jesus, but they do get upset with his *church*. His church is guilty of not representing him very well at times.

That's why I'm calling us to be representatives for Christ in both truth and grace.

One without the other is incomplete. We must walk in both truth and grace. If we are untempered in our attitudes about truth, we will become victimizers and harsh legalists and begin criticizing people for not walking in the truth (or at least our view of truth). If we over-emphasize grace, it becomes something less than godly in its character and makeup and becomes humanistic in its source. It leads to ignoring the very foundations of the issue of sin in people's lives.

There are many teachers and leaders in the body of Christ who know how to strike the right balance between truth and grace. One of my favorites is John Piper. He writes about and communicates the counsels of God in a way that is very palatable. He doesn't have any prickly parts. He doesn't slander other groups or cut down other teachers to make his point. He just straightforwardly teaches the word of God. I respect that.

Another theologian whom I admire in this regard is J. I. Packer. Packer associates with many Christians who may differ with him on specific points while agreeing with them on the main and plain issues of Scripture. He is not sectarian, but he has contributed time and effort to many inter-denominational projects. The following quote illustrates Packer's irenic spirit in his attitude towards charismatic life and teaching:

> In his book, *Keep in Step with the Spirit,* James Packer…has made a special effort to study and understand the charismatic movement. He is glad to acknowledge wholesome features, even though some of them may have slipped into occasional excesses. He is also clear-sighted in discerning the dangers and insufficient safeguards in some forms of the movement. Surely this is material that non-charismatics would do well to read and ponder, lest they miss some part of the full gospel of Christ; charismatics also would do well to consider the dangers…in order to be sure that their life and worship do

not derail...[37]

Packer came by his accepting attitude that hard way. In 1966, Martyn Lloyd-Jones began calling for evangelicals within the Church of England to leave because in his view the Church of England was incapable of maintaining a sound doctrinal position.

> This caused great distress to men like John Stott and Packer, who were persuaded that their ministry was to be pursued from within the church. [The controversy] caused a serious estrangement between Packer and Free Church evangelicals and made his work much more difficult. It was especially painful for him to be at odds with Lloyd-Jones, whom he described as "the greatest man he had ever known."[38]

The pursuit of truth with a de-emphasis on grace creates legalists who become pejorative and critical of those who do not believe or exercise the truth exactly as they do. This hyper-critical attitude is usually most clearly identified with the term "fundamentalism." However, just because a person identifies himself as a fundamentalist doesn't mean he is, by default, narrow-minded and argumentative. Nevertheless, under the rubric of "defending the truth" some fundamentalists have left a bad taste in the mouth of both believers and unbelievers who have assumed that all Christianity is represented by a vocal and angry minority.

Most of us in the body of Christ have bumped into some of these folks, and we've been bruised in the process. "You should (or shouldn't) baptize this way!" or "You should (or shouldn't) speak in tongues!" And it's always done with vehemence and an angry argumentative spirit. I've walked away from some of those exchanges shaking my head.

When you listen to people, listen not only for *content*, but for *intent.* The substance of their critique may even be valid to some degree. But are they "making every effort to keep the unity of the Spirit through the bond of peace" (Ephesians 4:3), or is their goal to divide and negate brotherhood and relationship within the church?

Again, overemphasizing truth can produce legalism. It can result in a mentality in which advocates become light on grace and heavy on truth.

---

[37]Walter A. Elwell, editor, *Handbook of Evangelical Theologians*, Grand Rapids, Michigan: Baker Books, 1993, 386.
[38]*Ibid.*, 381.

You may revel in the great truths of Scripture, adhere to systematic, logical systems, and be able to help people see treasures from the Word of God. But a dogmatic legalistic mentality will tend to cause you to stand aloof from the needy and the broken and prevent you from even being able to see them. An attitude that demands that others believe exactly the way you do will separate you from your brothers and sisters.

Paul exhorted the Philippian Christians: "Do everything without complaining or arguing, so that you may become blameless and pure, children of God without fault in a crooked and depraved generation" (Philippians 2:14-15).

GRACE LENSES

If you're heavy on grace, and light on truth, there are problems there too.

I don't intend ever to leave the truth of Scripture. And I also don't intend to leave the grace of the Lord Jesus Christ. That means we'll cut slack for people and give them room for growth. We'll also confront in love and dialogue about problems. But we'll do it with love, grace, and the desire to redeem, encourage, and strengthen.

We can read the bible through "grace lenses," and we should practice the grace oriented passages, because they form an essential New Testament emphasis as well as reflect our heritage in the Vineyard. For example: "Be kind and compassionate to one another, forgiving each other, just as in Christ God forgave you" (Ephesians 4:32).

But at the same time we can't disobey the more demanding truth passages such as "…continue to work out your salvation with fear and trembling" (Philippians 2:12).

Being grace orientated does not mean we shrink back from giving correction where it is needed. We pray for and shepherd a person who has sexually aberrant behavior, but we don't release him to practice that behavior among the flock. We have to deal with his problem in a way that profits him *and* protects the body. We don't want to encourage by default certain kinds of behavioral problems that would in some way hurt others in the body of Christ. At the same time, we want to deal as lovingly and as carefully as we can with anyone who comes towards Jesus and the church.

GRACE AND TRUTH IN ROMANS 14

Paul makes an application of the need for a balance between grace and truth in Romans 14. In this passage he gives us some reasons for not judging other Christians on debatable questions.

The problem was meat. Apparently there were two groups who were polarized over the issue of eating meat. One group (the "strong") had no problem eating meat. This group was probably the Gentile majority. Another group (the "weak") had a big problem with eating meat. These Jewish converts, a minority in the Roman church, were still sensitive to Jewish dietary restrictions. Since the meat available was undoubtedly "unclean" according to Jewish customs, they chose to be vegetarians. Moreover, they were scandalized by the thought of other Christians eating meat.

For Paul the issue was this: How do we preserve the unity of the Spirit in the bond of peace between these two groups without offending anyone's conscience and without compromising the gospel.

In a Word: "Accept!"

The first verse says, "Accept him whose faith is weak, without passing judgment on disputable matters." Later in this epistle he writes: "Accept one another, then, just as Christ accepted you, in order to bring praise to God" (Romans 15:7).

Paul continues in verse two: "One man's faith allows him to eat everything, but another man, whose faith is weak, eats only vegetables." People in the body of Christ with different levels of faith and maturity will have varying degrees of tolerance for other believers. In this context, there were people who could not eat the "cheaper meat" because it had been dedicated to idols, and they couldn't get over that. So Paul counsels the Roman Christians to accept people like that. Serve some vegetables with dinner and consider not eating meat yourself when you're around these individuals to make it easier for your brother. The underlying teaching here is to accommodate the graduations of agreement in the faith. In his letter to the Ephesian believers Paul pleaded: "Make every effort to keep the unity of the Spirit through the bond of peace" (Ephesians 4:3). Unity always requires some effort.

We're brothers! Don't be argumentative in your spirit. Don't focus on points of disagreement or debate over the externals of the Christian life. "We're more godly because we baptize three times forward and one time backward. You only sprinkle and don't dunk."

Matters such as these as disputable; they are not core to the faith. We can't allow minor issues to polarize and paralyze us. They ought not to be held up as the standard for fellowship with other believers. The higher path is to walk above these things and to deal lovingly with brothers and sisters who, for one reason or another, are "weak." It doesn't mean you're more godly; it just means that you intend to be and that you want to walk in the counsel of Scripture.

Look at verse 3: "The man who eats everything must not look down on him who does not, and the man who does not eat everything must not condemn the man who does, for God has accepted him." Again Paul introduces the concept of acceptance, this time referring to how God has "accepted him," the man who eats everything. You're not superior. You're not more spiritual because you do one thing and don't do another. Therefore, don't judge your brother. Did someone appoint you junior Holy Spirit? Jesus told us that in Matthew 7:1: "Do not judge, or you too will be judged."

We are to personally choose to obey our own inner convictions that are based on the revelation of God's word, remembering that our freedom is God-given. We're free to do or not to do, but we're never free to condemn those who take the other position. "Who are you to judge someone else's servant? To his own master he stands or falls. And he will stand, for the Lord is able to make him stand" (v.4). We're never free to judge.

We're to strive to see God's gracious working in our brothers and sisters. We're to put on "grace lenses" and look for the good things that we can commend and affirm in them. In verse 10 Paul strongly condemns two sinful attitudes: judging a brother, and looking down on a brother.

AVOIDING CONTROVERSIES

One might say, "Aren't there any limitations? Are we advocating total license?" No. I'm not licensing people to do anything they want to do. Within the context of Scripture, we already have some very clearly marked behavioral standard, practices, and policies. Instead of judging our fellow Christians, Paul tells us to "make up your mind not to put any stumbling block or obstacle in your brother's way" (v.13).

Speaking to the brother whose faith and conscience have allowed him to enjoy freedom in a certain area, Paul affirms the great commandment:

love. "If your brother is distressed because of what you eat, you are no longer acting in love. Do not by your eating destroy your brother for whom Christ died."

As the church of Jesus Christ, we've been called to walk on the higher plane of grace and truth. We should consider the opinions of fellow believers on minor matters. Few Christians today dispute whether or not meat should be eaten. And yet, many of us allow ourselves to get caught up in controversies that swirl about the Christian community today. These controversies take up inordinate amounts of time and energy. Should a congregation use contemporary music for worship or use only hymns in 4-4 time? Should there be dancing during worship or not? Should we forbid the raising of hands during the service? Paul's admonition is clear: "being right" is not the most important thing. Paul was convinced that no food was unclean in itself, but

> [a]s one who is in the Lord Jesus, I am fully convinced that no food is unclean in itself. But if anyone regards something as unclean, then for him it is unclean. If your brother is distressed because of what you eat, you are no longer acting in love. Do not by your eating destroy your brother for whom Christ died (Romans 14:14-15).

UNITY

We have a responsibility for building peace among other believers. How can we as pastoral leaders in the Vineyard share a spirit of unity with others in the body of Christ despite having different views on certain practices? Paul, speaking to the whole assembly in Rome, to peoples on both sides of "the issue" said, "Let us therefore make every effort to do what leads to peace and to mutual edification" (Romans 14:19).

STAYING FOCUSED: THE VINEYARD AS A CENTERED SET

July 95 – February 96, Volume 3, Issue 3

"Finally, all of you, live in harmony with one another; be sympathetic, love as brothers, be compassionate and humble" (1 Peter 3:8).

The recent circumstances evolving in Toronto have caused me to reflect on the need to review some of the past teachings that I've done in the hopes that doing so will clarify three basic questions that are being asked.

- In light of the recent separation with the former Toronto Airport Vineyard Church from the Association of Vineyard Churches, it might be appropriate to answer the question, "What exactly is the Vineyard?"

- Did we follow due process in our dealings with the administrators of the Toronto Church? Or were our actions capricious or arbitrary?

- What are those essential aspects of ministry that a committed Vineyard pastor is called to?

WHAT IS THE VINEYARD?

In the beginning years of the Vineyard movement I often described who we were and how we were to relate to others by referring to a sociological grid based on what is called Social Set Theory. Social Set theory, among other things, describes aspects of group dynamics and how individuals perceive their relationships to a group. Social Set Theory postulates that people interrelate to each other in bounded, centered or fuzzy sets. Allow me to review briefly the teaching concerning this theory.

Bounded, Centered and Fuzzy Sets

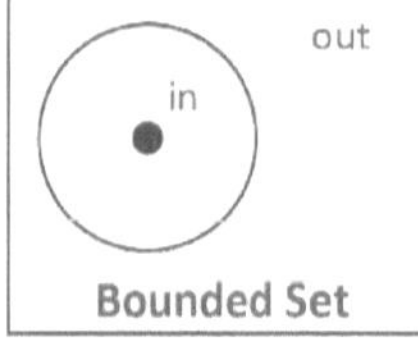
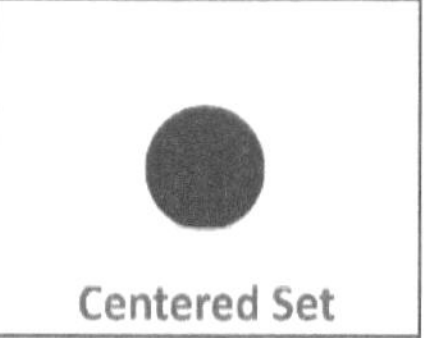
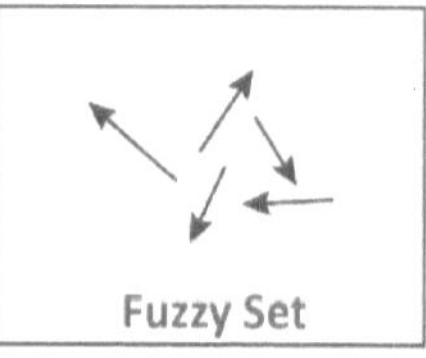

Bounded Set	Centered Set	Fuzzy Set
Based on faith & practice, clear who is in, who is out: rigid	Focus on defined core values: flexible	No organisational centre: formless

Bounded Set

Bounded sets make it easy to know whether you are in or out because they generally have clearly articulated lines of demarcation in both faith and practice. Traditions and people who exist in bounded sets, while safe in their clearly demarcated boundaries, are at risk of becoming dogmatic and harsh with brothers and sisters.

For instance, people who think in bounded sets might approach the issue of baptism with more righteous insistence that their particular mode is correct even though they cannot document this clearly in Scripture. It is tragic when an issue like baptism is used as a weapon against fellow Christians. Unfortunately, people who think and relate in bounded sets are often at risk of this type of behavior.

Centered sets and the Vineyard

The Vineyard is a young movement. In our early years, our detractors accused us of having an "anything goes" mentality and no boundaries. Yet, even when the movement was in its infancy, I purposely steered us away from either divisive dogmatism (bounded set) or a fuzzy ("anything goes") way of relating. Instead, I directed the movement towards the key values and practices we hold most dear. We were and are intent on being a centered set group.

In the context of the Vineyard as a growing movement, I purposely set out to center our movement around an orthodox/evangelical theology and, for the most part, practice. For instance, our Christology, our view of the importance of the bible, the high value we place on conversion by faith only, the doctrine of the fallen state of man, the importance of preaching a gospel of reconciliation (2 Corinthians 5:11-21), all fit into the core elements of orthodox/evangelical Christianity that we intentionally wanted to center our movement on.

The value of intentionally maintaining a centered set on orthodox/evangelical Christianity is not hard to see in practical terms. Take the issue of baptism. Controversies rage over which view or mode is correct: infant baptism, baptism after conversion, baptism by immersion or baptism by sprinkling. A centered set approach maintains a theology that stresses the core belief – baptism is biblical and important - without dictating a particular method or model for administering this rite.

Theologically, the Vineyard holds to the historical appreciation of baptism while allowing a degree of latitude about how it is to be administered. Thus, we discourage our people from dogmatically using their particular approach as a pretext to divide or distance themselves from their brothers and sisters.

Another area is eschatology. I've said in the past that I really don't care if your belief concerning the Rapture is pre-, mid-, or post-; it is possible to support all three interpretations biblically. We want to affirm that the doctrine of the Rapture is biblical, but we don't want to use our interpretations as a club to bludgeon a brother or sister, or teach that the other two views are non-Christian or non-scriptural. We want to avoid argumentative diatribes (2 Timothy 2:23).

As a centered set movement that attempts to be open and flexible, one key boundary we teach is the allowance of a great deal of personal latitude and practice as long as the teaching or practice is founded in church history and basis evangelical doctrine. When a person stands on a position that is clearly articulated within the Church, then I'm willing to abide with him or her taking that position. But I am not so open when an individual's stand cannot be defended with orthodox/evangelical theology and practice.

Fuzzy Set

Fuzzy sets aren't centered. People who relate in a fuzzy set have no central communality. The primary reason they get together is the enjoyment they get from simply being together. Fuzzy sets often precipitate the developing of relationships and organization and may develop into a centered set but there is no guarantee this will happen.

Many people around the world relate in these "fuzzy set" kinds of ways. The commercial that features a Jamaican group singing, "Let's all get together and feel all right," expresses this well. Getting together for itself sake is key; the core of their relationship is not a common allegiance to an agreed upon direction, set of beliefs or principles. This is viewed by the participants as being more free.

The Vineyard perspective on theology and experience

I designed the graph in Diagram #2 to illustrate to a gathering of Vineyard pastors in Manaki, Canada (July 1994), how certain aspects of renewal, even those that have historical precedence, could lead us away from the "main and plain" things of Scripture and to warn them about the danger of getting away from classic, historical Christian orthodoxy and ortho-praxy.

A secondary goal of my instruction to that group was to communicate my desire that the Vineyard elevate the importance of fellowship and openness with brothers who may have a slightly different interpretation or church practice than we do.

For example, I think it is difficult to support the practice of people being "slain in the spirit" from the Scripture. The infilling of the Spirit, on the other hand, is clearly illustrated and articulated. It is not my duty to convince those who teach and practice this otherwise. Therefore, in the interest of brotherhood, I choose to remain silent on the subject.

However, if someone said that there should be no falling down, I would say, "Wait a minute. You're now moving into a non-biblical position." The New Testament has numerous examples of people and even demons falling before Jesus and the power of God (Matthew 17.6, Mark 3:11, John 18:6, Revelation 1:17). There's a difference in my mind between being weak in a position and being non-biblical.

Easy in, easy out?

As diagram #3 shows, it is relatively easy to move towards a centered set organization. There are relatively few boundaries to jump over.

It sometimes happens, though, that because the boundaries are flexible and not rigid and because the allegiance is to a set of core values, beliefs and practices at its center, the only way to determine who is "in" and who is "out" is by the direction they are headed. Are they moving towards or away from the center?

In the case of the former Toronto Airport Vineyard, there was a growing realization that they were not in fact moving towards traditional Vineyard core values and practices but were moving away from the center, in my opinion.

WHAT WE CAN AND CAN'T AGREE ON

I have, in the past, emphasized those things we can all agree on. I have purposely stayed away from discussing those things that I would not agree on or find problems with. Those things can, in my mind, be called "extra- or non-biblical."

I'm going to name a couple of them in this letter for the purpose of clarifying to you the differences about the things I could and would bless and the things that I would hold at a distance and have difficulty with. These things do exist in the Body of Christ and I feel no responsibility to try to correct brethren outside our movement who hold these viewpoints. I simply would not merge our vision, theology and practice with theirs.

I am at peace to let brethren follow certain viewpoints and teachings and practices, as long as we don't have to accept them as bona fide ourselves when we cannot accept them based on biblical evidence, theological precedents or historical examples in the orthodox/evangelical Church.

Angels

A good example of this is the focus and exaltation of angels sweeping through not only our culture but the Church as well. A number of books, in both secular and Christian markets, tell of encounters with angels.

Some have even developed a doctrine that angels heal. These healing angels, so the doctrine says will – at our beckoning or request - touch people and heal them.

I have difficulty with that on several levels. First, this pseudo-theology assaults the integrity and the veracity of Scripture and undermines a believer's basic confidence in the office and ministration of the Holy Spirit. Scripture refers to God the Holy Spirit alone as healer. Even in the activity of Jesus Christ himself we see the Holy Spirit activating the healing process in peoples' lives (Luke 4:1, 4:18, 5:17).

It is bad enough when earnest and well-meaning Christians accept this specious theology for themselves, but I become very concerned when they then attempt to foist it onto others. We cannot and do not allow that type of behavior.

Spiritual warfare and territorial spirits

Another type of non-biblical teaching that's widespread today is this notion of territorial spirits and the necessity, through intercession, of assaulting them and drawing them down from their positions in and over cities and peoples, and in so doing, (the assumption is) preparing the way for the gospel.

Many well-meaning people are teaching these ideas. They do so on very skimpy biblical, theological or historical grounds, in my opinion. Whereas Ephesians 6:12 talks about wrestling with principalities and powers, there aren't, insofar as I know, any examples in Scripture in which anyone wrestles with principalities and powers. Scripture portrays Satan tempting Jesus in the desert; Jesus does not intentionally provoke Satan (Luke 4:1-13).

Furthermore, there are no examples of the apostles perpetuating this practice.

Last of all, I'm not aware of any significant historical Christian leader, whether Catholic or Protestant who has encouraged this kind of activity.

"New thing"

Another area that I have great difficulty with is the assumption that I've heard from prophetic people in charismatic and Pentecostal circles who often, using a King James language style, prophesy that God is about to do a "new thing". They often quote (or misquote) texts from the Old Testament to buttress their views. Advocates of this type of so-called spiritual warfare with principalities and powers view it as new weapon for the advance of the Church in these last times.

Whereas it was valid in the Old Testament for Prophets to be looking towards a "new thing", it bothers me when people have the notion that God, in the Church age, is going to do a "new thing". This teaching cuts across the import of the work of our Lord Jesus. Hebrews 1:2 portrays Jesus as the final Prophet. He came and delivered the ultimate message. He brought to an end the necessity for "new things".

Leaders throughout the history of the Church did not develop or discover "new things"; they simply recovered a greater revelation of what Christ had already done. For example, Augustine's teaching of the City of God and the importance of the kingdom of God was not new; it was a revelation from God about things already in the bible.

Martin Luther is another example. He didn't write Romans 5:1; God simply revealed to him the essential teaching of salvation by faith and faith alone. These people rediscovered truth already contained in Scripture that had been buried, often by the traditions of men and by the confusion that comes with religious practice as it overlays truth of Scripture.

Summary

My point in saying all of this is simply this: there is no "new thing" and there will be no "new thing." The only "thing" is the exaltation of Jesus, the waiting for his imminent return, the winning of the lost, and the establishing of the Church and nurturing of the same while we wait. You see, Jesus was and is the "new thing." Yes, there have been cycles of renewal and discovery throughout the history of the Church, but there are always rediscovery of old things, not a revelation of new things.

All this has been to say that the Vineyard is a centered set movement; we allow certain latitude and freedom while holding to a core set of values and practices. We haven't changed.

ISSUE OF GIVING DUE PROCESS TO AIRPORT VINEYARD

The answer to the question of whether we gave due process to the former Toronto Airport Vineyard is "Yes" and "Yes, but..."

I believe we followed due process in our dealings with the former Toronto Airport Vineyard in that we repeatedly emphasized to them in personal encounters and public exchanges the guidelines that were acceptable to us. The Board of the Association of Vineyard Churches developed those guidelines at great expense at a special meeting called for that purpose. (There was no Canadian AVC then.)

John Arnott says that he didn't understand the nature or intent of the documents that we sent to him. Yet when much of the leadership in the Vineyard (all the Regional Overseers helped draft the guidelines) received these documents they took to heart the pastoral directives I communicated.

One wonders what more we could have done to ensure that the former Toronto Airport Vineyard leadership take the guidelines more seriously. We sent the right signal; evidently it simply did not show up on their radar screen.

The pastoral team at the Toronto Airport Vineyard admitted receiving copies of those guidelines. They also admitted that they did not consider those documents as directives but more as informal guidelines. Hence, while they implemented many changes according to the guidelines, many on the staff simply filed them and did not familiarize themselves thoroughly with the contents.

We also followed due process when I wrote many papers on the topic in which I gave pastoral direction for the handling of it.

Furthermore, John Arnott says that the Association of Vineyard Churches didn't tell them of the problems AVC was having with certain practices they promoted. They were told but evidently not in ways that were meaningful to them. Again, most of the Vineyard pastors understood perfectly well the serious nature of those guidelines.

He further says that neither John Wimber nor anyone else communicated with them. At least five RO's attended the meetings in Toronto and discussed areas of concern with John and his leadership staff. Furthermore, I wrote several editions of *Vineyard Reflections* on this specific subject.

As I reflect on all that transpired I confess that given the serious nature of our misgivings of what was transpiring at the Toronto Church, I myself or perhaps Todd Hunter could have called John Arnott personally and made absolutely sure he understood those guidelines. Could he have not done the same with us? I acknowledge some degree of failure (possible on both our parts) and say, "Let's not allow our difference to hinder our good will or the work we do for the kingdom."

ESSENTIAL ASPECTS OF MINISTRY OF VINEYARD PASTORS

In the final section of this *Vineyard Reflections* I want to bring to your attention a series of questions I developed that you might ask yourself if you are wondering whether you are in tune or not with the general counsel of the Vineyard at this time. These are not trick questions nor are they meant to trip you up. They simply ask you is you can affirm those essential aspects of our core values, beliefs and practices.

Do I endeavor to:

- Build churches centered in the activity of teaching the Word of God?

- Build churches centered in the activity of worshipping the Lord your God with all your heart and might?

- Build churches in which care for the poor is prominent?

- Build churches where equipping the saints is an on-going reality?

- Build churches in which you endeavor to live in Christian unity with the Body of Christ around you?

- Build churches that serve the Body of Christ around you through renewal, equipping or other means?

- Build churches that plant other churches?

One positive result of all this is that it has caused us to re-examine who we are as a movement. I frankly like what I see. What happened with the Toronto Church is regrettable. We can redeem some of the pain and confusion if we move forward, firmly committed to preaching the Word and doing the works of Jesus.

UNITY AND WITHDRAWAL

of Endorsement from the Toronto Blessing

July 1996, Volume 3, Issue 4

"In necessary things, unity; in doubtful things, liberty; in all things, charity," Richard Baxter (1615-1691).

We value unity. We are convinced that all who belong to Christ are one in His Body, the Church. We aim to maintain unity by honoring all who call on Jesus' name and by seeking reconciliation with all parts of the Church.[39]

I've been asked dozens of times in the last six months mostly by people outside our movement, why, if the Vineyard values unity so much, would the Association of Vineyard Churches withdraw its endorsement[40] from the former Toronto Airport Vineyard Fellowship (now the Toronto Airport Christian Fellowship TACF) and thereby break the unity we value?

This question belies a tremendous concern for unity among members of the body of Christ. I respect and share that concern myself. The question also reveals some incorrect assumptions about unity among Christians,

---

[39]"Theological and Philosophical Statements of the Association of Vineyard Churches", 25.

[40]On December 13, 1995, the leadership of the Association of Vineyard Churches, with the full support of its board, announced in a personal meeting with the leadership of the former Toronto Airport Vineyard (TAV) that it was formally withdrawing its endorsement from the church and its activities. A subsequent written announcement made this decision public.

As we expected from such an announcement, there was a media "feeding frenzy" of sorts over this issue. Magazines such as Charisma, Ministries Today, Christianity Today and the National and International Religion Report, and many others, reported AVC's decision and the former TAV's responses. The Letters to the Editors columns of these magazines are still printing letters decrying the move as an obvious and unjust attack on unity in the body of Christ while others support the decision.

assumptions I would like to address in this issue of *Vineyard Reflections*.

We'll begin with a brief survey of unity in the bible. Then I will analyze several common misconceptions about unity among the body of Christ. Finally, I will use the situation between the former TAV and AVC and the latter's withdrawal of endorsement from the former as a context for discussing the difference between spiritual unity – which all believers in Christ have – and organizational unity – which believers under different authority structures have in varying degrees.

UNITY IN THE BIBLE

The bible, especially the New Testament, places a strong emphasis on unity among believers. As I will shortly point out however, there is no one single definition of unity in the New Testament. In fact, several different levels of unity are evidenced. Unity is discussed throughout both the Old and New Testament.

- *Unity in the body of Christ begins in God's own nature and heart.* "Hear, O Israel: The LORD our God, the LORD is one" (Deuteronomy 6:4). Jesus echoes this theme in John 17:22, when he says, "I have given them the glory that you gave me, that they may be one as we are one."

- *Unity of the body of Christ was created by God through the Cross.* "But now in Christ Jesus you who once were far away have been brought near through the blood of Christ. For he himself is our peace, who has made the two one and has destroyed the barrier, the dividing wall of hostility, by abolishing in his flesh the law with its commandments and regulations. His purpose was to create in himself one new man out of the two, thus making peace, and in this one body to reconcile both of them to God through the cross, by which he put to death their hostility" (Ephesians 2:13-16).

- *Unity among believers is a central theme of New Testament Christianity.* "Make every effort to keep the unity of the Spirit through the bond of peace. There is one body and one Spirit – just as you were called to one hope when you were called – one Lord, one faith, one baptism; one God and Father of all, who is over all and through all and in all" (Ephesians 4:3-6).

- *Unity of the body extends to all believers* (even the carnal Corinthians). "Brothers, I could not address you as spiritual but as worldly infants in Christ...The body is a unit, though it is made up of many parts; and though all its parts are many, they form one body. So it is with Christ. For we were all baptized by one Spirit into one body whether Jews or Greeks, slave or free and we were all given the one Spirit to drink" (1 Corinthians 3:1, 12-12).

The situation Paul addresses here with the Corinthians provides us with a good example of unity in Christ among Christians with widely varying levels of spiritual maturity.

- *Unity of the body of Christ witnesses to the lost about Christ's mission.* "My prayer is not for them alone. I pray also for those who will believe in me through their message, that all of them may be one, Father, just as you are in me and I am in you. May they also be in us so that the world may believe that you have sent me. I have given them the glory that you gave me, that they may be one as we are one: I in them and you in me. May they be brought to complete unity to let the world know that you sent me and have loved them even as you have loved me" (John 17:20-23).

- *Our final destination in heaven is a place of unity.* Jesus is waiting in heaven for one bride. "Let us rejoice and be glad and give him glory! For the wedding of the Lamb has come, and his bride has made herself ready" (Revelation 19:7).

- *Unity in the body of Christ is a weapon in God's hand against Satan and his kingdom.* The church united can overcome Satan, but a divided church cannot fully resist him. Division makes us weak (Luke 11:17-23).

FALSE ASSUMPTIONS

All believers in Christ are part of his body and form his bride. Not many disagree on this point. Others, though, harbor several false assumptions regarding unity:

- Unified *orthodoxy*: all members of the body of Christ should agree on every area of faith and doctrine.

- Unified *orthopraxy*: all believers should agree on every area of practice.

- Unified *organization*: Christians should be unified under one organizational structure. They infer from this assumption that Christians should never draw lines or separate from one another.

These assumptions fail to differentiate between the spiritual unity all believers have as members of Christ's body and organizational unity, which believers have in varying degrees. There are different levels of unity for different levels of relationship.

As an example, consider a family. A typical family consists of parents and children. Yet this single unit is really a subset of a larger extended family. Although the entire clan is unified by blood and marriage, each family is a separate entity, functioning under its own leadership structure. So while the entire clan is unified, there still exists varying degrees of unity between the families based on relationship, interaction, similarities and so forth.

I have found Dr. Wayne Grudem's approach to this issue helpful. He suggest we approach the issue of unity between Christians on a practical level through the matrix of separation, co-operation and fellowship.

In terms of separation, he says, "There are sometimes reasons why the outward or visible unity of the church cannot be maintained."[41] Although Grudem is careful to explain that each situation must be considered in its own context, there are basically three reasons for individuals and churches to separate: for doctrinal reasons, for reasons of conscience and for practical considerations.

Co-operation and fellowship refer to those passages in the New Testament that require Christians to forego all co-operation and fellowship with non-believers under certain circumstances (2 Corinthians 6:14).

The following chart graphically represents Grudem's matrix. Clearly, one has the highest degree of practical unity, that is, fellowship and co-operation without separation, within one's own church family. The graph shows that it is possible to have spiritual unity and not have complete organizational unity.

The Vineyard is a centered-set movement, which means we allow for a great deal of variety in matters of practice while holding to a core set of values and doctrines. We do not interpret unity to mean that all Christians should be united under one organizational or leadership structure. Unity

---

[41]Wayne Grudem, *Systematic Theology*, Leicester: Inter-Varsity Press, 1994, 878.

flows out of relationship, out of the life of the living organism that is the body of Christ.

Different Degrees of Unity (from AVC standpoint)

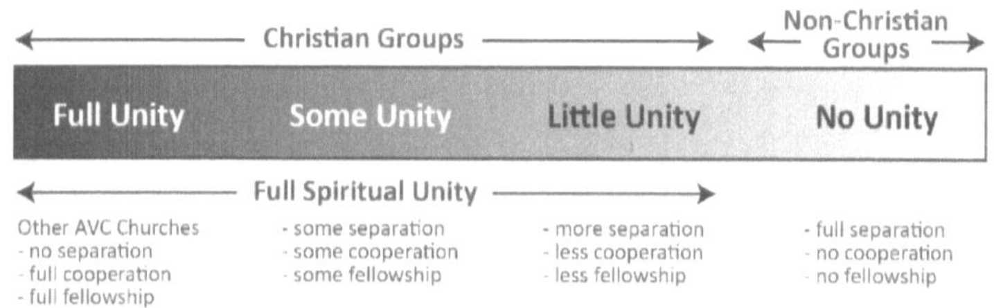

It is not my opinion that the body of Christ will or should become united under one organization, philosophy, theology or practice. Christians can be unified in basic orthodoxy and orthopraxy but not believe in one particular way, nor align themselves under one authority or leadership structure. One thing we cannot do, however, is to allow ourselves to become punitive and argumentative and therefore lapse into behavior that is prohibited in Scripture (2 Timothy 2:23).

SECTION II: UNITY, AVC AND THE FORMER TAV

Let me continue the discussion of unity as it relates to what occurred between the Association of Vineyard Churches and the former TAV.

In the light of discussion above regarding the New Testament emphasis on working for unity among believers, how can the Association of Vineyard Churches justify its withdrawal from the Toronto Airport Christian Fellowship?

The accusation that AVC excommunicated the former TAV is an obvious misunderstanding of excommunication and the issue of biblical unity, both spiritual and organizational. Excommunication has to do with repeated, unrepentant sin; it is an extreme, measure-of-last-resort, never done lightly.

When the AVC withdrew its official endorsement of the former AVC, it did so to make clear, on an organizational level, that it could no longer endorse what it could not exercise authority over. It did not excommunicate, withdraw the right hand of fellowship, break off communication, forbid its members to attend the former TAV, and so forth.[42] The following summarizes in a general way the degree to which AVC member churches fellowship and cooperate:[43]

- We will honor all previous commitments re: speaking engagements, conference dates, etc. As to future commitments, we will confer.

- We will free our people to associate with Toronto (attending, speaking in their events, etc.) just as we do with any other part of the body of Christ. All we ask is that the primary association of our Vineyard pastors/churches is with us and the vision that God has given us – anything less would lack integrity.

- We will take care in what we promote and ask the same of our churches and pastors. Practically this means that any Toronto Airport Fellowship Church speakers would need to fit within our context and direction if they were to be invited into one of our churches. It also means that our primary focus in renewal activities will reflect the main calling and direction of the Vineyard.

As Grudem points out, "[Churches] may decide to separate from [another] church if, after prayerful consideration, it seems that staying [together] will very likely result in more harm than good."[44]

If we return to the chart we used earlier, it becomes clear that AVC was simply exercising its right to establish some degree of separation on an organizational level between itself and the Toronto Airport Christian Fellowship. It does retain, as detailed above, some degree of fellowship and cooperation between the two groups.

As the chart shows, AVC and the Toronto Airport Christian Fellowship have changed their organization and fellowship.

---

[42]AVC leadership (ROs, DOs and APC) simply to prevent confusion about the withdrawal of endorsement and to not communicate a mixed message, have been asked not to minister at the Toronto Airport Christian Fellowship or have TACF leaders in their churches during this interim period. This policy will be reviewed at the AVC's annual board meetings.

[43]I thank Gray Best for this summary and the five following points.

[44] Grudem, *Systematic Theology*, 882.

The following points summaries my position on the subject.

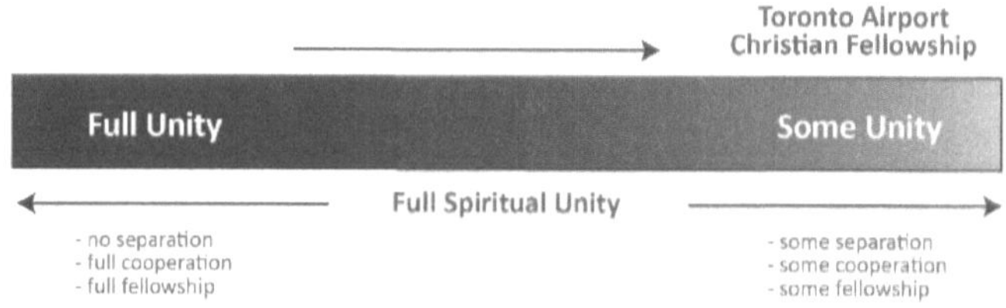

- We, as the Vineyard movement, believe that what has taken place in Toronto has been initiated by the Spirit. Many of us have been personally blessed and enriched through our contact with them.

- We do not believe, however, that Spirit-initiation brings immunity from the possibility of error. On the contrary, we are very aware of historical pitfalls (both theological and philosophical) that could seriously injure God's intention for this "blessing."

- As a result, we (as those given responsibility by God to pastor and protect those within the movement) have exercised our conscience and attempted to bring guidance and correction without quenching the Spirit. The key leaders at Toronto, because of what they believe to be the Lord's leading, found this guidance difficult to fully embrace.

- Being a "centered-set" movement our language during this process was primarily relational rather than legal in nature. We have apologized for every way in which that language confused the intent of our communication; we do believe, however, that we did communicate clear boundaries to them over a period of time.

- Through this process it became apparent that fully responding to our concerns would be a hardship to Toronto (they felt that God had spoken to them), which in turn was also a dilemma for us (we could not authorize what we could not exercise authority over.) That was the essence of our communication when we visited Toronto.

If they wanted to continue within the authority of our movement they would need to be convinced that it was the place in the body of

Christ that God had placed them, thereby trusting our leadership and receiving our correction – otherwise they would need to establish their own.

THREE FREEDOMS

I would like to conclude by outlining an approach to the issue of unity that I hope Vineyard leaders will find practical and helpful. It has to do with three freedoms: the freedom to promote, participate and pass.

I think we all ought to be quite careful about what we promote. That caution is partly due to my visibility, but it also reflects a value I hold dearly: pastors in the Vineyard are free to promote activities/people/events in the body of Christ as long as doing so meets the following criteria. Is the activity:

- deeply integrated into what I believe and practice?

- in strong agreement with Vineyard theology?

- in strong agreement with core Vineyard values?

- similar to our practices and emphases?

Vineyard pastors also have the freedom to participate. When making a decision of whether to participate in an activity or event, I ask myself:

- Is there strong agreement in the basics of the faith?

- Do we have agreement in broader values?

- Are there significant differences in practices or emphases?

Finally, I believe we have the freedom to pass. I pass on an invitation if

- I don't have faith for it (Romans 14:22).

- Accepting the invitation would violate my conscience.

- Accepting would in some way deter me from the work God has called me to do. Nehemiah's response to Sanballet (Nehemiah 6) is a good model for us. He refused to stop the work on rebuilding the walls of Jerusalem to meet with Sanballet.

We have a call of God on our lives to fulfill certain ambitions and things that God has given us to do. We accept the fact that God may have called others to certain things, which is fine. We bless them. But we need to stay true and focused on what our calling is.

To sum up: Exercising your freedom to promote, participate or pass does not break the unity of the body of Christ. We do not have freedom, however, to slander (Ephesians 4:15, 4:29, Galatians 5:13-15), denounce (Romans 14:3), attack (Galatians 5:13), judge (Romans 14:3), not love (1 John 4:19-20), strive over words (2 Timothy 2:14) or manipulate others into participation.

CONCLUSION

When we talk about the unity of the church in the sense of the horizontal, the church as it stretches back in time across the centuries, or as she spreads herself all around the world today, the truth is that the church, at least from our perspective, is not one.

Yet when God looks down vertically on the church from heaven, he doesn't see a fractionalized, broken church. From God's perspective, there's only one church. The New Testament depicts Jesus as the bridegroom, and the church as the bride of Christ (2 Corinthians 11:2; Ephesians 5:25-27, 31ff.; Revelation 19:7; 21:2; 22:17). Jesus loves the bride and can't wait to get her up to heaven.

You see we're one family, one church on our way to heaven.

I'll leave you with Paul's pastoral admonition to the believers in Ephesus: "Be completely humble and gentle; be patient, bearing with one another in love. Make every effort to keep the unity of the Spirit through the bond of peace. There is one body and one Spirit…" He goes on to say, "…prepare God's people for works of service so that the body of Christ may be built up until we all reach unity in the faith and in the knowledge of the Son of God and become mature, attaining to the whole measure of the fullness of Christ" (Ephesians 4:2-3; 4:12-13).

THE FIVE-FOLD MINISTRY

August 1997

I want to begin this *Reflections* article by first apologizing to you readers. It's been over a year since the last article, and on one hand I feel remiss. But on the other hand, I've been trying! This article is the most difficult article I can ever remember writing. If I didn't believe this topic was so important to the continuing health of the Vineyard movement, I would have abandoned it long ago.

I also want to thank many readers who have given input to this article. These are very complex issues. I'm trying to deal with a very diverse body of teaching in a way that is fair to their views, but also specific enough to be helpful to readers of *Reflections*. I've, therefore, sought the help of a diverse group of readers to sharpen my thinking, and I thank each one of you.

Vineyard is a church planting movement that actively seeks to discern what God is currently doing wherever we find His working in the Body of Christ. This philosophy of ministry exposes Vineyard churches to many different beliefs from various streams of thought within the church.

One the one hand, this keeps us honed because we are continually driven back to the Word of God as interpreted by the Spirit of God and to the historic church to ask: "Is this consistent with God's written Word, and with its historical expression through the centuries?" On the other hand, this openness can lead to a temporary drifting from the anchor of our historical beliefs and practices, and even a short-term distortion while the "fresh wind" is sorted through. I want to sort through some of this here in this article.

It's also very important to me how we view the larger church, and our reaction to it, whether the church is at "high tide" or "ebb flow". I want to love what Jesus loves, and He loves the whole church…always.

I believe some of the problems I'm going to address in this article have

177

arisen because of legitimate concerns on the part of some leaders about what they view to be nonfunctional church structures. I, too, share those concerns, but I also believe God has another plan to renew and revive His church.[45]

Adding still more to the confusion is that in the past two decades a number of valid biblical terms have now come to connote something different in the ears of the listeners than their biblical and historical usage. I don't believe that the altered meaning of the terms or the confusion arising from this was intentional, but it is never-the-less a problem that needs to be addressed in a growing movement like Vineyard.[46]

With these factors in mind, I want to first look at four commonly held beliefs supported by some in the charismatic and Pentecostal interaction with Vineyard. Then I want to draw five recommendations for ministries that reaffirm and clarify our Vineyard roots, both scripturally and historically, so we can continue to grow into the twenty-first century.

PART ONE

Four Commonly Held Beliefs

These ideas are held by what mainstream Pentecostals might generally call the Pentecostal extreme and to my knowledge do not represent the larger classical Pentecostal church.

In teaching on this controversial and diverse theme, I understand that I run the risk of appearing to some Vineyard readers as negative, even

---

[45]After observing the church and some of its nonfunctional structures, the church growth movement elected to ask and answer three penetrating questions: 1) Are the people equipped?, 2) Is the church mobilized?, and 3) Is the church growing qualitatively as well as quantitatively? I think these are excellent questions to ask. Later in this article I'll be giving "Five Recommendations for Ministries" that I believe are biblical, practical, time-proven, and useful for local church leaders to help alleviate some of these legitimate concerns.

[46]For instance, certain leaders began to use the word "Discipleship" as a proper noun. The "Discipleship Movement" redefined the term disciple to mean something that ultimately had to be largely abandoned because of the implications of its new meaning. When God, therefore, called me to disciple believers, I chose to use the more biblical term of "equipping" from Ephesians 4:12. I did this because it was functional, biblical, and not loaded with connotations of models and meaning I would have to correct and clarify.

though I am attempting to be neither polemical nor argumentative as I write. Please read the following section through *my* eyes, the eyes of an under-shepherd desiring to protect and re-focus, and not as a critic looking for arguments which can be used to hurt or injure others.

1. Restoring the New Testament Church

Some Christian leaders say the modern church needs to be brought back to a New Testament primitive experience. I don't entirely reject this. If, however, restoring the church means replacing the church, then I reject it. But if restoring means renewing all the church, then I accept it.

A fundamental and usually unspoken assumption of the view of these same leaders is the idea that we are now the unique recipients of the latter day work of the Spirit and that the Holy Spirit took a "leave of absence" from the church for the past nineteen centuries. This a-historical view misrepresents church history, in my opinion. The church under the administration of the Spirit has continued to grow and mature during the past nineteen centuries, albeit through ebbs and flows. I don't see any long parenthesis in which the Holy Spirit was absent from the church as I read church history.[47]

One can see the a-historical underpinnings of this view by the way in which it idealizes the early church depicted in the pages of the New Testament. One does not have to dig too deeply in Scripture to see the soil into which the early church was planted was clearly not ideal. Incipient heresies raged (Colossians), prejudice was rife (James), the church in Galatia struggled with a virulent strain of legalism, and there were serious divisions among the believers in Corinth, as well as the condoning of a major sin,

---

[47]I believe Peter's sermon on Pentecost marks this age as distinctively the Age of the Spirit from start to finish. "In the last days, God says, I will pour out my Spirit on all people. Your sons and daughters will prophesy, your young men will see visions, your old men will dream dreams. Even on my servants, both men and women, I will pour out my Spirit in those days, and they will prophesy" (Acts 2:17-18). We have been in the last days since Pentecost, and this is *still* the time of the outpouring of the Spirit as the Administrator of the church. Just to name one other example from Scripture, Paul compares the Old Testament ministry with the present New Testament ministry in 2 Corinthians 3. Paul emphasizes the "how much more glorious" ministry of the New Testament by characterizing it this way: "will not the *ministry of the Spirit* be even more glorious?" (3:8). I think that the scattered remnants of church history we have access to today demonstrate sufficiently that church history is replete with repeated outpourings of the Spirit.

incest (1 Corinthians), just to name a few.

My point is that the New Testament church was a mixed bag; it was glorious, but it was also laced with problems. I believe it's naïve to assume that early church Christianity was the high water mark of church history, but that things have gone badly since then. I'm aware that we have all of these, and more, evidenced in the church today. I'm just saying that the fact of these problems existing today does not call for rejecting the church and labeling it with some pejorative word.

These same leaders also assume that the leadership of the current church is self-serving. They seem to believe that the church is out of touch with the reality of the importance of the Gospel and has become focused instead on maintaining the existing community. In this rather pejorative view, the existing church is often characterized as "dead" or "old wineskins" and the supposedly "alive" church, is exhorted to "come out from among them". Again, this thinking is founded on a judgment that the church cannot be *renewed*; it must instead be *replaced* and the model for change is found primarily by looking backward, not forward.

To my mind, these ideas cut across several Scriptural values. First, the bible underscores the importance of endorsing and accepting leadership, submitting to it and thereby developing spiritual vitality together in dynamic fellowship.[48]

There is, secondly, the potential for those who hold this position to unintentionally immunize themselves from exercising the healthy habit of self-criticism and confession of sin. The church, according to this stance, needs to be restored, but what about those making this claim? Are they themselves above their own call to the church for repentance and restoration? Unfortunately, some may unwittingly communicate just that.

The justification some give for trying to take leadership in this area is communicated as "God told me" or "I had a visitation" and/or some other divine prerogative. To my knowledge, none have repented of their own activity in regards to any abuses they are now targeting in the church at large. For Israel at the time of Ezra, personal and corporate repentance led to renewal (Ezra 9:1-3).

Furthermore, a third Scriptural value these ideas contravene is that

---

[48] 1 Thessalonians 5:12-13 enjoins all believers to appreciate and esteem their leaders highly, and Hebrews 13:7, 17 adds to consider and imitate your leaders, and obey and submit to them since they watch over our lives.

believers are not to have judgmental attitudes.[49] In part these attitudes seem to flow from a lack of patience and forbearing with the church because they don't seem to recognize that the church, like its predecessors the Old Testament Israelites,[50] has a propensity to move away from intimate obedience to God toward a place where it could, and often did, pursue false gods.

In contrast to these views, it seems to me that old wineskins[51] can be renewed by water (sometimes a picture of the Word of God) and oil (a picture of the Spirit). I believe this can be observed in two realms: the natural and the spiritual.

I've seen this in the natural realm. My grandfather used to be a horse trader. Whenever he'd make a deal on a horse, he had a funny habit of asking that the harness be included in the trade. This request always drew odd looks because the weather and sweat had usually aged the leather

---

[49]This touches on a theme too large for this article. On one side we are clearly taught not to have judgmental attitudes toward the motives of others (Matthew 7:1-5; Romans 14:4, 10; James 2:13). On the other hand, however, we're not to suspend our critical faculties of discernment in the area of observable actions, teaching, prophecies, etc. (Galatians 6:1-2; 1 John 4:1; 1 Thessalonians 5:19-22; 1 Timothy 4:1,6). Paul warned the Ephesian elders that there would be both attacks from outside and heretical teaching from inside the church, and God's under-shepherds must be "on guard" (Acts 20:28-31). Maintaining the tension between these two is not always simple.

[50]For instance, in Judges, Israel lived out a four-fold cycle of apostasy and revival at least seven different times. SIN (a generation fell away into independence, forgot what God had done, and began doing what was right in their own eyes); SERVITUDE (in God's righteous anger against sin, He sent divine judgment through raiders who brought them into bondage); SUPPLICATION (in distress the Israelites finally humbled themselves, repented, and cried out to God for help); SALVATION (because of God's loving kindness and covenant faithfulness, He raised up judges like Othniel, Ehud, Shamgar, Deborah/Barak, Gideon, Jephthah, and Samson to deliver His people from their oppressors).

[51]The reader may ask if my position does not in fact contradict what Jesus taught in Matthew 9:17: "Neither do men pour new wine into old wineskins. If they do, the skins will burst, the wine will run out and the wineskins will be ruined. No, they pour new wine into new wineskins, and both are preserved." What do I think Jesus is saying here?
First of all, Jesus is not comparing the church to the New Testament church, because the New Testament church didn't exist then. He compared Judaism with the church, and says, in effect, "I've come to bring a new reality, and that new reality is not going to be attached, like a new cloth on an old garment, and/or given as new wine to an old wine skin." To take Jesus' teaching here and apply it to the church ignores the fact that he gave the church. The church, "Christ's Bride", is the new thing that was coming. There are times when the church is very close to God, as I've just mentioned, and times when it drifts away.

badly. But the seller would go along with it. He didn't want to appear foolish holding up a deal over a piece of old leather that wasn't worth much. But grandfather saw value that others didn't see.

After he got the harness home, my grandfather would walk around to the back porch of his farm house and soak it for a couple of days in a bucket of brine he had sitting there. After the brine had softened up the old leather, he would take it out, dry it off and then begin slowly rubbing linseed oil into the leather. I can remember him sitting in his favorite chair on the back porch after dinner, working the oil into those old harnesses, wondering why he cared so much about old useless leather.

It didn't take long before I saw why. After a couple of days of applying the linseed oil, that old leather would come back to life and sometimes appear like new again. Then grandfather would reattach the bit and hang it out in the garage to be used or sold. My grandfather didn't do it for the money; he simply enjoyed cooperating with the brine and the oil in renewing something that others considered useless.

I also enjoy cooperating with the water (the teaching of the Word) and with the oil (a new visitation of the Spirit) to see the renewal of "old wineskins", something that others may consider useless, but I value highly. This renewal through the Word and the Spirit is proof to me of the ongoing work of the Spirit in the church, and it will continue until the second coming of Jesus. The church is still the central instrument God uses for the advance of his kingdom.

That's why I believe the notion of the "dead" church is incorrect. If it's the church, it's alive because it belongs to Christ and is in Christ. Disobedience, encouragement of false doctrine, forgiveness, anger at God and men, all contribute to it being weak and sick. But for us to judge a church as dead because it is in low ebb spiritually seems to me to verge on sin. Jesus reserved for himself the right to judge the church (Revelation 2 and 3).

Sure, the church may need a resurgence of life; it may need a work of the Spirit that produces new life. That doesn't surprise you, does it? It shouldn't. The Old Testament is full of this ebb and flow cycle. Israel pulled away from God and then was drawn back time and time again. We also recognize this in church history where God raised up courageous men and women who led their respective movements out of such times of spiritual darkness and back to God. As a result, the church has been brought into a new place through a visitation of the Holy Spirit. Revivals bring new life at a time of a low ebb in the church, but don't give up on the church as dead.[52]

2. Re-establishing the Five-fold Ministry

A commonplace belief in this ideology is the assumption of the need for reestablishing the so-called five-fold ministry. When modern-day "Apostles" and "Prophets" take their rightful place, new forms, new wineskins, will be established, according to these ideas. The church will then be brought to a higher level of accountability, intimacy and spirituality than its predecessor. The church will then be able in this new state of empowerment to preach, pray, prophesy, heal, and do those things so effectively that it will precipitate the second coming of Jesus.

The misunderstanding is in part based on what is, in my opinion, an incorrect view of the "gifted equippers" given to the church in Ephesians 4:11 (see below for my understanding of these five ministries). I believe these five ministries have been extant in the church since the first century. As we study church history, there have been times when they have been more or less obvious, but not unavailable. These five ministries do not need to be *recovered* today, but *exercised* under the power and direction of the Spirit of God with humility and with a love and respect for the whole Body of Christ.[53]

Also underlying this assumption is again the idea that somehow the existing church is not spiritual and not in attendance to God. Yet, in my opinion, if it's the church, God is in it. And if it's not the church, it's not going to be renewed anyway.

Replacing old wineskins with new ones displaces structures and leaders and thus threatens existing churches and actually closes them to further renewal efforts. But isn't Christ the Supreme Head of the church? He is perfectly capable of disposing of and replacing leaders under the existing systems. In saying this I am not saying I approve of or am committed to all

---

[52]I do realize that there are false churches. There are many cult groups that may claim to be a church but whose teaching (if believed) will not save people, and there is little or no evidence of people who are genuinely born again.

[53]I don't believe that this is an exhaustive list, but representative. It's also very important to me that any practice of these five ministries is done in a manner of humility that exalts the Giver of the gifts, the Lord Jesus Christ, and not the recipients of the gifts in any kind of a self-exalting way.

existing systems of church polity.[54] I am just saying that I as leader of the Vineyard do not sense a call in correcting others in how they decide to do business in the Body of Christ.

I believe the church of Jesus Christ can be and is being renewed in this era and at this time. That doesn't lead me, however, to the conclusion that this renewal has been given because the existing church is so sinful that its structure and leaders need to be discarded.

The reader might ask: what do you think it means for Jesus "to remove your lampstand" in Revelation 2:5? Can the church reach that point where Jesus says, "This is no longer my church, and I remove it?" My answer is: "I don't know!"[55] Since it's His business, let's wait and see what He does. Jesus, after all, is the One who has "all authority" (Matthew 28:18).

3. Waiting For A "New Thing"

The third big issue that I hear over and over again is the prophetic announcement of something "new" coming. Prophecy of this nature can negatively affect the hearer. It can stir a desire for a Gnostic type of secret knowledge so that the believer can finally enter into some inner circle or be on the ground floor of some new move of God. This "new thing" or idea is usually supported with the logic that with this new information, wisdom, and power, the group will be better prepared to lead, nurture and care for

---

[54] I don't believe that the New Testament clearly teaches or demands any one, specific form of church government. I do, however, believe some forms are fraught with added problems. Having said that, I have no need to teach the Body as a whole or "correct" other forms of government which differ from Vineyard's. There is freedom here allowed in the New Testament, and other groups have a Master to give account to, and that's not me.

[55] I've listed three opinions, without comment or endorsement, just to give a flavor of the variety of interpretations. "The nature of the visitation is left unexplained; the threat is vague, but probably eschatological" (Nicoll, W. Robinson, Editor, *The Expositor's Greek Testament*, London: Hodder & Stoughton, 1897-1910, 351). "The reference is not so much to the Parousia as it is to an immediate visitation for preliminary judgment. Remember that Christ walks in the midst of his churches (2:1)," (Mounce, R.H, *The Book of Revelation*, NICNT, Grand Rapids: Eerdmans, 1977, 89). "If they do not heed, dire consequences are sure and swift. I will come is in fact in the present tense 'I am coming.' John sees it before his eyes. If the church does not heed the injunction Christ will remove its lampstand, which appears to signify the total destruction of the church. A church can continue only for so long on a loveless course. Continuing on that course means ceasing to be a church." (Leon Morris, NICNT, *The Gospel According to John*, Grand Rapids, Michigan: Eerdmans, 1971, 61).

the cause of Christ. Then they'll be in a better place than their predecessors to usher in the second coming of Christ. There is the inherent tendency to wait, rather than to actively do the stuff now. Jesus told us to occupy until He comes.[56]

My first problem with this idea is that nearly all the "new thing coming" prophecies used to support these claims are from the Old Testament.[57] But the new thing came! Jesus is the full, complete revelation of God, the exact representation of the Father's being (Hebrews 1:1-3). That "new thing" for all time was Jesus Christ the Messiah, revealed in radiant glory in the New Testament. And so, in my opinion, we should not expect a "new thing" to happen in the New Testament church era. It's all the reestablishing of "old things", or, in other words, continuing the ongoing ministry of Jesus (Acts 1:1).

I am not saying that God is not stirring the church in renewal. It's clear to me that the established Pentecostal groups emerging in this century have probably done more for evangelism and church planting than any other group in this century. But the assumption that there's new technology, technique, structure, or methodology to be generated via a higher spiritual experience in God is, in itself, suspect. And perhaps dangerous.

It can be dangerous because it can lead us away from Jesus, the Incarnate Word and from the bible, the written Word, to a place where subjective impressions and speculation are given more authority than they deserve. When we move from the practice of subjecting all prophetic words to the Word of God and in so doing elevate prophets (little "p") to Prophets (capital "P"), we move away from a New Testament understanding of gifts to understanding these gifted equippers as offices. We (the church) are urged to weigh and test the prophetic.

---

[56]"So he called ten of his servants and gave them ten minas. 'Put this money to work ['Occupy', KJV],' he said, 'until I come back.'" (Luke 19:13) The New Testament is, in my opinion, saturated with this concept to be actively engaged in the Master's business until he returns (for instance, the parables of the ten virgins, Matthew 25:1-13). As we anxiously look forward to the "not yet" fullness of the coming kingdom, we are still actively involved in daily drawing on the "already" of the kingdom "to destroy the devil's work" now (1 John 3:8).

[57]A commonly used verse is Haggai 2:9: "'The glory of this present house will be greater than the glory of the former house,' says the LORD Almighty. 'And in this place I will grant peace,' declares the LORD Almighty." Joel 2 is also commonly referred to, and the Old Testament tabernacle is also sometimes used as a blueprint.

A second problem with focusing our attention on a "new thing" is a tendency towards elitism. Elitism is fostered when those who are gifted form the special core who then dispense the new, revealed Truth to those on the outside.[58]

A similar situation developed during the Middle Ages in the Catholic church. The bible was at that time written in Latin (the Vulgate) and the priests, who were trained in Latin, were the bridge between the sacred and the uneducated secular masses. No doubt this situation developed over time. Perhaps the hierarchy of the Catholic church was simply trying to interpret the Word of God to the mostly illiterate church. But what it developed into was not quite so benign. Their special place of knowledge and power became in fact a weapon that the elite priestly corps used to separate the masses, who didn't have the "gift" of Latin, from God and the bible. This "gift" became a powerful tool to keep control over the source of power. The masses weren't able to enter into the "secret" places this knowledge provided.

As unhealthy fixation on one of the gifts to the exclusion of the others results in believers being classified according to their gifting level. This is clearly not a direction the church should go.

This type of thinking also violates a fundamental Vineyard value in that it reduces those outside the special core to a group who exist to receive what the core has to dispense. In other words, a reliance on the special corps of people to dispense the special revelations from God disempowers the church and turns God's army into an audience. Our goal in the Vineyard is to equip the church to be full members in the army of God. "Everyone can play" (that is, participate).

The final assumption is that with the development of the Apostolic and Prophetic offices (capital "A" and "P"), these "super-apostles" will be similar to, if not the same as, the Lamb's Twelve. This view is propagated uncritically by its proponents in that they do not clearly distinguish, in my opinion, between the Lamb's Twelve and the apostolic "legate"[59] (addressed further below).

While I believe there is lower-case apostolic ministry today,

---

[58]Edward Irving and the "Catholic Apostolic Church" illustrates the elitism that can be inherent in Apostolic claims.

[59]The word "legate" here is used to designate the group of *non*-Lamb's Twelve apostles. Throughout the rest of this article, I will use the term "apostolic function" for the functioning of the "little a" apostolic people.

1. I don't presume that they are going to displace the leaders of existing ecclesiastical structures today;

2. I don't believe any of them will write a new bible or communicate anything equal with Scripture since the canon is complete (Revelation 22:18-19);[60]

3. I also don't see them ruling or usurping power or even influence over the whole church (Revelation 4:9-11), and finally

4. I believe the purview of the apostolic function today is the same as in the New Testament: to win souls, make disciples and plant, nurture and set things right in churches over which they have spiritual authority.

Some who support the Five-Fold ministry use John 14:12: "I tell you the truth, anyone who has faith in me will do what I have been doing. He will do even greater things than these, because I am going to the Father," to support the idea that the age of the super Apostle/Prophet will come and be characterized by "greater things". But what does it mean to do "greater things", greater in quantity or quality?[61]

I do not believe in the assumption of some today that the prophets of the New Testament are the same as the prophets of the Old Testament. Wayne Grudem has demonstrated in a very thorough way why the Old Testament prophets became the New Testament Apostles, and the nature of New Testament prophecy.[62]

In the New Testament prophets did not speak with authority equal to the words of Scripture. For instance, Agabus' prophecy about Paul was nearly correct, but not entirely. Agabus stated that the "Jews of Jerusalem

---

[60]I don't personally know of anyone among those teaching this view who would say they are writing or speaking anything equal to Scripture. But I want to make this clear, because there are those who believe "apostle" always connotes "writing Scripture." By stating this point, I want to make sure there is no confusion on this very important point.

[61]The word translated "greater things" has been interpreted, in general, as *quantitatively* greater (greater in the sphere of influence, either numerically or geographically) as well as *qualitatively* greater (greater in kind, including eternal vs. temporary). This word is a comparative word which, according to Bauer, Arndt and Gingrich, can mean greater in extension, measure, quantity, intensity, rank, or importance, and they include the John 14:12 usage under "of intensity."

[62]Wayne Grudem, *Systematic Theology*, 1050-1056.

will bind" Paul, but it was in fact the Romans who put Paul in chains.[63] The New Testament epistles instruct believers to weigh, test, interpret, and then apply what is good in prophecies (1 Thessalonians 5:19-21, 1 Corinthians 14:29-38). If New Testament prophecy was always authoritative, they would simply be enjoined to obey it.

So, prophetic gifting is valid. But conceding that does not mean accepting the notion that these ministries become offices. In my mind there is no room within the Ephesians 4:11-13 verses to assume that the gifted equippers must mean offices which confer prerogatives, exclusive powers of grace, or structural authority over large portions (if not all) of the church.[64]

4. Continuing the Ministries and Gifts until Jesus Returns

I am fully in accord with the statement in the above headline. I do believe there is room in Ephesians 4:11-13 to support the notion that these ministry functions will continue until Jesus returns. Paul uses a strong temporal word, "until", in verse 13 to indicate, in my opinion, that the five gifts and their purpose would continue. I don't believe that this "unity in the faith" and "full measure of perfection" has yet been reached, so these gifted equippers are still needed.

I believe we can also argue cogently from other passages of Scripture that these gifts continue through this present day and will until Jesus returns.[65] I look forward to the ongoing expression of all five ministry functions in Ephesians 4:11 until the return of the Lord.

But how are these ministry functions to be exercised and expressed in the church today? That will be the question I want to answer in Part Two.

---

[63]See Acts 21:11, 22:29, and also Grudem's excellent argument in *Systematic Theology*, 1052-53.

[64]In commenting on a parallel text on gifts in 1 Corinthians 12:28, Gordon Fee, well-respected New Testament scholar, says, "At best we can say that the first three emphasize the persons who exercise these ministries, while the final five emphasize the ministry itself...That probably suggests that the first three items are not to be thought of as "offices" held by certain "persons" in the local church, but rather as "ministries" that find expression in various persons;" (Gordon Fee, NICNT, 619). I would agree with Dr. Fee on this parallel passage, although I usually use the word "function" to underscore their dynamic nature, instead of "ministry."

[65]In Acts 2:17-18, 1 Corinthians 1:5-7, 1 Corinthians 13:10, and 1 Corinthians 12-14, just to name a few passages, there seems to be the normal assumption that this is how the church functions, and I do not see anything in Scripture that says this has changed.

Conclusion

In my opinion, the church in the world today is going through another cycle of renewal (historic revival in some places, renewal in others). And as the church is a "work-in-progress", it's not helpful for the present day church to think it can exclusively evaluate itself. This is not to say that we shouldn't be self-critical. But I don't believe it is valid for us to write our own history. Ultimately, an era of the church must be evaluated by ensuing generations. A better question to ask is "What will they be saying a hundred years from today?" Or better still, "What will Jesus say?"

PART 2

Five Recommendations for Ministries

1. All Ministries Are (Should Be) Proven at The Local Church Level

It's my understanding that this is the norm in the New Testament where concrete illustrations are given. Let me illustrate it here with the first known missionary team, Barnabas and Paul.[66]

Barnabas proved his character and ministry in the local church at Jerusalem and also at Antioch. At Jerusalem Barnabas demonstrated his generosity and heart for the poor and was encourager to those around him. He was a discipler of men, seeing the best in others and acting on it. He was spoken of as a man of good and holy character, full of the Holy Spirit and faith, and a man who knew how to bring the lost to Christ. Barnabas was so highly trusted that he was sent out as a representative of the Jerusalem church to discern what God was doing at Antioch among Gentiles. Barnabas then became part of the leadership team in the Antioch church, and proved in this field again what he had already evidenced at Jerusalem.

Barnabas was also the one who sponsored Saul to the apostles on his short visit to Jerusalem about three years after Saul's conversion. Four or five years later Barnabas brought Saul from Tarsus to Antioch to help in the new church plant. Saul watched and learned and ministered together with Barnabas so effectively that non-believers saw Christ-like character in

---

[66]I spoke more completely on this in the Leadership Seminar sponsored by VMI, "Recognizing & Developing Leaders," September 1996.

the disciples in Antioch. They were first called Christians ("little Christ's") there. On Barnie's compassion ministry to Jerusalem, he took Saul along with him. Not only did they deliver the financial gift, but Barnie had a "with him" ministry time with Saul.

Here's my point. Saul had the best religious education available in his day, a very special, distinct call on his life, and was lavishly gifted. Even with all that, I believe this time in Antioch with Barnabas was a discipling and training time for Saul that was necessary for his own growth and also for the church at Antioch to recognize his readiness to be released for further ministry. In my opinion, it should be no different in the church today.

When competent ministers have chosen in the past to leave existing ministries and come to Anaheim (something we've usually discouraged), we have gone very slowly. There are times where some may say with their words or actions "hire me!" We respond by telling them to get involved in ministering through this local church. Sack groceries in benevolence. Minister to the poor. Pray for the needy. Give your life away freely to others. Become known in this church.

Three ex-missionaries now work with me on staff. All three returned from overseas to Anaheim at their own initiative and expense and were not promised anything except fellowship and training. Over a period of four years, I watched them. They all began with their families by sacking groceries to give to the poor. They have been faithfully involved in the life of the church since they arrived; they became known by us over the years. They weren't looking for a position, status, or a ministry, but looking to serve. When a need arose in VMI, I hired all three at separate times.

If a person is not doing the stuff effectively in and through the local church, it won't work just because they take a plane ride.

2. All Ministries Are (Should Be) Recognized by The Local Church

We all agree that only God can call someone as an apostle or a prophet or into any ministry. It is the sovereign Spirit who gives gifts to the church.

That notwithstanding, the local Body of Christ still needs to recognize and release all ministries, including apostles. The best known example is again the first missionary team of Barnabas and Saul in Acts 13:1-3. At his conversion, God had already called Saul/Paul to a ministry to Gentiles. The Holy Spirit Himself told the leaders that now was the time to set two aside for His work. But the church leadership fasted and prayed first, and then put their seal on this team by endorsing their character and ministry and confirming the timing. God does sovereignly call, but the local church recognizes and releases.

In my own experience in the church at Anaheim, I've been led a number of times to recognize gifted and emerging leaders. I'll just give two illustrations.

The first one is Monte Whitaker in the area of benevolence. Monte was a teenager when he heard a sermon I gave on the problem of the poor. Immediately afterwards he came to me and said he believed God had called him to minister to the poor. I don't know what his expectations were, but when I responded: "Great! Begin giving stuff away," he looked a little crestfallen. But that's exactly what he did.

He and his wife Brandi later moved to an area in Los Angeles and began daily giving out of their own resources. Monte would return home after work and find that Brandi had given away his extra shoes, or blankets and food to meet someone's need. Monte would also do much the same by giving his own lunch away, for instance.

I watched them and waited for eight years, asking God if it was time yet. Then the Lord acknowledged that it was time for Monte to be recognized as a benevolence pastor at Anaheim Vineyard.

The benevolence ministry at Anaheim grew, by the end of 1996, to where it:

- distributed over 1.4 million meals for 1996,

- dispersed approximately 32 tons of food a month,

- gave away over 51,000 items of clothing and blankets and 2,300 sundry kits to support the homeless,

- averaged several thousand decisions for Christ for the last few years through the evangelistic messages during the benevolence outreaches,

- has seven existing home groups and is preparing to plant four new Latino churches and one Vietnamese church among people we are ministering to in Orange County.

A second illustration is Todd Hunter. Todd and Debbie Hunter and another couple first came to us after they graduated from Calvary's Bible school. Both couples felt they had a call from the Lord to plant a church in Wheeling, West Virginia.

After a brief time with Todd, I made an assessment of what he needed to do for us to recognize and release him. First of all, my assessment was not based on what some would think is the obvious: *age*. In fact, I never look at age; I look for ministry maturity. Here is a sample of the objective evaluations I take:

1. Are they "already in motion;" going somewhere based on vision from God?

2. Do they demonstrate a hunger for God, evidenced by a strong desire for personal and professional growth (I look for teachability)?

3. Are they committed as a couple to ministry?

4. I test them: Can they risk? Will they initiate? Can they develop others?, etc.

I gave Todd some difficult assignments in a wide spectrum of practical ministries in the area of *formation*, including hospital visitation, junior children, and establishing and reproducing a home group. Todd passed every assignment with flying colors, demonstrating that he could evangelize, disciple, and reproduce leaders.

I also thought Todd's background needed to be strengthened in the area of *information* in areas such as church growth principles, planning and strategizing, and principles of leadership. I gave Todd tapes, books, and articles to digest, and we spent one afternoon a week discussing what he had learned. Todd says the principles he gleaned during those times together are still pillars in his perspective on ministry.

After just six months with us, we released Todd and Debbie to plant a church in Wheeling because Todd had proved himself in the local church here at Anaheim. In Todd's seven years in Wheeling, the church grew to several hundred, and he either was directly or indirectly involved in stirring up, training, or envisioning many church plants.

This didn't surprise me because he had first proven his ministry in the local church setting, and God had also given me a prophetic word for Todd that he had a call to lead leaders. Todd is now doing an excellent job in his present position as National Coordinator of AVC-USA, where he is engaged in what I believe to be the highest and best use of his life: as a leader of leaders.

I am not aware of any ministry in the Book of Acts or in the Epistles which is endorsed by God and yet not under the auspices of the local church. Roving, itinerant ministries (in our vernacular today, "loose cannons") who were not responsive to the authority of a local church soon became a problem in the early church. They were dealt with very specifically in the writings of the early Church Fathers.[67]

No matter what our giftedness, submission to the leadership of the local church is a hallmark of a Christian (Hebrews 13:17; 1 Peter 5:5). So the issue we are speaking to is not whether persons believe that they are an apostles, prophet, etc. God certainly must call, but this will be proven and recognized in the local church over time.

3. All Ministries, Including apostleship (little "a") Are (Should Be) Confirmed In The Field Over Time

We want to send people out who are released by the local church with a proven track record, but also who demonstrate the same standard in the field over time.

Some today are asking the wrong questions, in my opinion. "Have you seen the resurrected Christ? Have you been commissioned by the resurrected Christ?" These questions belong to the Lamb's Twelve. The Lamb's Twelve have no vacancies; the Lamb's Twelve was filled in the 1st century.

Here are some questions I believe we should be asking. Is there a proven track record in the field? Can I talk to some of your converts who are still "going and growing" through a local church?

The phrase "show me your puppies and I will give you your papers" came out of this kind of a context where I wanted to see the ministry proven in the field over time. In the particular situation where this phrase arose, that pastor now has his "papers" because he showed me his "puppies". There was fruit in his ministry.

But even if someone has an extraordinary fruitful apostolic (little "a") call and ministry today, that does not mean that he has a so-called Apostolic office that, as I've said, confers prerogatives, exclusive powers of

---

[67]How to deal with itinerant teachers was already a problem before the end of the first century (see 3 John 5-12). In 11:1-12:5 in the Didache, one of the writings from the Church Fathers probably dated in the 2nd century, detailed instructions for examining the traveling teachers were given, including the length of stay (not more than two or three days), what they're to teach, how they're to be supported, their character, and what they can take when they leave. 12:5 states: "But if he does not wish to cooperate in this way, then he is trading on Christ. Beware of such people" (J.B. Lightfoot, translator, *The Apostolic Fathers*, edited and compiled by J.R. Harmer, London: MacMillan, 1893, Second Edition, 155-157). Cooperation with the local church by the traveling teachers was important to this 2nd century writer.

grace, or structural authority over large portions of the church. It's my opinion that the only apostles today are little "a"-apostles, the modern day equivalent of the first century apostolic function.

We should be asking, "What is the fruit of your apostolic ministry?" and focusing on the description of the New Testament apostolic function in the broad sense. In my understanding a proven track record is the primary evidence of the reality of someone's call, along with the full endorsement of the releasing church.[68]

4. All Ministries Serve (Should Serve) The Purposes of Winning the Lost and Establishing Churches

Winning the lost and planting churches was the primary description of the apostolic function of the first century, and is the ongoing function of apostles (little "a") today. This is, I believe, God's heart and the reason gifted equippers were given to the church.

The immediate context of Ephesians 4:11-16 bears this out. Verse 12 states that the gifted equippers are to "prepare God's people for works of service".[69] Why are they to be prepared? "So that" is a statement of result or purpose. Giftedness or ministry is not an end in itself, but is to bring about the results that "the body of Christ may be built up". The result is the growth of the Body of Christ.

---

[68]Some missions advocates today assume that the churches at Antioch and Jerusalem had no oversight of the first mission team that they encouraged when they released Paul and Barnabas. They've been heard to say that Paul and Barnabas were not sent "out" but sent "off." It's their presumption that the change in prepositions justifies their conclusion that a traveling, church planting missionary team is equivalent to a local church requiring no outside authorization or accountability. In my mind this interpretative position ignores that Barnabas was sent to Antioch by the Jerusalem church when they first heard of the move of God at Antioch (Acts 11:22). It also ignores the discipleship training dynamic of Barnabas with Saul/Paul (see Part II, #1 in this article). The result was, in my opinion, that both were recognized functionally among "prophets and teachers" by the Antioch church (Acts 13:1). Thirdly, the team returned to Antioch after the first two missionary journeys. As I read the related texts (Acts 14:26-28; Acts 15:30: 18:22-23), I believe there was ongoing relationship that implies much more than being sent "off," but an accountability that implies they were sent "out."

[69]The noun *katartismos* means 1) to bring a broken bone into proper alignment (i.e. "bring people to wholeness in Christ, real depth of healing, not band-aids," 2) to establish and lay a solid foundation (i.e. "establish a launching pad, not put on a lid for control," and 3) to train others with/for skills (i.e. "not information, but transformation in ministry").

I believe the immediate context would point primarily to *qualitative* growth (maturity). It's an important function of gifted equippers to help every person in the Body of Christ to "grow up before he grows old" and to "learn to play nice".

But *quantitative* growth (numerical) is certainly not excluded in the Ephesians 4 passage and is the bull's eye of the New Testament church. "Going" and "growing" were the flip side of the coin for Jesus and for Paul.[70]

The larger context of the Book of Acts also supports this conclusion. A quick reading of the Book of Acts which focuses on the "growth" passages will paint a clear picture of a growing, thriving, penetrating church with the apostles at the cutting edge.[71]

5. All Ministries Are (Should Be) Exercised In Humility And With Love For The Whole Body

It's not just important what we do, but it's equally important how we exercise these "services" or *diakonias*. At times there seems to be more emphasis on the gifts of the Spirit than on the fruit of the Spirit. All the ministries should be exercised in fair, evenhanded treatment of people.

Even Paul's Apostolic ministry did not necessarily mean the Apostle chose to exercise full authority in all places and in every situation. At times he chose not to use his full authority. Paul acknowledged that his Apostleship meant that he was not to burden the people, but to be "gentle among you, like a mother caring for her little children."[72] What a picture of a self-giving, tender attitude in exercising authority and giftedness.

Paul's ministry was based on the care, love and relationship of a father, and not just on calling or Apostleship. For example, God had used Paul to bring the gospel to Corinth and lay the church's foundation there. Although he recognized and even used his Apostolic authority, Paul preferred

---

[70]Jesus gave His disciples as representatives for the church the Great Commission, which includes ongoing church planting, Matthew 28:18-20. Wherever Paul and his missionary team went, churches, which could reproduce other churches, were released as the team moved on to further evangelize and plant churches. One specific illustration is Acts 19:8-10 where the result of Paul's teaching for two years in Ephesus was evangelism and church planting.

[71]The following verses in Acts will at least whet your appetite: Acts 2:41; 2:47; 5:33; 6:1; 6:7.

[72]1 Thessalonians 2:6-7. Look also at Philemon as an example of not using his full authority, and also 1 Corinthians 9:1-12 as he relinquished his right for financial support.

to appeal to the Corinthians as a spiritual father.[73] Because Paul had established the church, he claimed a special relationship with the Corinthians. This enabled Paul to speak to them with a boldness that might not have been appropriate with other churches (for instance, the churches in Jerusalem or Rome, both of which had been established by others).

One test, in my opinion, is if a person is willing to take a demotion in the same spirit as a promotion. For instance, I've had some people who can't understand why I stepped away as Senior Pastor of a large church while I could still breathe. They don't understand. I never owned this church. The Anaheim Vineyard was never my church. In the same way the Vineyard movement was never my movement. I'm still working for God, rendering service where I can, and that service is in a different arena now than before. Now it's mostly behind the scenes with leaders through faxes and telephone calls. I don't mind what I do, just so I have a piece of Jesus' kingdom work. I'm change in God's pocket; He can spend me any way He wants. I joined up with nothing, and I intend to go out with nothing but Jesus. That's a good deal. After all, isn't Jesus what we all joined up for?

We respond to God and His sovereignty, and let others recognize God's work in us. "Let another praise you, and not your own mouth: someone else, and not your own lips" (Proverbs 27:2). I've always been wary of people who go around calling themselves by some high-sounding title. If it's really true, others will be able to figure it out without reading it on out business cards. Even the crowns we have in heaven will not be worn, but cast at Jesus' feet in recognition of whose they are (Revelation 4:10). There is only one "man" in the kingdom, the man Christ Jesus, and we will adore Him for all eternity.

"Teacher", "pastor", "evangelist", "prophet" and "apostle" are not titles to bear or wear, but a stewardship to exercise in humility and love towards the whole church. Jesus loves the whole church, and so should we. The New Testament emphasizes functioning and serving the church, not claiming an office or calling oneself someone.

Paul says "So then, men ought to regard us as servants of Christ and as those entrusted with the secret things of God" (1 Corinthians 4:1). When Paul rehearsed to the Ephesian leaders some of the values he based his life and ministry on, he said "I served the Lord with great humility and with tears...Guard...all the flock of which the Holy Spirit has made you

---

[73]1 Corinthians 4:14-16; see also Galatians 4:19 for a similar response in another situation.

overseers" (Acts 20:18,28). Gifted equippers are given to the whole Body to serve it in humility and love.

Summary

God has richly and creatively gifted the church from its birth until today. I love what God wants to do. But all ministries, in my opinion, must be proven and released through the local church, confirmed in the field, give rise to the extension and expansion of churches, and be exercised with Christ-like humility and love for the entire Body of Christ. That's how gifted equippers can cooperate in this generation with the Ascended King to continue "all that Jesus began to do and teach" (Acts 1:1). Let's serve Jesus together as long as God gives us breath.

DEFINING THE FIVE-FOLD GIFTS

Context

Ephesians 4:7-16 speaks of gifted equippers who are given to the church as Christ apportions grace to them. But it's very important to note that the context assumes, in my opinion, a discipled person, who first of all understands his position, identity and calling in Christ (the "then" or "therefore" in verse 4:1 refers back to the first three chapters and our calling by grace).

Paul then exhorts these gifted equippers to live a life characterized by a practical outworking of that truth in their own lives. They are "to live a life worthy of the calling" as a "prisoner for the Lord" (v. 1). Paul further describes this walk with works like humble, gentle, patient, forbearing, loving, unity (vv. 2-6).

Not only are these gifted equippers to make consistent choices to "put on" Christ-like character, but Paul goes on to instruct them *not* to "live as the Gentiles do, in the futility of their thinking" (v. 17). Paul practically samples specific areas to "put off," such as lying, anger, stealing, unwholesome talk, bitterness, brawling and slander, and lists a corresponding Christ-like response to "put on" (4:20-32).

As a young Christian I was taught "God will *not* use an unclean vessel." Furthermore, those who are clean, godly and well established in the discipline of Scripture will likely have a longer, greater quality (and perhaps quantity) of ministry.[74]

In summary, the gifted equippers of Ephesians 4:11 are also to have the godly character of Ephesians 4:1-6 and 17-32 with a track record of relating the truth of God's Word to the needs of their lives. This very brief contextual introduction does not do justice to how important I believe this subject of character is.

Introduction

Ephesians 4:11-16 has been foundational for the ministry of the Vineyard since its inception. It lies at the very heart of our emphasis on equipping and releasing the Body to do the works and the words of Jesus.

The gifted equippers in Ephesians 4:11 are given by Christ to the church for the purpose of equipping the saints. These five designated areas of ministry are more *functions* that *persons* perform, and not any sort of offices, although some commentators, in my opinion, are not careful in their use of terms (possibly because they are often more thinkers than doers).

In my opinion, though, neither the text nor the context of Ephesians 4:11-13 warrant us to assume that the gifted equippers must mean offices which confer exceptional prerogatives, exclusive powers of grace, or structural authority over large portions (if not all) of the church.

Paul is teaching that *equippers* are Christ's gift to the church, and these *equippers* are to function in the following ways through the gifts the risen Christ has given:

Apostles

The word apostle simply means a "sent one," and in the New Testament has both a broad and a restrictive use.

An apostolic function – the broad sense of "apostle" – 2 Corinthians 8:23; John 13:16

An apostle (little "a") is one sent forth to win souls and make disciples, plant and nurture churches, and set things right in churches over which they had spiritual authority. This was often attended by signs and wonders

---

[74] I believe this ignores biblical evidence of God doing exactly that in Scripture (i.e. Sampson, Barak, Judas, etc.). Furthermore, church history (ancient as well as contemporary) is replete with unclean vessels who God obviously uses.

(Barnabas: Acts 11:22-26; 13:2-4; 15:22; Silas: Acts 15:22-23; Timothy, I Thessalonians 3:2-3). These first century apostles include among others: Barnabas, James, Silvanus (Silas), Epaphroditus, and Timothy (Acts 14:14; Galatians 1:19; 1 Thessalonians 1:1 with 2:6; Philippians 2:25. Other church planters throughout church history have been called apostles because of their work in specific area of ministry (Ansgar, Cyril, Carey, etc.).

The Lamb's Twelve (possibly including Paul) – the restrictive sense of "Apostle" – Mark 3:13-19; Matthew10:1-4

Apostle (with a big "A") would include all the characteristics of apostle (with a little "a"), plus these Apostles were specifically commissioned by Jesus (Acts 1:2-3; Galatians 1:1), saw the resurrected Christ (Acts 1:22; 1 Corinthians 15:5-8), and some were used by God to write Scripture (Ephesians 3:5; 2 Peter 3:15). They ceased with the death of John, and last of the Twelve, and are the ones who will rule in heaven (Revelation 21:14).

Prophets

A prophet is one through whom the gift of prophecy is consistently manifested. This person is used by God to communicate what God wants the community to hear concerning a specific situation. He/she is a spokesman for the Spirit, receiving direct revelation from God.

Old Testament prophetic ministry

Old Testament prophets were sent by God (Haggai 1:13, Obadiah 1:1) and spoke and wrote words which had absolute divine authority (2 Peter 1:19-21, Numbers 22:38; Exodus 7:1; Jeremiah 1:9). To believe or disobey an Old Testament prophet was to sin against God Himself (Deuteronomy 18:19; 1 Samuel 8:7; 1 Kings 20:36). Old Testament prophets were at times the most powerful and dominant ministry in the Old Testament, even reproving, rebuking, and challenging Israel's national leaders: priests, judges, and kings (1 Samuel 15:26; 1 Kings 17:1). Old Testament prophetic ministry ceased with the last and greatest of the Old Testament prophets, John the Baptist (Luke 1:76; Matthew 11:9-13), and most of these ministry functions were passed on to the Apostles (compare "Apostles" above), not to the New Testament prophets.

New Testament prophetic ministry

New Testament prophets spoke words which God had laid on their hearts for strengthening, encouraging, and comforting the Body (1 Corinthians 14:30). Their words were never prefaced in the New Testament with "thus says the Lord" and did not always come to pass (Acts 21:11, "Jews would bind Paul", 22:29, Romans put Paul in chains). The recipients of prophecy, therefore, needed to test, weigh, interpret and then apply what was good (Paul and his journey to Jerusalem, Acts 20:23; 21:4-13: also 1 Corinthians 14:29, 1 Thessalonians 5:19-22, Acts 11:27). New Testament prophets operated under church government (1 Corinthians 14:29-31).

Evangelist

An evangelist is one who proclaims the simple message of salvation to those who are non-believers with the effective result that men and women become disciples of Jesus and responsible parts of the Body of Christ. Paul, for instance, knew that he had an obligation to preach the Good News to all men because he was debtor, compelled by love, and that the gospel was the only power that could set captives free (1 Corinthians 1:17-19, 9:16-18, Romans 1:14-17). An evangelist may have an itinerant ministry, but there is no evidence in the New Testament that they were not under the authority of a local church (Matthew 28:18-20; Acts 21:8; 2 Timothy 4:5).

Pastors or Pastor-Teacher

A pastor is one who keeps watch over the flock and provides for their spiritual needs by leading, feeding, and protecting the sheep put under his care (Hebrews 13:17, 1 Timothy 5:17, Acts 20:28). A pastor does this through hard work, admonishing with God's Word, and modeling a godly life because he will give an account to God for this responsibility (1 Thessalonians 5:12-13, Hebrews 13:7, 17). There is no greater joy than to see and hear God's people are walking according to his truth (3 John 3, Hebrews 13:17). This may by a hyphenated word along with teacher, since teaching is a primary function of a pastor and in the original language teacher has no article (unlike the other functions) and a different connecting word is used.

Teachers

A teacher is one who provides for the spiritual needs of the flock by accurately unfolding the mysteries of the Word and relating them to the needs, opportunities, and mysteries of life. Teachers don't just tell but train the Body to think like the bible writes so their thinking processes will be transformed to become more like Christ (Romans 12:1-2, 1 Corinthians 2:9-16). The teaching ministry was foundational for the early church (Acts 2:42), a requisite for pastors (1 Timothy 3:2, 5:17), and something they needed to work hard at (2 Timothy 2:15) because of the purpose and function of the Word of God (2 Timothy 3:16-17) and also because of the warning to teachers in James 3:1.

Conclusion

If "fruit that will last" (John 15:16) and "equipped to serve" (Ephesians 4:12) are the goals, then how should we weigh expectations? Here are some *suggested* questions to ask for each of the five functions.

- *Apostolic function* – How many disciples and churches are there as a fruit of your ministry?

- *Prophetic function* – Do the prophetic words benefit others? How many believers are equipped to prophesy?

- *Evangelistic function* – How many have been won and brought into the life of the church? How many evangelists have been trained and released?

- *Pastoral function* - How many people have been equipped for life and ministry? How many are able to help others in the same way?

- *Teaching function* – How biblically accurate, personally helpful, and culturally current is the teaching? How many teachers have been equipped and released?

DISCIPLINING FALLEN LEADERS

We have a responsibility to call for fallen leaders' true repentance, accountability, and a proved character before they are restored to leadership.

Paul anticipated the emotional and spiritual bind of Christians whose leaders failed. In the first letter to Timothy he wrote that elders (our leaders) are "worthy of double honor," yet when they sin, they should be "rebuked publicly, so that the others may take warning". (1 Timothy 5:17–20; also 5:1). Paul is saying that we should always approach elders with honor and respect even when serious accusations are brought against them.

God calls us to humility in these difficult situations for two reasons.

First, He is concerned that we respect the office of pastoral leadership.

God leads his body through delegated leaders – men and women whom he calls and anoints. To denigrate the office is to undermine Christ's lordship over his body.

Second, any challenge to ordained authority, even to leaders who have sinned grievously, opens Christians up to the sins of pride and rebellion. There is scant distance in our hearts between legitimate outrage over other's sin and our personal pride and presumption.

David's attitude towards Saul is an excellent example of how we should treat fallen leaders. David avoided speaking against Saul, though Saul brought false accusations against him and tried to kill him. When David learnt of Saul's death, a death brought on by unfaithfulness to the Lord (I Chronicles 10:13–14), he "mourned and wept and fasted" over "the Lord's anointed" (2 Samuel 1:12, 16). David was especially careful to guard his tongue when referring to Saul. Second Samuel 1:20 warns Israel against broadcasting the scandal of Saul's life to the surrounding nations, "lest the daughters of the uncircumcised rejoice."

Nevertheless, leaders do fall. And Scripture teaches that we must treat their sin in a serious and far more significant manner than non-leaders' sin. Why? Because leaders' sin, when improperly treated, is like a contagious disease, quickly spreading throughout the entire body of people they are ministering to. Unfortunately, there are other ramifications to leaders' sinning.

Besides the obvious embarrassment and shame that come with exposure of seedy acts, fallen leaders betray their followers' trust, damaging a God-ordained bond between them and the people they influence. And especially damaging is the disrepute brought on the pastoral calling itself. Faithful pastors have found it more difficult to lead in recent years, due to the well-publicized failings of prominent leaders. Through no fault of their own, their office has been tarnished.

Under these circumstances we shouldn't be too surprised that many Christians are confused, hurt, and even cynical about leadership. But the problem isn't merely emotional; Christians are divided over how to treat fallen leaders. One thing is certain: the crisis in Christian leadership directly or indirectly affects *every* Christian.

So, how should we in the Vineyard treat our failed leaders, especially those guilty of sexual sin and other ethical wrongdoing?

RESTORATION?

The treatment of fallen leaders is based on God's treatment of all sinners: the cross. At the cross, forgiveness and reconciliation are extended to all those who trust in Christ. Implicit to the work of the cross is restoration of the fallen, the establishment of fruitful lives and ministries in God's kingdom. Leaders are no different.

The bible contains several examples of fallen leaders who were restored. In the Old Testament, David was restored after he abused his power and position in having an affair with Bathsheba and murdering her husband. Moses returned to lead Israel out of Egypt after committing murder and running away. In the New Testament, Peter was restored after he denied Christ three times.

There is no question in my mind that fallen leaders can be restored. But saying restoration is possible raises a more difficult and complex question: what qualifications must they meet before they can be restored?

Immediate restoration?

When leaders fail we have a responsibility to love, forgive, and receive them back into the body of Christ, as we would any repentant sinner. But does genuinely forgiving them mean they should remain leaders? If we fail to return leaders to office, does that mean we don't love them, that in fact we still hold their sin against them? In other words, does immediate restoration to ministry automatically accompany forgiveness? I think not.

If the individual sin itself were the only obstacle to leadership, restoration would be tied exclusively to receiving forgiveness. But far too often individual sins reflect the more troublesome problem of a flawed character. For this reason, repentance and forgiveness are prerequisites for *entering* the restoration process, not qualifications for *completing* the process.

The bible requires fallen leaders to step down from ministry at least temporarily because they no longer meet the moral qualifications of an overseer, qualifications that are much higher for leaders than for other Christians. They are no longer "above reproach...temperate, self-controlled, respectable, ...and (having) a good reputation with outsiders..." (1 Timothy 3:1–7; also Titus 1:6–9).

These character qualities are known with certainty only over the long haul. (That's why leaders are called "elders" and not "youngers.") Fallen leaders need time to reestablish their character as they grow in patterns of faithfulness, righteousness and accountability.

PUNISHMENT?

An ability to understand or accept the unique character of Christian leadership leads to erroneous conclusions about restoration.

Recently I read an article in which the author argued that, like a corrupt businessman who serves his prison sentence, once a fallen pastor has been "punished" he should be given a "second chance." The author illustrated his point by describing how quickly a former executive was hired after serving prison time for illegal securities training. The writer even went so far as to say fallen leasers may be better than those who haven't tasted serious sin!

He asked, "Does the secular world understand forgiveness better than we do?" I think not. The author confused restoration with punishment. He failed to recognize that the restoration of a leader involves the rebuilding of his character, not the successful completion of a penal sentence.

Christian leaders *are* different from the world's leaders. Many doctors, for example, do not follow their own advice. But we don't expect doctors to personify health. We go to them for expert advice and knowledge about medicine. But pastors who fail to embody the moral and spiritual values that they preach undermine their message of personal transformation through Christ. Paul could say, "Follow my example," because he followed "the example of Christ" (1 Corinthians 11:1). Christian leaders expertise and advice are only as genuine as the quality of their character.

Fallen leaders also must recognize that they are not the only ones in need of healing and renewal; the people they lead have also been hurt. The leaders have violated a sacred trust, and trust is the very foundation of their leadership. Once destroyed, trust may take years to rebuild again.

Fallen leaders must overcome many obstacles before they are restored, which complicates our relationship with them while they are working through the consequences of sin. So, to know how to treat a fallen leader we must know the path to restoration, for we will walk it with them.

The following guidelines capture the main elements of restoration in the Vineyard. They are the clear, biblical criteria that must be fulfilled before we will allow a leader to resume his or her ministry.

THE MAIN ELEMENTS OF RESTORATION

1. The leader must exhibit the fruits of true repentance

Scripture offers clear, concrete guidelines from which we can discern true repentance. The Greek word translated as "repentance" in English versions of the New Testament is *metanoia* which means literally, "changing one's mind." The first step of changing one's mind about sin is *admitting we have done something wrong.*

Admitting sin isn't merely feeling bad about being found out; it's deep remorse over sin. This involves true confession, acknowledging sin to all who have been sinned against and who may have been hurt by it. Of course, true confession starts with God. Does the fallen leader willingly divulge all of his sins, or does he appear only to tell those things in which he has been caught? In other words, is he hiding anything?

In Psalm 32, David describes the relationship between confession and forgiveness:

> When I kept silent, my bones wasted away through my groaning all

> day long. For day and night your hand was heavy upon me; my strength was sapped as in the heat of summer. Then I acknowledged my sin to you and did not cover up my iniquity. I said, "I will confess my transgressions to the Lord" – and you forgave the guilt of my sin. (vv. 3–5)

David couldn't go on hiding his sin, for left unconfessed it was becoming a spiritual cancer.

As David demonstrates, confession is to God first. But for the fallen leader confession must also be to the arena of his ministry, which for David was all of God's people – the nation of Israel and the church. First Timothy 5:20 says that elders are to be "rebuked publicly." What exactly does Paul mean by a public rebuke? To rebuke is to reprimand, to scold in a sharp way; the fallen elder is told to stop his sinning, now. Paul also says the rebuke is to take place among people against whom the fallen leader sinned; elders have a public ministry, so they are to be corrected in public. Implicit to a public rebuke is the fallen leader's confession of grief over his sin.

The need for a "public" rebuke always raises questions of *how* public it should be. As I wrote above, the repentance should be to the arena of the leader's ministry. For example, a fallen small group leader in a local church would repent to his fellow small group leaders and the members of his small group. A local pastor, however, would repent to his entire congregation. An evangelist or pastor of international repute would need to make his sin and repentance known to leaders from all over the world.

This passage isn't saying a leader owes a detailed confession, though it does raise questions about how much detail a fallen leader should reveal. Many Christians think it is inappropriate to require fallen leaders to confess their sins explicitly, that somehow this invades their "right to privacy." But leaders forfeit their right to privacy when they accept God's call; their lives are supposed to be examples of what they teach, living testaments of God's grace. Part of being an example is coming clean with sin.

For example, Paul rebuked Peter and Barnabas publicly (Galatians 2:11–14). And what about Nathan and David in the Old Testament (2 Samuel 12)? We know everything about these leaders – the good and the bad. God isn't as concerned about protecting fallen leader's reputations as either they or we are.

Confession to follow elders – those directly responsible for a fallen leader's discipline and care – must be specific and complete. They need to know details so they can determine how to approach restitution and restoration. But the broader audience doesn't need explicit detail, though the confession must clearly acknowledge the nature of the sin. If the fallen leader is vague about his sin, misunderstanding and gossip may follow him the rest of his life.

True repentance is motivated by brokenness of heart and the desire to protect God's people – not the desire to retain position and power or to cover up sin. After the prophet Nathan confronted David for his abuse of power and privilege, David said:

> The sacrifices of God are a broken spirit; a broken and contrite heart, O God, you will not despise. In your good pleasure make Zion prosper; build up the walls of Jerusalem (Psalm 51:17–18).

David's concern was for Israel's glory, not his position as king. His repentance was true.

The second mark of repentance is a firm and spoken *renunciation of the sin*. Proverbs 28:13 says, "He who conceals his sin does not prosper, but whoever confesses and renounces them finds mercy."

Renunciation means a willingness to do *anything* to stop sinning.

This is what Jesus had in mind in Matthew 18:8–9 when he told the disciples to cut off their hand or pluck out their eye if either caused them to stumble. He wasn't telling them literally to cut off a limb or poke out an eye; he was saying that no action was too extreme in avoiding sin.

The third mark of repentance is *reconciliation*. In Matthew 5:23–25 Jesus instructs us, before worshipping God, to seek reconciliation with someone we have wronged. Reconciliation involves taking responsibility for our sin, confessing to the person we have wronged, and asking for his or her forgiveness. For the spouses of leaders guilty of sexual wrongdoing, reconciliation is usually a complex and long-term process. It is also the most critical step of repentance, one that requires much of the leaders' energy and attention.

An important part of reconciliation is a willingness to make *restitution* for harm done to others. Zacchaeus, the corrupt tax collector (all tax collectors were corrupt in those days), responded to Jesus' call by offering to make restitution: "Look, Lord! Here and now I give half of my possessions to the poor, and if I have cheated anybody out of anything, I will pay back four times the amount" (Luke 19:8). Zacchaeus' act of restitution embodied faith in God; Jesus pronounced him saved that very moment.

Restitution frequently involves more than money. For example, a pastor guilty of sexual wrongdoing owes restitution to his congregation or organization; he must fix broken trust through open repentance and a humble willingness to do whatever is necessary to repair the harm. How is this done? In the very least, by patiently understanding that the people need time to heal from broken trust.

Sometimes an organization may owe restitution for sin committed by the fallen leader when he acted on its behalf. For example, the leader may have had extramarital affairs with women from other churches or he may have misused others' funds. The organization will need to ask for forgiveness, rebuild broken bridges, and, in some instances, pay financial restitution.

Fallen pastors who truly repent are broken by the experience. Their public lives become transparent; they are no longer willing to live a lie around other Christians. When it comes time to confess their sins to the congregation, there is no sense of their covering up anything. They recognize that they betrayed a trust and brought scandal on the people of God, and they are willing to release their ministerial influence over the people. They no longer find their identity in their pastoral position. They are now truly broken before God.

2. A momentary moral lapse is treated differently from habitual, cunning and deceptive sin that reflects a seriously flawed character

There is a significant difference between the consequences of momentary sin that comes from a one-time temptation and sin that is prolonged and flagrant. An isolated act of passion must be dealt with differently from long-time, pre-meditated sin. The former, though serious, may be repented of and dealt with more easily than long-term sin. The latter represents a seriously flawed, immature character that usually requires many years – if ever – to reclaim.

I once knew a pastor named Bill (not his real name) who had a difficult marriage. His wife was like Gomer, the adulterous wife of the prophet Hosea in the Old Testament. Yet Bill remained faithful to his wife, despite her flirtatious manners.

Bill's marriage caused him to suffer periodic bouts with depression and loneliness. One day, when in the midst of one of these emotionally difficult times, Bill gave in to temptation and had sex with a woman he was counseling. The minute she left his office he phoned one of the elders and confessed everything to him. The elders called a meeting that evening, and Bill repeated his story, then turned in his resignation. He also asked if he could confess his sin to the entire congregation.

Bill's elders wisely refused to accept his resignation, instead placing him on a leave of absence. He was allowed to confess to the church and ask for forgiveness. The elders determined that Bill's problem was not part of a long history of sin or the result of a serious character flaw. Rather, it was a one-time failing, under stressful circumstances, of a good man.

The elders recommended that Bill receive time off for counseling to work through his troubled marriage and moral failure. Six months later, Bill returned as pastor, and he has faithfully served the congregation ever since. The church was able to accept Bill back immediately, because they understood the circumstances surrounding his sin, felt his brokenness, and sensed he wasn't hiding anything from them.

Secret Sin

Fallen leaders with a long history of serious sin face a far more difficult and longer road to restoration than Bill. They must overcome habit patterns of cunning, deception, and secret sin built up through years of disobedience – sin that they are unwilling or unable to control.

The length and complexity of the restoration process is tied directly to the length and nature of the sin. Commenting on this, John White and Ken Blue, in their book *Healing the Wounded* write,

> People who abuse power are changed progressively as they do so. In abusing power they give themselves over to evil, untruth, self-blindness and hardness without allowing themselves or anyone else to see what is happening. The longer the process continues, the harder repentance becomes.

Because of this, nipping sin in the bud is especially important for the restoration of leaders. Many fallen leaders with a long history of secret sin never make it back into the ministry. When they truly repent, the severity and effects of their sin are so great that they have forfeited the privilege of leadership. If they do make it back into leadership, the process takes many difficult years. (There is much more I could write about this process, but space limitations prevent me from doing so.)

3. The fallen leader must be submitted to and accountable to other leaders throughout the entire restoration process

There is no recovery process for a leader with a hardened heart, but there are many paths back for the truly repentant. I have outlined the biblical steps of repentance, but most rank and file church members aren't close enough to their pastors to discern the difference between false and true repentance, especially if they are members of large churches. The pastors may have all the external marks of repentance, but still suffer from serious character defects and concealed sin.

For this reason we must rely on the judgment of other leaders, men and women to whom the fallen leader is accountable. Is the pastor willing to cooperate with and submit to other leaders in the restoration process? (And are these leaders capable of standing up to him?) The fallen leader must be willing to be guided, directed, taught...to do *anything* that they think necessary to set his life in good order. If the fallen leader chooses to stand "alone before God" and reject other leaders' authority, he is a dangerous man.

A purpose of a leader's restoration is the formation of mature character. A mature character is confirmed only by a track record of resisting sin and walking faithfully with God, family, and brothers and sisters.

In the case of a leader who has a momentary failure, a proved character may be restored in a relatively short period of time. Those overseeing the process aren't dealing with major flaws and corruption – though an individual act usually reveals significant character problems. In fact, much time usually is required to bring reconciliation with a spouse or to make restitution.

ACCOUNTABILITY

More serious sins and character flaws require longer track records of righteousness. For someone who has been unfaithful for years, the process required long-term counseling and prayer. The key element for success is accountability; other leaders must be free to scrutinize the fallen leader's life and discern whether true change has come, both for his benefit and for the benefit of those he may lead one day.

The mechanics of restoration work a variety of ways. Most established denominations and churches have precise disciplinary procedures spelled out. The Vineyard is no different. The process is overseen by Vineyard leaders from the local body or leaders from outside the body, depending on the position and visibility of the fallen leader. If the fallen leader is a senior pastor or has a significant ministry outside of the local church, extra-local Vineyard pastors will oversee the restoration process.

We need to be careful, though, about relying too rigidly on disciplinary procedure. Each case is unique, requiring the love of God and Spirit-led wisdom for healing and restoration. The mechanics and oversight of the process are not as important as a willingness to submit on the part of the fallen leader, and a willingness to confront and hold accountable on the part of the overseeing process.

Christians cannot afford to sit by passively when their leaders fall. We have a responsibility to maintain an attitude of honor and respect towards them, avoiding gossip and bitterness that tears apart the body of Christ and brings scandal on the Gospel. But we also have a responsibility to call for fallen leaders' true repentance, accountability, and a proved character before they are restored to leadership. How Christians treat their fallen leaders today will determine the vitality of the church as we enter the twenty-first century.

SELECT BIBLIOGRAPHY

Peter Berger, *The Homeless Mind: Modernization and Consciousness*, New York, Random House, 1973.

Edith L Blumhofer, *The Assemblies of God: A Popular History*, Springfield: Radiant Books, 1985 or Gospel Publishing House, 1985.

James Dunn, *Jesus and the Spirit*, London, SCM, 1975 or Westminster: John Knox Press, 1980

Jonathan Edwards, *Some Thoughts Concerning the Present Revival* of *Religion in New England*, (1743), Reprint Services Corp, 1817.

Jonathan Edwards, *The Religious Affections*, Sovereign Grace Publishers, 2001, or *Religious Affections: A Christian's Character Before God*, Bethany House Publishers; Reprint edition, 1996. This can be obtained online at http://www.ccel.org/ccel/edwards/affections.html

Susan T. Foh, *Women and the Word of God, a response to Biblical Feminism*, Phillipsburg, N.J., Presbyterian & Reformed, 1979, or Baker, 1981.

Michael Green, *I Believe in the Holy Spirit*, Grand Rapids: Eerdmans, Revised edition, 2004.

L. Grant McClung, Jr., Ed., *Azusa Street and Beyond: Pentecostal Missions and Church Growth in the Twentieth Century*, South Plainfield, N.J., Bridge, 1986, or Bridge Publications, 1986.

John Piper and Wayne Grudem, *Recovering Biblical Manhood & Womanhood: A Response to Evangelical Feminism*, Wheaton, Ill., Crossway Books, 1991.

Hanna Whitall Smith, *The Christian's Secret of a Happy Life*, Barbour Publishing, April 2006. Can also be obtained online at http://www.ccel.org/ccel/smith_hw/secret/files/secret.htm

Howard Snyder, *The Radical Wesley and Patterns of Church Renewal*, Downers Grove IL: InterVarsity Press, 1985.

Carol Wimber, *The Way It Was*, Hodder and Stoughton, 1999.

John Wimber & Kevin Springer, *Power Points*, London, Hodder & Stoughton, 1990.

John Wimber & Kevin Springer, *Power Healing*, London: Hodder and Stoughton, 1986, or HarperSanFrancisco, Reprint edition, 1991.

John Wimber, *Power Evangelism,* San Francisco: Harper, 1986, or Trafalgar Square Publishing; New edition, 2000.

A Skevington Wood, *The Burning Heart, John Wesley: Evangelist,* Bethany House, 1978.

BIBLIOGRAPHY

Leith Anderson, *Winning the Values War in a Changing Culture*, Minneapolis: Bethany House Publishers, 1994.

E. W. Blumhofer, *The Assemblies of God: A Popular History*, Springfield, Mo., Radiant Books, 1985.

Guy P. Duffield, *Pentecostal Preaching: Lectures from the L.I.F.E. Alumni Preaching Lectureship*, 1956.

James Dunn, *Jesus and the Spirit*, London, SCM, 1975.

Jonathan Edwards, *Some Thoughts Concerning the Present Revival*, 1743.

Elisabeth Elliot, *Shadow of the Almighty*, San Francisco: Harper & Row, 1958.

Walter A. Elwell, ed., *Handbook of Evangelical Theologians*, Grand Rapids, Michigan: Baker Books, 1993.

Gordon Fee, *The First Epistle to the Corinthians, New International Commentary on the New Testament*, Grand Rapids, Eerdmans, 1987.

Wayne Grudem, *Systematic Theology*, Leicester, Inter-Varsity Press, 1994.

Michael Green, *I Believe in the Holy Spirit*, London, Hodder & Stoughton, 1975.

Walter C. Kaiser, Jr. *Quest for Renewal*, Publisher not known.

Donald McGavran, *Understanding Church Growth, 3rd Edition*, Grand Rapids Michigan: Eerdmans, 1990.

William Hendriksen, *New Testament Commentary: Exposition of the Pastoral Epistles*, Grand Rapids Michigan: Baker Book House, 1979.

Carl F. H. Henry, "Dare We Renew the Controversy Part II: The Fundamental Reduction," *Christianity Today*, June 24, 1957.

J.B. Lightfoot, translator, *The Apostolic Fathers*, edited and compiled by J.R. Harmer, London, MacMillan, 1893.

L. Grant McClung, Jr., Ed., *Azusa Street and Beyond: Pentecostal Missions and Church Growth in the Twentieth Century*, South Plainfield, N.J.,

Bridge, 1986.

W. R. Moody, *The Life of Dwight L Moody, by his son W.R. Moody,* London, Morgan & Scott, 19?

Leon Morris, *Tyndale New Testament Commentaries, The Revelation of St. John,* Leicester, Inter-Varsity Press.

Leon Morris, New International Commentary on the New Testament, *The Gospel according to John,* Grand Rapids, Michigan: Eerdmans, 1971.

Mounce, R.H. *The Book of Revelation, New International Commentary on the New Testament.* Grand Rapids: Eerdmans, 1977.

Nicoll, W. Robinson, Ed., *The Expositor's Greek Testament,* London, Hodder & Stoughton, 1897-1910.

The Works of John Wesley, Vol. III, Oxford, Clarendon Press, 1975-1983.

John White, "Prayer and Renewal" course, Canadian Theological Seminary, 7/1/91.

Wimber, Carol, *The Way It Was,* London, Hodder & Stoughton, 1999.

Wimber, J. & K Springer, *Power Healing,* London: Hodder and Stoughton, 1986.

Wimber, J. *Power Evangelism,* San Francisco: Harper, 1986.

A Skevington Wood, *The Burning Heart, John Wesley: Evangelist,* Bethany House, 1967.